The Age of Exuberance

The Making of Britain
1066–1939

General Editor: Andrew Wheatcroft

The Norman Heritage Trevor Rowley
The High Middle Ages Trevor Rowley
The Age of Exuberance Michael Reed
The Georgian Triumph Michael Reed
The Transformation of Britain Gordon Mingay

The Age of Exuberance
1550–1700

Michael Reed

Routledge & Kegan Paul
London, Boston and Henley

First published in 1986
by Routledge & Kegan Paul plc
14 Leicester Square, London WC2H 7PH, England
9 Park Street, Boston, Mass. 02108, USA and
Broadway House, Newtown Road,
Henley on Thames, Oxon RG9 1EN, England

Set in Linotron Palatino, 10 on 12pt
by Input Typesetting Ltd, London
and printed in Great Britain
by The Thetford Press Ltd
Thetford, Norfolk

Library of Congress Cataloging in Publication Data

Reed, Michael A.
The age of exuberance, 1550–1700.

(The Making of Britain, 1066–1939)
Bibliography: p.
Includes index.
1. Great Britain—Civilization—16th century.
2. Great Britain—Civilization—17th century.
3. Great Britain—Description and travel—To 1600.
4. Great Britain—Description and travel—1601–1700.
5. Landscape assessment—Great Britain.   I. Title.
II. Series.
DA320.R44   1986   941.05   85–11845

British Library CIP data also available

ISBN 0–7100–9803–0 (c)

To Philip

Contents

Illustrations

Illustrations

Figures

Acknowledgements

Many people have contributed unstintingly of their time,
learning and skill to the making of this book: I am grateful
to them all. Professor Havard-Williams has continued his
support and encouragement. Mrs S. Hulland has allowed
me free access to her researches into her family history,
and Mrs J. P. Hey has typed successive drafts with
unfailing care, accuracy and good humour. Alan Cameron,
of the Department of Manuscripts at Nottingham University, helped me to Plate 6. Mrs P. A. Halfpenny, Keeper
of Ceramics in the City Museum and Art Gallery, Stoke
on Trent, helped me to Plate 15, and Miss Extance, of the
Cambridge University Committee for Aerial Photography,
went to great trouble to find Plate 17. My thanks are also
due to Andrew Wheatcroft and to other members of the
staff at Routledge for their unfailing interest in the
progress of this book. Other debts are more particularly
acknowledged in the appropriate place. Only my wife
knows the true cost of this book, and only she can
appreciate the full significance of its dedication.

I am very grateful to the following for permission to
reproduce copyright materials. Plates 1, 5, 14, 15, 34, 61,
64, 66, 67, 68, 69, 71 and 74 are by courtesy of the British
Library; Plate 47 is reproduced by courtesy of the Trustees
of the British Museum; Plates 4, 7, 12, 22, 42 and 53 are
by courtesy of Aerofilms Ltd; Plates 16 and 60 are Crown
Copyright and are reproduced with the permission of the
Controller of Her Majesty's Stationery Office; Plates 8, 28,
30, 33, 35, 41, 51 and 54 are Crown Copyright and are
reproduced with the permission of the Royal Commission
on Historical Monuments, Scotland; Plates 26 and 27 are
also Crown Copyright and are reproduced with the
permission of the Royal Commission on Ancient and
Historical Monuments in Wales; Plates 19, 20, 21, 23, 25,
29, 31, 32, 36, 37, 38, 43, 44, 45, 46, 49, 52, 56, 58, 59, 65
and 73 are reproduced with the permission of the Royal
Commission on the Historical Monuments of England;
Plates 2, 9, 10, 13, 17, 48 and 50 are in the Cambridge
University collection, copyright reserved, and are reproduced with the permission of the Committee for Aerial

Acknowledgements   Photography; Plate 11 is reproduced with the permission of the Leicestershire Museums, Art Galleries and Records Services; and Plate 6 is reproduced by courtesy of the trustees of the will of Earl Manvers and the Library of the University of Nottingham; Plates 40 and 72 are published with the permission of A. F. Kersting; Plate 70 is published with the permission of Northamptonshire Libraries; Dr Mary Reed supplied me with Plate 18; and Plates 24, 57 and 62 were taken by Philip Reed; Plate 39 is reproduced with the permission of Hereford City Libraries and Plates 3, 55 and 63 are from my own collections.

General editor's preface

To the archaeologist, the notion of material culture, of a society exemplified by its artefacts, is commonplace. To historians it has traditionally had less appeal, although Professor Fernand Braudel's *Civilisation matérielle et capitalisme* marks a foray into unknown terrain. The intention of this series, which follows chronologically from another of more directly archaeological approach,* is to see the history of Britain from the Norman Conquest to the Second World War, partly in human terms – of changing cultural, social, political and economic patterns – but more specifically in terms of what that society produced and what remains of it today.

Few themes run with consistency through the history of the British Isles, save the land itself. This series seeks to show the way in which man has shaped and occupied the country, and how society has been moulded by the opportunities and constraints imposed by the landscape. The broad theme is of man's interaction with his environment, which is carried through the series.

As editor, I have tried to allow each author to write his approach to the subject without undue interference. Ideally, such a study would have appeared as a large single volume but we have sought to make the divisions less arbitrary by allowing authors to cover a broad body of material in more than one book. Thus the volumes dealing with the medieval period come from the same hand, as do those spanning the sixteenth to the nineteenth centuries.

The two centuries of which Michael Reed writes in this book present a paradox. They are crammed with incident. The power of the Church was broken in both England and Scotland, and the institutions of the secular state, Crown and Parliament, began a set of conflicts which dragged on through these years. A civil war was fought. One king, Charles I, lost his head in an act of ceremonial and judicial revenge, while his younger son, James II, was forced to

Britain before the Conquest, 5 vols, Routledge & Kegan Paul, 1979–81.

take flight. Even the boundaries of the state were dramatically enlarged with the personal union of England and Scotland under James Stuart, the first of England and the sixth of Scotland. Yet despite all these events the pattern of life remained largely unchanged; moreover, many of the developments of these years – economic, social and political – had their origins in earlier periods. Thus the drainage of large areas of lowland Britain in the seventeenth century was prefigured by the great drainage works of the medieval period. And the great disruption of intellectual life which sprang from the religious reformation had notable late medieval precursors. The distinctive character of this epoch lies not simply in the changes themselves, but in their range and cumulative effect.

Eighteenth-century savants often dismissed the excesses of the years after 1500 as the product of an excess of enthusiasm, of a lack of controlling moderation and discipline. Michael Reed describes it as 'exuberance' which is a more exact definition. It was a period in which the boundaries of what was thought possible, or acceptable, were being tested and changed. This exuberance is manifest in the rapid growth in domestic building and in landscape change, which is well demonstrated in this book, as well as in the whole realm of intellectual and political life. Michael Reed makes a convincing claim that it is this ferment, the willingness to explore new ideas and new opportunities, even in fields hitherto forbidden, which provides the common factor within the hectic and often contradictory events of these two centuries.

Andrew Wheatcroft

Preface

In 1898 one of the greatest of English historians, Frederick Maitland, published one of his most seminal books, *Township and Borough*. He took as his point of departure the drawings made in 1688 by David Loggan of views of Cambridge from the east and the west, using them to explore the history of the development of the medieval town, both physically and as a legal entity. He did not, however, exhaust Loggan's drawings. Indeed it was not his intention to do so. He used them to explore the past. They can also tell us a great deal about the present, the world which is represented in them. It is the object of this book, a pigmy on the shoulders of a giant, to take these same drawings and use them to explore the nature of the physical environment of men and women living in the sixteenth and seventeenth centuries – those men and women, riding, walking, sitting, working and at play so vividly realised in Loggan's drawings, reproduced here as Plate 1. This book is not a social and economic history of Britain in the sixteenth and seventeenth centuries, although the landscape is shaped by men and women at work and at play in society. There are yet further factors at work. Men's ideas and ideals shape their environment as well as their hands and their tools, and it is the exploration of these ideas that adds richness and depth to the landscape. The skyline of the view of Cambridge from the west, the bottom half of Plate 1, is dominated by the chapel of King's College. Immediately to its left is the tower of St Mary's church, and to the left again is the library of Trinity College. In the foreground is a farm wagon laden with corn and with a boy asleep on top. Together these items contribute to the fabric of the landscape. To explain their presence fully would require a history of the western world. This book is an introduction to that history.

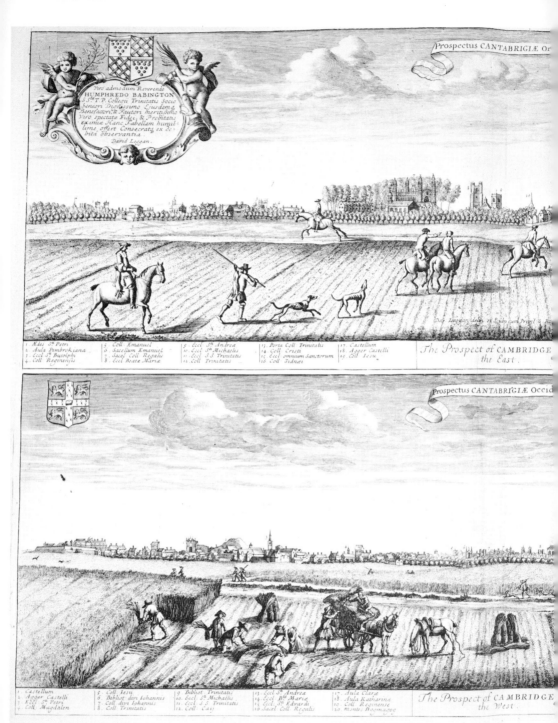

Viro admodum Reverendo
HUMPHREDO BABINGTON
S.S.T.P. Collegii Trinitatis Socio
Seniori Dignissimo Ejusdemq,
Benefactori & Fautori meritissimo
Viro spectata Fide, & Probitate
eximia Hanc Tabellam humil
lime, offert Consecratq, ex de-
bita observantia.
David Loggan.

The Prospect of CAMBRIDGE the East.

1. Ædes S.ti Petri	5. Coll. Emanuel	9. Eccl. S.ta Andreæ	13. Porta Coll. Trinitatis	17. Castellum
2. Aula Pembrokiana	6. Sacellum Emanuel	10. Eccl. S.ti Michaelis	14. Coll. Crusti	18. Agger Castelli
3. Eccl. S.ti Butolphi	7. Sacel. Coll. Regalis	11. Eccl. SS. Trinitatis	15. Eccl. omnium Sanctorum	19. Coll. Iesu
4. Coll. Regiensis	8. Eccl. Beatæ Mariæ	12. Coll. Trinitatis	16. Coll. Sidner	

The Prospect of CAMBRIDGE the West.

1. Castellum	5. Coll. Iesu	9. Bibliot. Trinitatis	13. Eccl. S.ta Andreæ	17. Aula Claræ
2. Agger Castelli	6. Bibliot. divi Iohannis	10. Eccl. S.ti Michaelis	14. Eccl. B.tæ Mariæ	18. Aula Katharinæ
3. Eccl. S.ti Petri	7. Coll. divi Iohannis	11. Eccl. S.S. Trinitatis	15. Eccl. D.ti Edvardi	19. Coll. Regiense
4. Coll. Magdalen	8. Coll. Trinitatis	12. Coll. Caij	16. Sacel. Coll. Regalis	20. Montes Regionacog

xvi

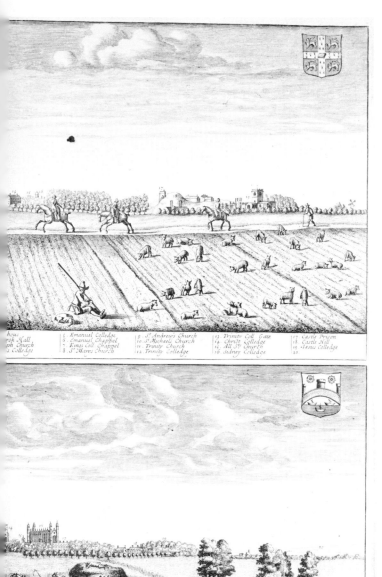

Plate 1 Views of Cambridge from the east and the west, drawn by David Loggan and published in 1688. These two views form the starting point for the account of the British landscape in the sixteenth and seventeenth centuries which is the subject matter of this book

Britain in 1550: the land and its people

The landscape of Britain had, by the middle years of the sixteenth century, an immensely long and complex history behind it. In one sense this history begins with the beginning of the world itself, since the underlying geological structures of the landscape form the stage upon which the men and women who moulded the landscape lived out their lives, and within the next few pages we must look very briefly at the shape and structure of this stage. The perspective may however be considerably foreshortened by focusing for a moment on the last time there was a clear break in the history of the landscape, something which occurred at the end of the last Ice Age, a mere twelve thousand years ago. Plants, animals and men recolonised the land as the ice retreated; these elements have been here ever since, shaping and modifying the landscape as men wrestled with the problems and opportunities it presented to their efforts to make a living. Farms, fields and temples were to be found at least five thousand years ago, with all that this implies for a structured, organised society with disposable wealth and technical resources. Large areas of Britain had been cleared of the primeval woodland, and the Derbyshire and Yorkshire moors, the Lake District fells and the chalklands have been open, largely treeless country ever since. (See Plates 2 and 4.) It is of course impossible accurately to estimate the population of Britain in prehistoric times, but an informed guess might suggest that there were as many as six million people living in Roman Britain. This may be an underestimate rather than anything else, but it is certainly more than were living in the whole of Britain in the middle decades of the sixteenth century.

With the collapse of Roman power, many of the external features of Roman civilisation, villas, baths, made roads, town houses and drains for example, were abandoned and fell into decay for want of the technical knowledge to keep them going, but in no sense does the coming of the English represent a new beginning in the history of the landscape, since it is now clear that they adopted many features of the Romano-British landscape, the cultivated arable land,

1

1 Map showing
Highland and Lowland
Britain

for example, and some territorial boundaries, and the
names of hills and rivers, always among the most permanent elements in the palimpsest which is the landscape.
By the middle decades of the sixteenth century much had
been added to and altered in this landscape, new administrative divisions such as counties and parishes, although
often adopting very ancient boundaries, many new settlements, churches, farmsteads and windmills for example.

There are both churches and a windmill on Plate 1. But much was very ancient in the sixteenth- and seventeenth-century landscape, and it is this sense of continuity from the past which must always be borne in mind when reading the following pages.

The underlying geological structures of Britain are in outline very simple, in detail immensely complex. The oldest rocks lie in the north and the west of the island, newer and younger ones overlying these ancient strata as one approaches the south and the east. Archaeologists have for half a century now used the phrases 'Highland' and 'Lowland' Zones to mark off in very broad terms the differences between the north and the west on the one hand and the south and the east on the other. It is however most important to appreciate that the terms 'Highland' and 'Lowland' are but convenient shorthand expressions, useful to point a broad contrast, but dangerously misleading when applied at a microscopic level since they obscure the fine detail and the regional variation which give to the landscape and its history its undoubted fascination and its rich historical density.

The Highland Zone is a region of old, hard rocks which weather very slowly to produce thin, infertile soils. But although the rocks themselves are very ancient, and some in the Isle of Lewis are among the most ancient to be found anywhere in the world, their topography today is comparatively recent, since they have been sculpted, moulded and shaped by the immense forces exerted by successive ice sheets, sometimes as much as five thousand feet thick. The ice sheets and their glaciers gouged out valleys, planed mountains and scraped the landscape bare of soil. The mass of debris carried in a glacier acted like a huge sheet of very coarse sandpaper, and the mountains of central Wales, the Lake District and the Highlands of Scotland still bear the scars.

As the glaciers melted so they dumped their debris, sometimes in huge piles, blocking drainage and forming lakes. Sometimes this debris has formed heavy but fertile soils, as the boulder clays of midland and eastern England, sometimes only thin, sandy soils, as in the Breckland of Norfolk. Even in those areas of southern England where the ice did not reach, and it seems to have advanced no further than the line of the Thames, the intense cold of periglacial conditions had a very similar effect upon the landscape. Thus the surface skin to the landscape has been moulded almost everywhere by the comparatively recent effects of the ice, and the glacial drift is of immense import-

3

Plate 2 An aerial view of Rannochmoor, Perthshire, illustrating the bleak, heavily glaciated landscape of large areas of the Highland Zone

ance since it provides the soil on which men grow their crops and graze their animals. (See Plate 1.) It provides root-hold for trees and the raw materials for bricks and hence the basis for the homes in which men live. If the soil is rich and fertile, they will live well, if it is thin, poor or badly drained, they will live accordingly. This thin skin owes its origins to the actions of the glaciers, and their role in shaping the underlying structure of the landscape cannot be over-emphasised.

But beneath this glacial drift, which in some parts of southern England may be hundreds of feet thick and in the Highlands of Scotland altogether absent, lies the solid geology, the rocks laid down over aeons of geological time. These rocks can be just as important as glacial drift in the history of the landscape. They provide building stone, for example; and since, in the days before the transport revolution of the late eighteenth century the movement of stone was always difficult and expensive, these underlying strata form the bases for the differences between the built environments of the Cotswolds, the Lake District, the Dark Peak and the White Peak, and they yield the raw materials for flint churches in Norfolk, flint cottages in the Chilterns and granite farmhouses in Devonshire.

These underlying geological strata also provide minerals: coal, iron, lead, zinc, copper, tin, silver, even gold at Dolauchothi. Coal and iron are quite widely distributed throughout Britain and have been worked since prehistoric times. The other minerals are by and large to be found only in the Highland Zone, in Cornwall, Devon and Somerset, in Wales and Derbyshire, the Pennines and the Lake District, and less commonly in the Scottish Highlands. The lead mines of Mendip and the Peak District have been worked at least since Roman times, and the tin mines of Cornwall were known to the Phoenicians. The presence or absence of minerals, by making mining possible or impossible, has had a profound effect upon the evolution of the landscape.

The Highland Zone, as an area of mountains in the north and west of Britain, has a difficult climate compared with that of the Lowland Zone. It faces into the Atlantic. The Gulf Stream may modify climatic extremes – after all Britain is in the same latitude as Labrador – but the western coasts of the Highland Zone have to endure the full force of Atlantic gales, with strong winds, heavy seas and salt spray to contend with, so that much of Cornwall, for example, is almost as treeless as Lewis, and sand blows are not uncommon. Leland found early in the sixteenth century that St Ives was 'sore oppressed' with sand, and several medieval churches have been lost, St Constantine for example, and St Enodoc.

The prevailing wind direction in Britain is from the south-west, and rain-bearing winds encounter the mountain masses of the Highland Zone immediately they cross the coast. This means that the Highland Zone is a region of heavy rainfall, much cloud and comparatively little sunshine. Heavy rainfall means that soils are quickly leached, losing such plant nutrients as they may possess, and a hard impervious 'pan' may develop below the surface, impeding root formation and drainage. In these conditions the only cereal that will ripen is oats, and the poor transport of the sixteenth and seventeenth centuries meant that it had to be grown wherever possible if men and their animals were to eat at all. The growing season is short, and is made shorter by altitude. Mean temperature is reduced 1°F for every three hundred feet, and the growing season is shortened ten days for every 260 feet.

5

Altitude also means that much of the rain falls as snow, and in some parts of the Highlands, especially on the north slopes of Ben Nevis, snow will survive the summer. The result is that although the high rainfall may encourage the growth of grass and the pastoral farming which is based on it, other environmental factors mean that cattle often have to be stalled during the winter months and the pasture on the uplands is coarse and rank, with large areas of bog and heather.

Plate 3 This cottage, near Monks Risborough, in Buckinghamshire, shows the decorative use of flint as a building material, set in square panels with brick surrounds to doors and windows

The preceding paragraphs have of course been at a level of generalisation that conceals the wide range of variation to be found within the Highland Zone. Sheltered south-facing valley slopes, in Teesdale for example or in Spey-side, could provide very congenial conditions. Stock raising in central Wales and the southern uplands of Scotland could be very profitable, and some of the islands of the Inner Hebrides enjoy an exceptionally mild, sunny climate, Tiree for example.

The Lowland Zone, again in very general terms, is characterised by low rounded hills, deep rich soils and a comparatively mild climate. In the eastern part of England the climate is quite dry, and so lack of water can become a problem on the chalklands (see Plate 4) and in the Breckland of Norfolk. Rivers are often broad and slow-moving, so that adequate drainage become very difficult, especially along the coasts and estuaries. Thus there were in the sixteenth and seventeenth centuries extensive areas of marshland along the coasts of Kent, both shores of the Thames estuary, the Somerset Levels and the tidal stretches of the Severn, much of the Lancashire coast, the

Plate 4 Westbury Hill, Wiltshire. Cultivation has reached both the brow and the foot of the scarp, but the steep slopes of the scarp itself are left to grass and scrub

lower reaches of the Trent and both shores of the Humber, and above all in the region of the fens of Lincolnshire and Cambridgeshire. These marshlands were not bleak watery wastes. They supported a society which had long learned to exploit the opportunities for stock raising, fishing and wild fowling which the marshland presented. The Broads of Norfolk were also in existence by this time, but they are entirely artificial in their origins, being formed by the flooding of extensive peat cuttings in the late fifteenth century.

There were still, in the sixteenth and seventeenth centuries, extensive areas of woodland in Lowland Britain, but in no sense were these woods an untamed wilderness. Wood was a valuable commercial crop and often carefully managed. Much of the woodland was Royal Forest in the legal sense in that it was a tract of countryside subject to the Forest Laws, designed originally to preserve cover for the deer and hunting for the king. By the middle of the sixteenth century however the timber was more valuable than the deer, and many Royal Forests were badly neglected, especially those at any distance from London and Westminster. James I was the last English king to be passionately fond of hunting and he rarely moved outside the south-eastern corner of England after 1603.

This then, in outline at any rate, is the stage upon which the men and women of the sixteenth and seventeenth centuries in Britain acted out their lives. It presented them with an extraordinarily varied range of choices and opportunities, problems, difficulties and hazards, although they were by no means the passive victims of environmental forces. Rather were they active exploiters of the opportunities which lay within the range of their ideas, skills and technology.

There is yet a further facet to the exploitation of the physical resources of the landscape, one which can be easily overlooked, and this is climatic change. The period from the fourteenth to the late nineteenth centuries has been called the Little Ice Age, as it appears to have been both wetter and colder than the periods immediately before and after, although there were milder periods early in the sixteenth century, in the 1630s and the 1730s. Summers were wet, cool and cloudy, especially in the late sixteenth and the late seventeenth centuries, and winters were dry and often very cold. The Thames froze over at London Bridge a dozen times in this period. There were bad harvest failures in the 1550s, the 1590s and again in the 1690s, especially in Scotland where famine conditions led to high mortality and the population may have fallen by as much as 15 per cent. In these crisis years the role of the weather, especially excessive rainfall in the summer months, was crucial, and topographical factors in the north and west merely aggravated the situation.

High summer rainfall may also have meant that many small streams carried a greater volume of water than they do today, and this may go some way towards explaining the location of watermills, many of which appear to be situated on very small, sluggish brooks. The development of river navigation in the late seventeenth century may also owe something to this climatic deterioration, and it may have contributed to the problems of flooding in mines of every kind, thus stimulating the search for effective draining methods and the invention of the steam engine. Of course not all summers were uniformly wet and cool. As we shall see, bargemasters on the Thames found drought a problem in some years, and when the Dutch artist Willem Schellinks visited England between 1661 and 1663 he records visiting Sir Arnold Braems at Bridge Place where there was a vineyard yielding two to three hogsheads of wine each year. Nevertheless it is clear that climatic change is a factor which cannot be ignored in the evolution of the landscape.

We must now turn to the people who lived and worked in sixteenth-century Britain and the ways in which they organised themselves between the cradle and the grave.

There are no accurate population statistics for Britain before the nineteenth century. There are however a number of sources, including parish registers, ecclesiastical censuses, the Hearth Tax records and a handful of what appear to be complete listings of all the inhabitants of individual parishes, from which it has proved possible to make some estimates as to the numbers of people living in sixteenth century Britain.

The population of England in the 1540s may have been about 2.75 million, and by 1600 it may have reached a little over 4 million. There was a high birth rate compared with that at the end of the twentieth century, normally over 30 per 1,000, and also a high death rate, usually above 20 per 1,000, but this on occasion could go sky high. Plague was the most feared disease in the sixteenth and seventeenth centuries, but it was by no means the only killer. Medicine could make no impact at all upon disease of any kind and so influenza, dysentery, typhus, typhoid, smallpox, tuberculosis and measles all went totally unchecked and all could kill. Infant mortality rates were particularly high, with perhaps a quarter of all children born dying before they reached their first birthday. The average expectation of life at birth was rarely much more than forty.

Only in the very small segment of the population which made up the nobility and country gentry was there a tendency towards early marriage. In the population as a whole men may have been on average about twenty-seven when they first married, and women about twenty-six. This means that many women spent the most fertile ten years of their lives unmarried, thus reducing significantly the

9

number of children which they could bear. Certainly there
were very large families, with a dozen or so children, but
they were the exception rather than the rule, with five or
six being a more usual pattern. In sum, England had a
younger population than it has at the end of the twentieth
century, with perhaps 30 per cent under fifteen years of
age, a much lighter dependency burden than is to be
found in many developing countries today, where
commonly 40 per cent or more of the population is in this
age group. At the other end of life, it is likely that elderly
dependents, that is people over sixty, formed no more
than about 10 per cent of the total.

People were not distributed evenly over England in the
sixteenth century. The majority lived to the south of a line
from the Severn to the Wash, although by the end of
the century numbers were already beginning to thicken
around Manchester, Leeds and Newcastle upon Tyne. The
largest town by far was London, with perhaps 250,000
inhabitants in 1600. Norwich was next, with about 20,000
by the middle years of the seventeenth century. York,
Bristol, Newcastle upon Tyne and Exeter may all have had
about 10,000 at the end of the sixteenth century, Coventry
and Salisbury about 6,000, Canterbury and Ipswich about
5,000, and the township of Manchester perhaps 2,000.
Towns in the sixteenth and seventeenth centuries
remained very small and their connections with the
countryside very close.

Much less is known of the population of Wales, but it
has been estimated that there may have been about
278,000 inhabitants in 1536, and perhaps 380,000 by 1600,
thinly and fairly uniformly distributed, with perhaps
Glamorganshire as the most populous county. Welsh
towns were uniformly small. Cardiff may have had a thousand inhabitants in the middle of the sixteenth century,
Swansea perhaps the same. They had probably not
doubled in size by the end of the seventeenth century.

There are no sources at all from which to estimate the
population of Scotland before Webster's census of 1755,
when there were probably 1,265,000 inhabitants, and Edinburgh had a population of 47,570. To say that Scotland
may have had a population of about 1 million at the end
of the seventeenth century is therefore no more than a
guess. Edinburgh probably had about 40,000 inhabitants,
Glasgow about 12,000 (see Plate 5), and Dundee, Aberdeen
and Perth had perhaps 4,000 each. Scottish population
was concentrated in the Central Lowlands, along both
shores of the Firth of Forth, the Tay estuary and the north-

east coast. Elsewhere numbers were thinly distributed. It was only in the eighteenth century that population growth in the Highlands became a problem.

Men, women and children are not, however, merely peas in a statistical pod, to be counted by demographic historians concerned only with numbers in the aggregate and with long-term trends at national level. They are social animals, who organise themselves into groups in which their basic needs may be the more conveniently met, and

Facies Civitatis GLASCOÆ ab Austro. The prospect of the Town of GLASGOW from y̆ South.

associations in which their more intangible desires for intellectual and spiritual satisfaction may be fulfilled. The basic unit of social organisation is the family.

Plate 5 A view of Glasgow, drawn in 1693 by Thomas Slezer. It illustrates the small size of the town at this time, confined as it was to the north bank of the Clyde

The family in sixteenth- and seventeenth-century Britain had a structure in many ways quite unlike that of modern Britain, together with a much wider range of functions. As far back as documents allow us to penetrate the family in Britain has been a nuclear one, composed of a man, his wife and their children. Only very occasionally do individual families have other relatives living with them, and then it is usually an elderly grandparent who is retired and perhaps incapable. As we have just seen, one of the characteristics of pre-industrial population structure is a high death rate, with an average expectation of life of

11

about forty. This means that the proportion of elderly people in the population was low, and so there were comparatively few elderly people to be provided for. A common way of doing this was for a man to stipulate in his will that his widow should occupy a stated portion of the matrimonial home after his death, with free access to the garden, the privy and the water pump, and perhaps the right to keep a servant. In this way a widow could live in the son's house, but she would constitute a second, independent, household, and there is some evidence to show that, particularly in towns, such subdivision of a large house could become permanent.

The nuclear family of man, wife and children was not very large. The average household size in England was probably less than five in the seventeenth century. An average can of course cover very wide differences, and in fact it is very likely that more than half of the population lived in households with more than six members, with the implication that there was also a significant proportion of single-person households. There are certainly plenty of well-authenticated examples of families with very large numbers of children, a dozen perhaps or fifteen, but they are the exception rather than the rule. Three, four or five children is a much more likely number, the nature of pre-industrial population structure making not only for a high birth rate, but also for a high death rate in that pitifully vulnerable first twelve months of life.

Where the pre-industrial family does differ noticeably from the post-industrial one is in the addition of servants and apprentices to complete the family and make it into a household. Most households had both servants and apprentices, and most men and women could expect to spend much of their adolescence and young adulthood in service. It was a very common practice to send children away, sometimes at a very early age indeed, into another family in order to be brought up and educated. Frequently the two families were related in some way. Sometimes these children were formally apprenticed, sometimes they were not. Apprenticeship was often for seven years, during which time the apprentice could expect to be instructed in the mysteries of his trade by his master, and this was the only form of technical instruction available for almost every trade and profession, including barber-surgeon and attorney. Only physicians, clergymen and barristers had any other form of professional training. Apprentices were not permitted to marry until their period of service was completed, a further restraint upon natural fecundity. A young man would then hope to be taken on as a journeyman by a master-craftsman, when he would live in his household, until he had sufficient money and experience to set up as a master himself, marry and establish his own household.

If family and household was the most important unit in pre-industrial society, then the adult married male head of household was its most important member. In general terms the family as an institution provides for the legitimate production of children, for their education and social placement and for the physical support of all its members. In all of these functions the role of the head of the household was crucial. He was expected to support his wife and children, and if as a consequence of his neglect a child should die then he would be guilty of manslaughter at the least. He was expected to see that all the members of his household went to church regularly, and his responsibility for their moral and spiritual welfare and for their obedience and good behaviour as citizens were stock themes for innumerable moralists and preachers and several Acts of Parliament throughout the sixteenth and seventeenth centuries. His wife occupied a very subordinate role. She could own no property herself and was considered very much the inferior partner in a marriage. Only when she became a widow did she assume many of the responsibilities of her deceased husband, and again there are numerous well-authenticated examples of widows taking over their husband's business and running it very successfully for many years.

For support in many of his functions the head of a household could look to the kinship network, both his own and that of his wife. This was quite informally structured, and there was just as much family strife and bickering as there is today, but relatives, and often quite distant ones, were also often much more supportive than those today, not least because they also could foresee an occasion when they might need help. It was through the kinship network that families looked to place their children as servants and apprentices, to find openings in the church, opportunities in trade and manufacture, for loans in time of need, and for consolation and often more material support in time of sickness, disaster or death. In other words the sixteenth- and seventeenth-century family and its kin was school, employment agency, bank and social security fund all in one.

The household was also the most important economic organisation in Britain in this period. Almost all trade and

13

manufacture was carried on at home. The journey to work was almost unknown, save in such occupations as mining, building, shipbuilding and carrying. Shoes, clothes, textiles, nails, household and farm implements, guns and knives, were all made at home, and forges, workshops and looms were an integral part of a house.

Finally, the family was the unit for social placement. In a hierarchical society such as that of sixteenth- and seventeenth-century Britain birth and kinship were all-important in determining educational opportunities, social status and employment prospects. Contemporaries placed great emphasis upon degree and order within the social hierarchy as a bulwark against anarchy, but in fact there were no legal barriers to social mobility. William Harrison, writing in 1577, divided English society into four categories: gentlemen, citizens or burgesses, yeomen and labourers. But there were no clear or fixed lines of demarcation between these categories, the terms themselves lack precision and were frequently applied on a subjective basis by the neighbours of those men who in their eyes had achieved the status indicated by the label of yeoman or gentleman.

Gentlemen as a category included the nobility, and these were the only members in society whose rank had legal recognition. They were frequently very wealthy indeed, and their landed possessions gave them an influence in society out of all proportion to their numbers. Even at the end of the sixteenth century there were no more than about fifty hereditary noblemen in England. Of gentlemen as such, Sir Thomas Smith wrote in 1582:

> In these days he is a gentleman who is commonly taken and reputed. And whosoever studieth in the universities, who professeth the liberal sciences, and to be short, can live idly and without manual labour and will bear the port, charge and countenance of a gentleman shall be called master.

In other words, gentlemen were often accepted on their own terms, and this was particularly true of Wales, where there were very large numbers of poor gentlemen intensely proud of their pedigrees but with little else to support their pretensions.

Citizens and burgesses formed the ruling groups in towns. They were often very prosperous and in due course they would hope to buy property in the country with a view to making their way into the ranks of the gentry, and this was frequently achieved, especially by their sons.

Yeoman is another ambiguous status indicator. It can mean a prosperous farmer who owns at least part of his farm. It was also a term used in towns of craftsmen who were well-established but not yet in the first rank of urban society. Thus there could be yeomen-blacksmiths and shoemakers as well as yeomen farmers.

In the last group Harrison lumped day labourers, poor husbandmen, artificers such as tailors, shoemakers, carpenters, bricklayers and the like, copyholders and the poor. Again the terms are ambiguous and the divisions blurred. He goes on to note that there were no slaves or bondmen in England. In this however he was mistaken since even as he wrote surveys were being made in different parts of the country and a number of bondmen were discovered, at Leominster, for example, and at Winslow; whilst at Helston, in Cornwall, it was noted in 1576 that Henry Hicke, deceased, a bondman in blood, had had three sons and two daughters. The two daughters had become free upon their marriages, according to the custom of the manor, but the sons were still bondmen, and one in his turn had had five sons and two daughters, all of whom were bond in blood.

In Scotland, however, bondage was actually extended during the course of the seventeenth century. An Act of 1606 forbade anyone to employ a collier or salter unless he could produce a certificate to show that he had been released by his previous master. This was ratified in 1660, and then interpreted in the courts to mean that a man, on accepting employment in a coal mine or salt pan, thereby became bound for life. This was further extended by 'arling', giving a small present to a collier and his wife when a child was christened in return for an undertaking to bring him up as a miner. By the end of the seventeenth century, the majority of Scottish coal miners had been reduced to serfdom.

Any categorisation of society, even so traditional a one as that of Elizabethan England, fails to do justice to the subtleties of social placement, regional and local variations, and the processes of change as a new generation replaces the old. The social structure of sixteenth-century England was a slowly moving organism, not a rigid, immutable caste system.

The social structure of sixteenth-century Scotland differed in a number of important respects from that of contemporary England and Wales. First of all the contrast between nobles and lairds on the one hand, and their tenant farmers on the other was much more marked than it was south of the border, and this finds physical expression in that numbers of substantial stone-built

15

houses of the landed proprietors still survive in the Scottish landscape today, but none of the cabins of their tenants. A few Scottish noblemen were wealthy, even by English standards. Many lairds were poor. There were sometimes fairly prosperous tenant farmers, especially in the Lowlands, but their sub-tenants, whether called crofters, cottars or grassmen, were often wretchedly poor, and nearly as badly off as the landless labourers and servants.

The larger Scottish burghs were in the sixteenth century headed by well-to-do merchants and burgesses, with tradesmen and craftsmen immediately below them. Such men often formed but a small fraction of the population of a burgh, the majority being 'unfreemen', that is servants, journeymen, unskilled labourers and the poor, indeed anyone who was not an admitted burgess.

There was, throughout Scottish society, a much greater emphasis upon kinship and service than there was even in England. Bonds of kinship bound together men of very different social status, in the Lowlands as well as the Highlands, and these relationships were given formal expression in a peculiarly Scottish institution, the 'bond of manrent', a pledge of service in return for protection, a form of obligation that no ranks in Scottish society were too proud to enter into. Ties of this kind certainly contributed to the violence and lawlessness which were endemic in sixteenth-century Scotland. They also meant that society, when under stress, would split, not horizontally, as in England, but vertically. Blood was more important than class at this time.

If the family and household was the unit of society in which a man or woman was born and spent almost the whole of his or her life, there were nonetheless other social organisations which had a claim upon his or her loyalties and affections.

The first of these is the parish. At the end of the fifteenth century the parish was essentially a unit of ecclesiastical organisation, with a parish priest at its head. The parish church was often the largest and most permanent building that many countrymen would know, and it was here that those profoundly significant events of everyone's life would take place: baptism, marriage and burial. The church was also the centre of many other activities such as church ales, parish feasts and festivals, even markets and fairs. Many of these came under increasing attack by the more censorious of Protestant reformers, but they had by no means all vanished by the end of the seventeenth century. During the course of the sixteenth century the parish became increasingly used as a unit of administration and local government, with the vestry meeting almost the governing body of the parish. Churchwardens, overseers of the poor and surveyors of highways were all chosen by the vestry at its Easter meeting, accounts of previous office holders were examined and rates levied.

Parishes could vary enormously in size. In large towns such as London, Bristol and Norwich they were measured in square yards. In remote districts of the Pennines, the Lake District, central Wales and the Highlands of Scotland they were measured in square miles. It was well into the twelfth century before the whole of Britain could be said to be divided up into parishes, and even then some parish boundaries were left vague and imprecise, especially where they crossed moorland or marsh. Thus many parish boundaries were quite new, but others are undoubtedly very ancient, with the very real possibility that they originate in territorial divisions dating from prehistoric times. Some parishes had two or three centres of population and these often had a chapel of ease to save parishioners a long journey to the parish church. Sometimes these chapels of ease were split off to form new parishes. We shall see this happening in the East End of London in Chapter 7; an Act of Parliament of 1708 created a new parish in Birmingham and appointed twenty commissioners to build the new church of St Philip designed by Thomas Archer and finished, save for the top of the tower, in 1715. As new parishes were created in response to population growth so others were amalgamated as the consequence of population decline, and we shall also look at examples of this in Chapter 7.

By the end of the sixteenth century the parish was the humblest unit of both ecclesiastical and secular political organisation. The next rung in the ecclesiastical ladder was the deanery, followed by the archdeaconry and then the diocese, with a bishop at its head. The boundaries of the dioceses in England and Wales were fixed by the beginning of the twelfth century, the bishopric of St Asaph being established in 1141. When the monasteries were dissolved Henry VIII had a number of schemes for creating new bishoprics but in fact only five, Bristol, Gloucester, Oxford, Peterborough and Chester, were created, a sixth – Westminster – lasting only ten years. The bishoprics varied enormously in size, from Rochester, confined to the western third of Kent, to Lincoln, which still stretched from the Humber to the Thames, in spite of losing perhaps a quarter of its area to the new dioceses of Oxford and

Peterborough. England and Wales were divided into two
provinces, the archbishoprics of Canterbury and York.

There were also bishoprics in Scotland but the history
of individual dioceses is much more fluid than it is in
England and Wales, and even at the end of the twelfth
century it seems likely that only Glasgow and St Andrews
had any substantial administrative organisation. Scotland
was unique in western Europe in having no archbishop
until one for St Andrews was created in 1472 and a second

2 Dioceses in England
and Wales

for Glasgow in 1492. Bishoprics throughout Scotland were
formally abolished in 1638, revived in 1661 and finally
abolished in 1689.

As a unit of civil administration parishes were subject
to the authority of the county Justices of the Peace. These
have a long history in England, dating back to the end of
the thirteenth century, and by the end of the sixteenth
they were the principal local agents of the Crown with
wide-ranging criminal and administrative responsibilities.

Justices were country gentlemen appointed by the Crown
by means of the Commission of the Peace, and the Crown
could drop them as quickly as it appointed them. It was
the Justices of the Peace who saw to the detailed administration of the poor law, the repair of roads and bridges,
urging, cajoling and bullying parish officials to carry out
their duties properly in just the same way that the Privy
Council urged, cajoled and bullied the Justices to do their
work properly.

Counties as territorial divisions in England have a very
long history, although the boundaries of Lancashire,
Cumberland and Westmorland were not defined until after
the Norman Conquest. In Wales the story is quite
different. Counties on the English model were first introduced by the Statute of Rhuddlan of 1284, when Flintshire,
Anglesey, Caernarvonshire, Merionethshire, Carmarthenshire and Cardiganshire were created, almost invariably
by amalgamating and regrouping the ancient Welsh
administrative units of cantref and commote. The rest of
Wales remained in the hands of the semi-independent
Marcher lords with jealously guarded privileges and juris-
dictions, including the right to levy private war. Many of
these lordships were forfeited during the Wars of the
Roses; and in 1471 Edward IV was able to establish the
Council of the Marches of Wales to begin the long, uphill
task of bringing law and order into the lordships –
although it was not until Rowland Lee became President
of the Council in 1534 that it began to be really effective.

In 1536 Wales was united with England by the Act of
Union. English law and methods of administration were
introduced, and English was made the sole language of
official business of every kind. The lordships were then
grouped to form the counties of Denbighshire, Montgomeryshire, Radnorshire, Breconshire, Glamorganshire,
Monmouthshire and Pembrokeshire. Their boundaries
often used very ancient boundaries indeed. Thus Radnorshire comprised the former kingdom of Rhwng Gwy a
Hafren, Montgomeryshire the medieval kingdom of
southern Powys, Denbighshire incorporated northern
Powys and three cantrefs of the Perfeddwlad, and Breconshire the ancient kingdom of Brycheiniog and the cantref
of Buellt. Thus, although the Welsh counties are comparatively recent in their creation, they do in fact incorporate
and perpetuate elements from a very ancient landscape
indeed.

It took some time for the details of the 1536 Act to be
applied, not least because its operation was suspended by

19

a royal proclamation in February 1537, and further changes
were made by the Act of 1542. The first Welsh Justices of
the Peace appear in 1541, and the first complete lists of
Justices for all the Welsh counties, old and new, only in
March of 1543. The twelve counties were also grouped
into four sets of three, and the work of the Justices in each
group was subject to the supervision of the court of Great
Sessions, which had been at work since 1284 in the earliest
four shires. It met twice a year in each shire of the circuit.

3 Wales after the Acts of
Union

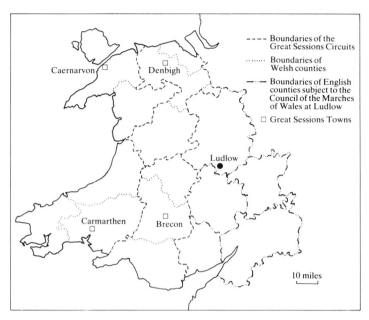

Monmouthshire was excluded from the court of Great
Sessions and instead was incorporated into the English
assize system. The Council of the Marches of Wales
continued to function from its headquarters in Ludlow,
and its authority was extended not only to the whole of
Wales but also to Shropshire, Herefordshire, Worcestershire and Gloucestershire. It was not finally abolished until
1688.

Shires in Scotland have their own history. They originate
in the castle-area attached to each royal castle, built from
the time of David I onwards as successive Scottish kings
sought to extend their control over the country. This
occurs first in what are now the Lothians, where Linlithgow, Edinburgh and Haddington had royal castles
which became the centres for sheriffdoms. Once a royal

castle had been built then a burgh quickly grew up under its protection. Counties such as Peebles, Berwick, Roxburgh, Selkirk, Aberdeen and Banff originated in this way. In 1360 David II granted to the earl of Douglas and his heirs all the lands in Galloway between the Nith and the Cree. This was the origin of Kirkcudbright, which is strictly a stewarty rather than a county, because the Douglas then appointed a steward to administer the area for him. Royal authority was established only very slowly in the Highlands and Islands. Almost the whole of northern Scotland was administered, if that is the word, from Inverness. Only in 1631 was Sutherland split off from Invernesshire, and Caithness and Ross-shire in 1641. Cromarty, consisting of about fourteen small patches of territory scattered across Ross-shire, remained a separate county until the nineteenth century.

Attempts made by successive Acts of the Scottish Parliament between 1587 and 1661 to introduce Justices of the Peace on the English model into Scotland were largely unsuccessful before 1700, and the Scottish counties were ruled on behalf of the Crown by the sheriff, an officer with very wide powers of justice, administration and finance, powers enhanced by the fact that the office was usually heritable in the family of a territorial magnate.

The county was for most parts of Britain the administrative unit immediately below the Crown, although, as we have seen, in Wales and the four English border counties the Council of the Marches had a superior jurisdiction. There was a similar council in the North of England. The Council of the North originated in the last decades of the fifteenth century and was formally constituted by 1537. It had similar responsibilities for law and order in the border areas with Scotland. It simply disappeared at the outbreak of the Civil Wars and was never revived.

However to represent the pattern of administrative structures as a simple hierarchy leading from parish to county is to be guilty of gross over-simplification. There were a host of other bodies and organisations competing for the services, money, loyalty and attention of sixteenth- and seventeenth-century men and women. One of the oldest of these was the manor. By the middle years of the sixteenth century the manor court was beginning to lose much of its authority as a petty criminal court, being increasingly confined to the regulation of the cultivation of the open fields and the registration of transfers of copyhold land, and when enclosure took place it lost even these responsibilities and became moribund. Manorial

boundaries sometimes corresponded with parish boundaries, more frequently not. There could be two, three or
more manors in a parish, and often their lands were so
closely intermingled that a village assembly was necessary
to manage the open fields. We shall see something of the
manor at work in the next chapter.

The equivalent of the manor in Scotland was the barony.
This was ruled by the barony court, presided over by the
lord's bailie or steward, with a clerk who was always a
notary in attendance and the dempster who pronounced
the sentence of the court. The lord at first had almost
absolute jurisdiction in matters both criminal and civil,
including everything relating to the tenure of the land
within the barony and the performance of the services due
from the tenants. It was by means of the barony court that
improving landlords pushed through their changes in the
latter part of the seventeenth century. These powers were
only gradually whittled down during the sixteenth century
as the Court of Session for civil causes, established in
1532 following a papal bull, began gradually to extend its
authority. There was no central criminal court for Scotland
until the office of Justice-General was created in 1514.
Various attempts to improve the administration of criminal
justice in Scotland came to fruition with the establishment
of the High Court of Justiciary in 1671–2. Another legal
institution which was of considerable importance in
sixteenth-century Britain was the incorporated town,
called a borough in England and Wales, a burgh in Scotland. However borough institutions are so intimately
connected with towns as such that they are best left for
consideration in Chapter 6.

This wide and diverse range of local and regional courts
and institutions, each with its own authority, powers and
officers, was supervised to a greater or lesser extent by
national courts and institutions.

In England the national law was the common law, so
called because it applied throughout the king's dominions.
By the opening decades of the sixteenth century it was
administered by men, often of profound if rather narrow
learning, trained at the Inns of Court, men sometimes of
great political and social influence. The profession
expanded rapidly during the sixteenth century, and well
before the end of the century it had become usual for
country gentlemen to spend a year or two at one of the
Inns as part of their general education, although with no
intention of taking up the law as a profession. The
common law was administered through three courts. The

Court of King's Bench dealt with matters in which the Crown was directly concerned, and especially with criminal cases. Secondly, the Court of Common Pleas was concerned with all suits between private parties. Thirdly, there was the Exchequer of Pleas. This court was originally concerned only with revenue cases, but during the sixteenth century, by offering speedier remedies than those available in Common Pleas, it rapidly extended its jurisdiction. From 1579 it was fully assimilated into the common law system and its judges joined those of the other two courts on the assises, when judges from all three courts toured the country on circuit dispensing justice in the county towns and scrutinising the work of the Justices of the Peace.

There were yet further courts. By the sixteenth century the common law had become immensely technical and very rigid. It was in order to overcome these manifest defects and to dispense justice based upon reason and the merits of the case that Chancery, hitherto the principal administrative organ of the Crown, began in the fourteenth century to hear petitions, and by the sixteenth century a formal court of law had emerged, aided immensely by its willingness to hear cases concerning copyhold land, something which the common law courts refused to do.

The Court of Star Chamber was essentially the creation of Cardinal Wolsey and an extension of the powers of the King's Council to deal with the grievances of the subject. Only members of the Privy Council, together with the two chief justices of Kings Bench and Common Pleas, could sit in the Court of Star Chamber. As a court it was flexible, swift, largely free from technicalities, and hence very popular. It dealt primarily with cases in which riot and violence were alleged, including in due course libel and slander as being likely to lead to a breach of the peace, and this is why so many of the cases arising out of enclosure and anti-enclosure disturbances found their way into this court. Another extension of the King's Council was the Court of Requests. It was in existence by the 1530s, primarily as a court designed to give justice to men who were too poor and unimportant to obtain it elsewhere. It was both cheap and swift. However it came under increasing attack later in the sixteenth century from the common law courts, and in 1599 the Court of Common Pleas declared that 'it had no power of judicature'. This was not the end of its useful life, but it did shake its authority to such an extent that in 1643 it simply stopped functioning.

In 1565, Sir Thomas Smith, one of the leading statesmen of the day, wrote 'the most high and absolute power of the realm of England consisteth in the Parliament'. Two points need to be made about this claim. First of all Parliament consisted of three parts, Crown, Lords and Commons, and the consent of all three was necessary before legislation over-riding every other authority and claiming obedience from all could be passed. Secondly it acquired this authority only in the sixteenth century, with the Reformation Parliament of the years 1529–36 the turning point. Henry VIII, by requiring it to legislate on such weighty and momentous matters, gave Parliament, and especially the House of Commons, a significance and a permanence it had not hitherto enjoyed. Even so, it still remained with the Crown when to summon Parliament and when to prorogue or dissolve it.

The composition of the English Parliament changed considerably during the course of the sixteenth century. At the time of Henry VIII there were fifty-two bishops and abbots in the House of Lords. Henry removed thirty-one abbots at the dissolution of the monasteries, and added five new bishops, but the twenty-six lords spiritual were very much in a minority from mid-century onwards, when there were some fifty or sixty temporal lords.

The numbers of the House of Commons grew dramatically during the course of the sixteenth century. At the opening of the reign of Henry VIII there were 296 members. By the close of Elizabeth's there were 462. Some of this increase came when 31 members were added for Wales and Cheshire, being made up of one member for each county and one for each county town except Merioneth. Monmouthshire however acquired two county members and two members for the county town. For the period from 1536 to 1558 there were also two members for Calais. But the real increase in the number of members was due to the creation of boroughs with the right to return members to the House of Commons. Boroughs were incorporated or re-incorporated entirely at the initiative of individual towns, and especially at the prompting of those local country gentry who hoped to be able to secure the new seats for themselves, and in this they were eminently successful, especially in the small boroughs where the franchise was very restricted, with perhaps no more than a dozen burgesses entitled to vote, so that local influence and patronage were usually successful in obtaining the election of a suitable member.

Each English county was represented by two members, chosen by the forty-shilling freeholders, a very much larger electorate than was to be found in any borough, and so county elections could rarely be influenced to any great extent, although this did not prevent the leading county families from managing the elections wherever possible. The Crown could exert decisive influence in only a minority of constituencies and so there were always members who could be outspoken and critical, and management of the House called for considerable political skill, especially when it came to money. Even Henry VIII recognised this and did not always get his own way by any means, since from well before the 1530s the Commons had established the right to freedom of speech – that is the right of members to say what they liked, within the limits of decorum – about the matters put before them. From the 1560s however they increasingly began to demand the right to discuss, not only what was put before them but also anything and everything which they considered to be of interest or concern for the kingdom as a whole. Elizabeth fought this extension of the right to freedom of speech throughout her reign, more especially when it touched the matter of her own marriage and its implications for the succession to the throne, or when it touched foreign policy, trade and monopolies and her role as supreme governor of the Church of England. By the end of her reign her control over the House was running thin and both James I and Charles I, who lacked her political skill and quickly forfeited the respect of the members, lost control altogether.

Wales and England were united by the Acts of 1536 and 1542 and became politically one nation, so that the Parliament of Westminster legislated for both countries. Scotland however was quite independent, and in spite of the union of the Crowns of England and Scotland in 1603 she would remain politically separate from England until the Act of Union of 1707. Only then did the Scottish Parliament come to an end.

The Scottish Parliament differed in a number of important respects from the English. It was made up of three estates, the clergy, the nobility and representatives of the burghs, together with about eight great officers of state and it always sat as one chamber. When it first met it chose the committee of the Articles, usually about eight representatives of each estate. The committee then decided upon the details of legislation, which in any case had almost always been handed down to it by the king, and

25

Parliament then reassembled to accept this legislation
without further discussion. Thus in 1633 Parliament
accepted 168 statutes in one day since bills were read only
once. Nevertheless, in spite of its severely limited powers,
its assent to legislation was almost always considered
necessary, and nor did very tight control by the Crown
prevent opposition from forming and making its voice
heard.

The composition of the Scottish Parliament also showed
some change during the course of the sixteenth century.
An Act of 1428 provided for the election of members from
the counties, but this was never put into operation.
However at the Parliament which met in 1560 at a particularly confused point in Scottish affairs over a hundred
lairds suddenly put in an appearance, claiming to do so
under the terms of the 1428 Act. This situation was regular-
ised by a further Act of 1587, which provided for the
election of two members from each county, save that
Kinross and Clackmannan should return only one member
each. The franchise was confined to freeholders worth 40s.
'of the auld extent', that is, land held of the Crown by a
traditional valuation. It was not until 1661 that it was
widened to include feuars.

As far as the towns were concerned it was only the
Royal burghs that had the right to representation in the
Scottish Parliament. In 1500 there were about forty but by
1700 there were 66. It was usual for each burgh to send
one commissioner, although on several occasions one or
two burghs sent two, and it was only in 1621 that it was
finally established that Edinburgh alone should have the
right to send two. Burgh commissioners were chosen by
the burgh councils, which were very small, self-perpetu-
ating oligarchies, giving plenty of scope for the exertion
of pressure from the Crown.

Scottish abbots and bishops sat in the Scottish Parliament, but because Scottish monasteries were not formally
dissolved their representation was not suddenly with-
drawn. Instead they continued to sit, either as genuine
abbots or else as lay commendators, and when they died
successors appeared until the erection of the abbatal estate
into a lay lordship brought the whole process to an end,
and for many abbeys this did not occur until early in
the seventeenth century. Episcopal representation went in
much the same way. When an individual bishop died he
might be succeeded by a clergyman of the reformed church
or by a lay titular holder. Bishoprics were not formally
abolished until 1638 and their representation continued in

this way until that date, and, briefly again between 1661 and 1689 when the episcopacy was restored.

The Scottish nobility numbered about thirty in the sixteenth century, but there was a massive increase in their numbers during the seventeenth century, many being lords of erection, that is the hereditary lay lordships created out of monastic estates; and by 1701 there were 154 Scottish noblemen.

The body responsible for the day-to-day administration of England and Wales was the Royal Council, chosen by the monarch and responsible only to him. It was Thomas Cromwell who turned this powerful but rather amorphous body into the Privy Council. Its numbers never exceeded twenty during the reign of Elizabeth. It was made up principally of the great officers of state. It could include other men, but Elizabeth in particular was always very careful in her choice of members of the Council. The Privy Council concerned itself with a very wide range of business, from grave matters of foreign policy to trivial details of poor law administration. It advised and reprimanded the Justices of the Peace. It investigated cases of alleged treason and minor breaches of the peace. The only restraint upon its power and authority was the monarch, who was not bound to accept its advice and could repudiate its decisions.

The Scottish Privy Council had even wider powers. It could legislate on its own authority and could override Acts of the Scottish Parliament. It had equally wide judicial powers and could hand down decisions that were legally binding on all concerned. The Scottish Privy Council had a larger nominal membership than did the English, although in practice only a handful of officers of state attended regularly. When James VI reached his maturity he treated his Council much more imperiously than ever Elizabeth did hers, and scolded and chided its members unmercifully. After 1603, when he left for England, he was able, as he claimed, to rule Scotland with his pen, and his Council became little more than an administrative body carrying out the royal instructions.

Finally, in the well-ordering of almost all of these institutions the ability, personality, sex and maturity of the monarch can scarcely be exaggerated. Henry VIII was a powerful, self-willed king who would tolerate no opposition. He was succeeded in 1547 by his only son Edward VI, who, by the time of his death at the age of sixteen in 1553, gave every indication of growing into a bigoted tyrant. He was succeeded by his unhappy elder sister,

27

Mary who, when she died in 1558, was succeeded by
her sister Elizabeth. None of the children of Henry VIII
themselves had children, and the problem of the
succession to the English throne was an important thread
in English politics from the 1530s to the death of Elizabeth
in 1603.

In Scotland there was no adult male king between the
death of James V in 1542 and 1584 when, formally at
least, James VI became head of church and state. In the
intervening years Scotland had to endure a series of
regents, save during the brief personal rule of Mary, which
proved so unsuccessful that she was forced in 1567 to
abdicate in favour of her infant son, James. James was the
great grandson of Margaret, the elder sister of Henry VIII,
who had married James IV, and he succeeded peacefully
to the Crown of England in 1603. It was only a personal
union of the two Crowns however. Political union did not
come until 1707. In 1603 James had two sons living and
the succession problem appeared to be solved.

This then was, in outline, the structure of Britain in the
middle years of the sixteenth century. Its geology and
soils, rivers, mountains and minerals form the raw
materials of the landscape, and provided its inhabitants
with a range of opportunities to be seized and problems
to be overcome. The ways in which men and women
organised themselves exercised a profound influence over
their interaction with the environment. Social organisations, from the family and household to the king in Parliament, are concerned with the distribution of power and
hence the regulation of access to resources. The open field
system of husbandry at its full maturity must have been
one of the most complex codes of practice governing such
access ever devised; a map of an open field village is a
first-rate diagrammatical representation of the code; and
surviving ridge and furrow are the concrete, relic evidence
that the code once existed and has now been superseded
by others. Similarly, the ruins of a long dissolved monastery represent a code of beliefs, moral standards and practices, for long devoutly held, which quite suddenly lost
their value and significance for large numbers of men and
women in sixteenth-century Britain.

In this way the landscape is shaped, moulded and
changed by successive generations, their ideas, skills,
assumptions and beliefs finding physical expression in
boundaries, fields, country houses, churches, even windmills. It is for this reason that the study of the landscape
must begin with its physical structure and then turn to

man in society. But it is impossible, even in the late twentieth century, for a generation to obliterate completely all trace of its predecessors in the landscape. It is the object of the remaining chapters of this book first of all to describe some of the more salient features of the landscape of sixteenth- and seventeenth-century Britain, secondly to explain their origins and purposes, and thirdly to point to at least a handful of survivors from this period into the late twentieth century.

Chapter two

The rural landscape of Britain

Britain in the middle years of the sixteenth century was overwhelmingly and profoundly rural. The great majority of its inhabitants drew their livelihood directly from the land and lived in houses with ploughed fields, meadow and pasture, commons or woods almost at their back doors, as Plate 1 reveals. Towns, as we have seen, were very small and more than one contemporary could suggest that only London really deserved to be called a city. Nevertheless, these are sweeping generalisations which conceal wide regional and local variations. Some towns grew rapidly in the sixteenth and seventeenth centuries, certainly faster than the national average as a whole, but even making allowances for this, it seems very unlikely that more than a quarter of the population was living in towns, however defined, at the end of the seventeenth century. Thus the lives of the great majority of the inhabitants of Britain during the period covered by this book were lived out in farmsteads, hamlets and villages, their horizons bounded by fields and trees, the harvest the most important subject of conversation in a way which today it is almost impossible to comprehend.

However, this intimate relationship of the great majority of the inhabitants of sixteenth- and seventeenth-century Britain with the countryside did not lead to any uniformity in their modes of thought or in the patterns of their lives. Quite the opposite. The variations in geology and climate outlined in the previous chapter mean that no two villages or farms, fields or woods are exactly alike. There is infinite variety, sometimes subtle, sometimes dramatic, in the rural landscape of today, after a century or more of increasing standardisation. In the sixteenth and seventeenth centuries the rural landscape was so diversified as to make any generalisation less than convincing. Nevertheless such generalisations must be attempted unless the reader would drown in an ocean of detail.

Over much of Lowland England, in a great belt of country from Dorset and Somerset in the south-west through to the coastal plains of Durham and Northumberland in the north-east, open field husbandry was widely practised and long-established. Under this system of farming the arable land of the village was divided up into a number of great open fields. Within each field the land was sub-divided into furlongs, and within the furlongs lay the individual strips. (See Plate 6.) This meant that the farm of an individual peasant proprietor lay, not in a single block of land surrounded by a ring fence, but scattered, strip by strip, throughout the full extent of the arable land of the community. A whole field was cultivated at a time,

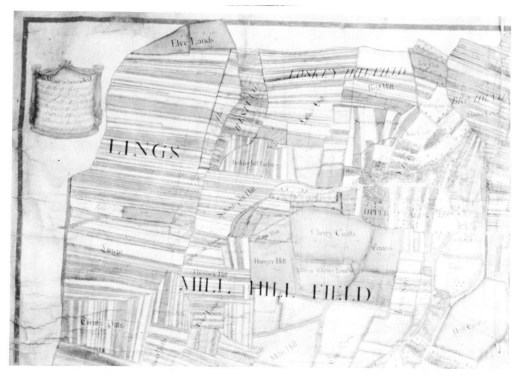

ploughing, sowing and harvesting being organised communally, and at least something of what this meant can be seen in Plate 1. When the crops had been gathered in, the livestock of the villagers were turned out on to the stubble to graze. A field would often lie fallow for a year after it had been cropped, although at Harvington, in Worcestershire, where there were four open arable fields in 1714, there was also a field called 'every year's land', which was cultivated every year. The livestock of the village would continue to graze over the fallow until it was time once more to begin to prepare the land for its next crop.

In addition to arable, each community had its own areas of meadowland, pasture, wood and common. Meadow

Plate 6 A photograph of part of an enormously detailed map of the open fields at Eakring, in Nottinghamshire, made in 1737

31

usually lay close to a stream so that there would be a good
growth of grass. This was mown to provide hay for winter
fodder. The location of an individual villager's strips in
the arable was fixed and permanent. Meadow was also
often divided up into strips, but it was quite usual for these
strips to be re-allocated by drawing lots at the beginning of
each season. Pasture provided permanent grazing for the
village livestock, which were often also turned into the
woods and commons. Woods however could also provide
villagers with fuel, with the wherewithal to repair their
houses and to make carts, fences, implements, tools and
furniture, whilst commons were often quarried for
supplies of stone, gravel and sand.

The organisation of an open field village of this kind
called for close and careful regulation of almost every
aspect of the agricultural year, this regulation being carried
out through a manorial court according to the terms of
village custom. Such custom had no validity beyond the
bounds of its own village, but it did embody the rules
governing the relationship of men with their environment
in that particular community. These rules were very
frequently committed to writing in the sixteenth and
seventeenth centuries, and such custumals, of which
several hundred must survive, provide an extraordinarily
detailed, vivid and intimate record of the manner in which
the members of the community thought that they should
allocate the available resources amongst themselves.

A community practising open field husbandry in this
way often lived in a nucleated group of houses and
cottages clustering about the parish church, their open
fields, woods and pastures lying all round them and stretching on every side to the parish boundary, since parish
and village frequently coincided, whilst the landscape was
at once more open, browner and far less tidy than it is
today.

This is the traditional, conventional open field village,
and it is certainly true that very many villages of central
England were, in the sixteenth and seventeenth centuries,
organised in this way. But the system was so complex and
so flexible that variation within this broad pattern was
almost infinite, and it is this variety that gives to each
village community its own fascinating uniqueness.

First of all the number of open fields into which the
arable could be divided varied considerably. Padbury, in
Buckinghamshire, and surely one of the most frequently
quoted examples of an open field village, had three –
Hedges, East and West Fields. But Prestbury in Glouce-

stershire had eight, and Tirley, in the same county, had nine, of which three, Northfield, Southfield and Nethersfield, were themselves divided into two parts. The township of Denwick, in the coastal plain of Northumberland, had four fields in 1624, and Cuxham in Oxfordshire had three; whilst Wotton Underwood, in Buckinghamshire, had five, although they were worked as three. Rushall, in Wiltshire, in the early seventeenth century, had some 850 acres of arable land. This was divided into about fifteen fields, the largest, Northfield, of about 185 acres, and the average about fifty acres each, each with about five furlongs in it.

Further, many parishes contained more than one village or hamlet, and each of these in turn could have its own arable fields. In Buckinghamshire again, Whaddon had three fields in the seventeenth century, whilst Nash, a hamlet within Whaddon parish, had its own three field system; and at Hanslope, also in Buckinghamshire, not only did Hanslope itself have its own field system, but also Greenend, Pindon End, Longstreet and Woodend Lane. Similarly, in Gloucestershire, the ancient parish of Bishops Cleeve included the hamlets of Woodmancote, Stoke Orchard, Gotherington, Southam and Brockhampton, each of which had its own field system. By way of contrast, Boddington, also in Gloucestershire, had several hamlets but only one set of fields, and in Marsh Baldon in Oxfordshire, four hamlets shared two open fields.

Nor does the number of open fields remain constant. Huish, in Wiltshire, had two arable fields up until the end of the seventeenth century when a third field was created out of the other two. Similarly, at All Cannings, also in Wiltshire, there were two fields at the beginning of the sixteenth century. During the course of the century a third was carved out of them, and by 1649 there were two more. At Great Corringham, in Lincolnshire, there were two fields at the beginning of the thirteenth century. By 1600 there were four, and in 1601 the number was reduced to three, and all this over the same area of land. It was done simply by redrawing the boundaries of the fields.

The fields themselves could vary considerably in size. The two original fields at All Cannings, mentioned in the previous paragraph, were about 750 and 500 acres in size, but at Hasfield, in Gloucestershire, the three main open fields were no more than thirty acres in extent. Similarly, although furlongs and strips seem to have been much more permanent in their layout than the fields into which they were grouped, individual strips could also vary a great deal in size, even within the same furlong. A detailed written survey of Chicheley, in north Buckinghamshire, made in 1557, shows astonishing variation in the size of the strips. In the Barlong field, Brouke furlong contained 110 strips, with a total area of 40½ acres, Nether Blacke lond had 52 strips, covering 20 acres, and Goosecroft furlong had 34 strips in 5½ acres. Many of the strips in the open fields of mid-sixteenth-century Chicheley must have been minute, but they were by no means unique. At Deerhurst, in Gloucestershire, for example, the strips in the open fields averaged no more than a fifth of an acre in size.

Further, the provision of meadow and pasture, common, waste and wood could vary enormously from one community to the next. In North Newnton, Wiltshire, the hamlet of Hilcott had four open fields for arable, perhaps 300 acres. There were three common meadows, totalling perhaps 18 acres, and two areas of common pasture, the Cow Leaze and a sheep pasture of about 20 acres. In contrast, Thornborough, in north Buckinghamshire, had in the early seventeenth century about a quarter of its area given over to common land. Some meadow lay near the stream which served as the boundary with Buckingham, and there were three other areas of lot meadow, but there does not seem to have been a tree anywhere in the parish. In Great Linford, however, another three field parish of about 1800 acres in north Buckinghamshire, there was, according to a survey of 1560, a wood of 61½ acres. This was carefully managed and coppiced regularly to provide a supply of wood: 15 acres had wood of two years' growth worth 4s. the acre, another 15 acres had wood of three years' growth worth 6s. the acre, whilst wood of seven years' growth was worth 14s. the acre. There were 1600 oaks in the wood, and 560 ash and elm trees, the loppings and shreddings of which provided the villagers with kindling. By way of contrast, the parish of Corse lay within Corse Chase, in Gloucestershire. It had three open fields at the end of the sixteenth century, and a fourth had already been enclosed, but two-thirds of the parish lay within the Chase, open, unenclosed and uncultivated, save in so far as it was used for pasture. By the second decade of the seventeenth century there had been much felling of the trees in the Chase, and all the woodland had disappeared by the end of the eighteenth century. Great Linford Wood, however, still survives today.

A survey of North Leigh, in Oxfordshire, was made in 1581, and the map in Fig. 4 is based upon this, together with further details taken from an account of 1651. Like all maps and surveys it can be misleading in that it presents the village frozen at one point in time, whereas in fact change, albeit slow, was almost continuous. There were, in 1581, no less than nine open arable fields, and it is very likely that they had been created by the subdivision of the two fields recorded in 1277, together with the

The rural landscape of Britain

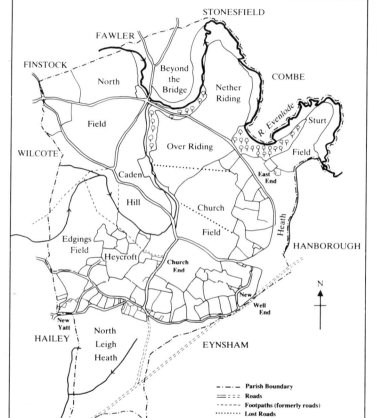

4 North Leigh, Oxfordshire. Acknowledgement: B. Schumer, 'An Elizabethan Survey of North Leigh', *Oxoniensia*, 40, 1975, pp. 309–324

addition of some land cleared from the woodland in later medieval centuries. One of the nine, Sturt Field, was cultivated only by the occupier of Holy Court Farm, and it seems very likely that this field had once been the manorial demesne. There was, in 1581, no resident lord of the manor. The remaining eight fields were divided into furlongs and strips, and were grouped into a very uneven three year rotation or season, in which 40 per cent of the arable was in one season, 37 per cent in the second and only 21 per cent in the third. But the furlongs and strips also varied considerably in size and the distribution through the eight fields of the lands of individual tenants was equally irregular, so that it would seem very unlikely that this rotation pattern in practice posed any real problems for individual farmers. The map also shows that much piecemeal enclosure had been taking place, accompanied by the conversion of some arable to leys. Of twenty-six farms in 1581 only two were freehold, the rest being copyhold, with the half yardland of about 15 acres of arable, a load of hay from the meadow and unstinted grazing on the heath, as the basic unit – although this unit had also been subjected to change brought about by enclosure, exchange and consolidation. Thus the community was essentially one of husbandmen, peasant farmers of only modest prosperity.

The only characteristic that North Leigh shares with ten thousand other communities in sixteenth- and seventeenth-century England is its uniqueness. Only at an almost meaningless level of generalisation can it be said to be a typical English rural community of this period. Nevertheless it does lie within the generalisations of the preceding paragraphs and so may serve at once to illustrate many of the points that have just been made and to emphasise the astonishing variety that individual communities can show within these broad generalisations.

But field patterns are only one part of the rural landscape of sixteenth- and seventeenth-century England, however fascinating their detail and their variety may prove to be. They were brought into being by men engaged about the humdrum business of making a living from the land within the terms and boundaries set by topography, by the limits of the technology of the time and by their own mental horizons. English society generally and rural society in particular was strongly hierarchical in the sixteenth and seventeenth centuries, ranging from cottagers through husbandmen and yeomen to gentlemen. The barriers, especially between gentlemen on the one hand and the rest of rural society on the other, were very real, but lacked any precise or formal definition, and so could be overcome by the lucky, the successful or the pushing, and were in any case subject to much variation over time and space.

To classify countrymen as cottagers, with perhaps no more than an acre or two of land to provide a meagre living when opportunities for earning a wage by working for their better-off neighbours failed; or as husbandmen, with a farm of perhaps 20 or 30 acres and an almost unending struggle to pay the rent; or as yeomen, with a substantial farm, much of it freehold, and sufficient money at least to be able to contemplate sending a son to the university; or as country gentlemen with as many villages as their tenants held strips – is to be as near, and as far, from the truth as the generalised picture of an open field village painted in the opening paragraphs of this chapter is to the reality revealed by closer study of individual communities. Such broad classification may impose some order upon an inchoate mass of evidence, but it also serves to conceal the infinite diversity of the human beings who had actually to make the open field system work. It is through the medium of probate inventories that we can penetrate to at least something of this humanity.

Probate inventories are lists of the personal possessions made shortly after a man's death by a group of his neighbours who, if they were conscientious, went through the rooms of his house and out into his farm recording what they found. Such documents are invaluable, and provide us with those little, hard pieces of concrete fact which bring to life the broad generalisations with which the historian has so often to work. Thus, when John Bowde of Ellesborough in Buckinghamshire, husbandman, died in January 1607, his neighbours went through his three-room cottage – it had only a hall, chamber and buttery – and then out into his farm, where they found 36 sheep, worth £9, wheat, barley and oats in a barn, a stack of peas and another of hay, together with 16 acres of wheat and rye in the open fields, worth £16, and a further 5 acres of tilth, land lying fallow but ploughed ready for sowing, worth 14s. All together he left goods worth £72 7s. 3d., a not inconsiderable sum. Another husbandman, Richard Coxe, at Cold Brayfield, also in Buckinghamshire, died in 1614 leaving personal possessions valued at £131. 3s. 8d. His house was much larger than that of John Bowde, and included hall, entry chamber, inner chamber with loft over, buttery and dairy house, and a kitchen. He had 8 milk cows, 6 heifers and 4 calves, £40 in grain and peas, 16 sheep and lambs and four pigs. The lease of his farm was valued at £10.

The impossibility of categorising human beings accurately or consistently is illustrated by the probate inventory of William Hartley, of Edlesborough in Buckinghamshire. He died in 1634, leaving personal possessions worth £53

17s. 2d., substantially less than the two husbandmen just described, and yet his neighbours called him yeoman. His house had hall, bedchamber and buttery, and he had nine acres of wheat and barley on the ground worth £18 10s., 12 acres of peas and oats, worth £12, and 10 acres of tilth, worth £5. Here is the three-field system, with its three-course rotation, actually at work. His only livestock comprised a horse, a cow and three pigs.

The dangers of classification become even more obvious if we look at the probate inventory of William Smyth, yeoman, of Newport Pagnell, Buckinghamshire, where he died in 1682. First of all, he lived in a town, but it was a town which still preserved its open fields. He had 24 acres in the tilth field, 19 acres and 3 roods in the breach field, and 23 acres, with the dung for them, in the fallow field. Here again is the open field system, its structures and its processes, laid bare for us, each field being at a separate stage in its cultivation. He also had cows, 2 weaning calves, 45 sheep and 12 lambs. But he was much more than just a peasant farmer, since he also dealt in lace, and probably organised its making; for he had £84 in lace in his house and £41 in lace thread and cash. In addition his debtors owed him £505 8s. 5d., and he died worth £843 2s. 2d., a considerable sum indeed. He was, however, by no means exceptional. Richard Barnwell, yeoman, of Willen, died in 1671, his personal possessions worth £1954 19s. 2d. He had livestock out to pasture in several north Buckinghamshire villages: 47 right breed ewes and 40 lambs in Weston, 63 wethers at Chicheley, 108 sheep and 24 lambs in Tickford Park, Newport Pagnell, 40 sheep agisted at Clifton Reynes, 30 acres of wheat and 30 acres of peas at Little Wolston, as well as pasture leased at Milton Keynes. Here is a man who has successfully exploited the demand of the London market for meat, wool, hides and skins to build up a personal fortune that a good many country gentlemen would have been very grateful for.

Variations within the broad pattern of the Midland open-field villages were the result of complex and subtle inter-reactions between men and their environment, where local differences of soil, slope and aspect, even from one end of a field to the other, could be of fundamental importance in swaying men's decisions as to the best way in which to exploit the opportunities offered. At the same time men had also to live with the long-term consequences of their own decisions, and they learnt, not only from their own past experiences, but also from the example of their neighbours. This slow diffusion of experience and example must be added to the environmental constraints to explain regional and local variations even within the Midland pattern; and it must lie, for example, behind the adoption in Wootton Hundred in Oxfordshire – a broad tract of rich, undulating land between the Cherwell and Wychwood – of the practice of dividing each of the two open fields characteristic of medieval townships in the area into two during the course of the sixteenth century; each field often

then became quite separate, with its own pattern of crop rotation.

Topography and experience could produce yet wider and more varied responses. The heavy claylands of central Norfolk and Suffolk were largely enclosed by the end of the seventeenth century, and a wooded landscape of small closes had almost no room for open arable fields. In contrast the lighter soils of western Norfolk were a network of large open arable fields and extensive heathlands linked by a complex system of sheep-corn husbandry in which large flocks of sheep grazed the heathlands and stubble, being folded at night on the arable

Plate 7 The thickly wooded yet intensively cultivated landscape of Warnham Heath, Sussex

39

to maintain the fertility of the soil on which barley was
the principal crop. In the Norfolk Breckland, where soils
were even thinner, patches of heathland were broken up
on a temporary, shifting basis, being cultivated for perhaps
five or six years together, before being allowed to revert
to pasture again. The same kind of shifting cultivation was
to be found on the thin sandy soils of Sherwood Forest,
in Nottinghamshire.

At the same time an entirely different terminology for
landscape features had evolved in East Anglia. 'Field' was
a word applied almost indiscriminately to a quite arbitrary
subdivision of the land of a township: thus in 1646 the
'Northefeyld' of Sporle with Palgrave, in Norfolk,
contained a hundred acres of woodland, 26 acres of
pasture and much enclosed meadow, but no arable. At
Walsham le Willows, on the heavy clays of High Suffolk,
there were in 1577 two manors totaling in all some 2,700
acres, of which 1052 acres were pasture, 328 were arable,
123 were meadow and 114 were woodland. There were
over twenty subdivisions, called 'wents', of the lands of
the township, but they seem to have had no purpose
beyond being convenient units for the preparation of a
written survey. They were divided from one another by
lanes, ways and brooks. There was some common pasture,
but almost no evidence that there had ever been any common arable. Instead everywhere fields and closes were
separated by hedges and fences and it is clear that tenants
had complete control over the way they used their lands.

Farms and fields in Kent and the Weald were everywhere enclosed. Fields were generally squarish and on the
large side in East Kent and Romney Marsh, but even here
the average field size was about 11 acres. In the Weald
fields were smaller, often irregularly shaped, and separated one from the other by thick hedges called shaws,
giving to the landscape the well-wooded appearance
which it still enjoys today. (See Plate 7.) Although there
were no common arable fields there were common
meadows and pastures, some of which were quite extensive – Blackheath Common for example was over 250 acres.
The landscape of this part of England was further
diversified by the development during the sixteenth
century of market gardening around Sandwich, Gravesend
and Greenwich, of orchards, especially for cherries,
between Gillingham and Faversham, and of hop gardens,
especially around Goudhurst.

The rural landscape of Cornwall differs yet again, and
there the subtle patterns produced by changes over time

in the response by man to his environment are particularly apparent. In some parts of Cornwall, around Zennor, for example, field boundaries are built of huge granite boulders, filled in and topped out with smaller stones. Such walls were almost certainly made as part of the process of clearing land for cultivation, and once built they would have been impossible to move. Their size and massive permanence, coupled with the fact that the fields they enclose are small and irregular but basically squarish in shape, lead many archaeologists to suggest that they are prehistoric in origin. Open, common arable fields divided into strips were to be found in medieval Cornwall – at Helston for example, and at Kilkhampton – but enclosure was already taking place by the opening decades of the sixteenth century to produce a landscape of rectangular closes with sinuous boundaries, clearly reflecting the shapes of the plots of land which were enclosed. Yet further enclosure, in the eighteenth and nineteenth centuries, from the waste and moorland, tended to produce a pattern of fairly straight field boundaries. Learning to recognise the layers in the Cornish rural landscape is one of the most fascinating and rewarding exercises for any landscape historian.

The coastal plains of Northumberland and Durham were characterised by townships with three open arable fields. Shilbottle, in Northumberland, for example, had three open fields in 1624: North Field of 341 acres, Middle Field of 268 acres and South Field of 349 acres. There were fairly substantial areas of wood, but very little meadow, and 1227 acres of common pastureland. In the Pennine uplands, however, a more rugged terrain, a harsher climate and acid and often poorly drained soils yielded vast areas of moorland pastures with only very restricted valley bottoms and south-facing slopes where small enclosed arable fields could be persuaded to yield thin crops of oats.

Of 288 townships in Cumberland, there is evidence from at least 220 of the presence at some time in the past of open fields cultivated in strips, and in many the common fields were still being added to up until the end of the sixteenth century. But again topography and climate exerted a profound influence over the ways in which this common arable was organised. Field and furlong seem to have been interchangeable terms and tenants could find their lands scattered in strips through some, although not all, of the furlongs. Only oats would ripen in the brief, cool summers of the Lake District, and when it was harvested cattle were turned into the stubble to graze until

41

it was time to prepare the land for the next crop. In other words the only fallow allowed to this infield land was the six winter months, and there is no trace of a three field rotation. In addition to the infield there was an outfield, divided up into sections called brakes or rivings. One or more of these brakes was cultivated until it was exhausted, when it was allowed to revert to rough pasture and the next plot was broken up. Oats had to be grown to provide food both for man and beast, but the mainstay of the Lake District farmer was his right of access to huge areas of rough moorland and fell pasture, often running into thousands of acres. Thus the manor of Castle Carrock, in the barony of Gilsland, extended in 1603 over 2615 acres, of which 1934 were commons.

Much piecemeal enclosure was taking place in the Lake District in the sixteenth and seventeenth centuries. The common arable fields of Carlisle had disappeared by 1600, and in that manor of Castle Carrock just mentioned there were in 1603 14 furlongs minutely subdivided into strips, with only a handful more than 2 acres in size; and yet in only two of these furlongs is there definite mention of arable, the rest being given over to meadowgrass ground and woodground. Not all of these strips were enclosed, but the furlongs themselves were small, perhaps 20 or 30 acres, and many of the abutments describing their locations speak of enclosures. There was also at least one close of pasture, of 24½ acres, shared amongst four tenants, so it is clear that enclosure did not everywhere mean occupation in severalty, or unshared tenure.

The arable was of the first importance in sixteenth- and seventeenth-century Britain. It provided grain for bread and drink, fodder for animals, and, as we shall see in the next chapter, an increasingly wide variety of specialised crops such as woad, madder, flax and hemp which yielded raw materials for industry. The arable could not be ploughed without the efforts of horses and oxen, which in their turn required meadow and pasture for their sustenance. This meadow and pasture also allowed the rearing of cattle to provide meat, hides, cheese, milk and butter, and sheep to yield wool, meat and milk for cheese. The relationship between arable and pastoral husbandry was close and intimate, and in the absence of cheap and reliable transport, one could not exist without the other, which is why men struggled to grow oats in the rain-swept valleys of central Wales, Cumberland and the Highlands of Scotland. They had to, if they and their livestock were to eat any cereal-based foodstuffs at all.

To have emphasised the importance of the arable and its inter-relationship with meadow and pasture is only right and proper. After all, the achievements of seventeenth-century literature, art, learning, science and music depended upon it. It can, however, give a misleading impression of a neatly and tidily cultivated Britain, an impression that would be very misleading. Vast areas of upland Britain, whether in Dartmoor, central Wales, the Pennines, the southern uplands or the Highlands of Scotland, were given over to rough grazing, bog and heather covered moorland, areas extending in many cases over tens of thousands of acres. When Hexham Manor and Allendale Common, in Northumberland, were finally enclosed in the nineteenth century, the award related to 40,322 acres. Much of this upland cannot be cultivated even today; the soils are too acid, the climate is too harsh, the growing season is too short, and so it is left to the sheep and the grouse.

There were however other districts in Britain where the arable formed only a subsidiary part of the landscape, and these were areas of woodland, marsh and fen.

By the middle years of the thirteenth century something like a third of the total area of England had been declared Royal Forest in the sense that it was subject, not only to the common law, but also to the Forest Law, a code designed to protect above all else the deer and the woodland that gave it cover. Such a huge tract of the country could not have been densely wooded, and in fact towns and villages, open fields and meadows were to be found everywhere within it. Nevertheless some parts were densely wooded, and although the Royal Forests were shrinking steadily from the middle years of the thirteenth century onwards, they still made up an important element of the sixteenth- and seventeenth-century rural landscapes. Shotover in Oxfordshire, Bernwood in Buckinghamshire, Salcey, Whittlewood and Rockingham in Northamptonshire, Delamere and Macclesfield in Cheshire were all Royal Forests at this time.

The medieval centuries were marked by much piecemeal clearing of the woodland in the Royal Forests. Sometimes the clearings would remain as small closes, often distinguishable even today on the map and the ground by their thick, sinuous boundary hedges. Sometimes the clearings were divided up into strips and incorporated into the open arable of a village. Whatever the fate of individual clearings the long-term results were the same: the slow, irreversible disappearance of the woodland. Although the

Royal Forests were in theory administered by royal officials, in fact central control was either very lax or non-existent for decades together, leaving the way wide open for corrupt or lazy officials to allow the destruction of trees, the enclosure and cultivation of plots of land and deer poaching to go almost unchecked. Edward Bostock of the Chamber in the Forest of Macclesfield and chief keeper of the Forest reported in 1638 that His Majesty sustained great damage in the keeping of his deer in the Forest because John Hallywell, one of the keepers of the Forest, together with two Derbyshire men, kept 300 sheep in the Backsydes, within a mile of the Chamber, and one of the principal summer feeding grounds for the deer. He reported many other enclosures in the Forest but seemed to be powerless to do anything about them.

By the last decades of the sixteenth century Royal Forests were almost everywhere in a sorry state. A survey of the Forest of Bernwood made in 1586 shows over half of the Forest, 2600 acres out of nearly 5000, enclosed. Large areas were coppice, from which the deer would have been excluded, and 700 acres were enclosed for sheep pastures. Three villages inside the Forest, Brill, Boarstall and Oakley, could turn their livestock into the woods to graze without stint, and several neighbouring villages claimed similar rights in return for quite nominal payments. A rather similar survey of the Forest of Delamere, in Cheshire, made in 1627, reveals a slightly better situation, with 8346 acres still open and unenclosed out of a total area of 12,672, but the number of timber trees was said to be sadly depleted. On the other hand the High Forest of Teesdale, said in 1647 to be 21 miles round, had by that date no timber trees left at all, no coppices or underwood, and the roe deer were utterly destroyed.

A similar story is to be told for the Forest of Bowland, high in the Pennines on the borders between Lancashire and Yorkshire. Here there was much small-scale enclosure and clearing in the sixteenth century, leading to the creation of a landscape of small hedged or walled enclosures, and isolated farms. At first these were of timber and thatch but by the beginning of the seventeenth century they were built of stone, in a landscape from which timber trees had all but disappeared; in 1556 there were said to be 1327 oak and ash trees, in 1652 there were only 96. Eventually the tenants came to an agreement with the Crown permitting them to enclose and improve upon a large scale, and some 10,000 acres of waste and moorland were enclosed and converted to meadow and pasture, a process which pushed the limits of cultivation to the 900 feet contour line, a point not passed even today.

There were however other areas of woodland outside the Royal Forests, and these, if properly managed, could be extremely valuable. Woodland can produce two types of wood. Most English trees, including oak, ash, elm, beech and hazel, can be coppiced very successfully. This entails felling the tree, and then allowing it to shoot from the root, or stool. The shoots are then cut when they have reached an appropriate size, and the cycle begins again. The young shoots are of course extremely attractive to grazing animals, and coppices need to be enclosed. The wood, when cut, can be used for an enormously wide range of purposes, depending upon its size, and hence age, when it is cut. Handles for every kind of domestic and farm implement, hurdles, fencing, spoons, plates and dishes, furniture, wood for carts, sledges and wheels, and firewood, can all be produced by coppicing, and the bark from oak can be used in tanning. Larger timber, produced by felling mature trees, would be used in house and ship building. A survey of Eymoor Wood, in Upper Arley, in Worcestershire, made in 1649, the property of the Dean and Chapter of Worcester cathedral, shows what a well-managed wood could be like. The wood covered 300 acres, divided into 21 coppices, with 1,558 timber oaks. The keeper lived in a timber and thatch house, and he was required to plant a hundred perches of quickset every year until the entire wood had been newly quickset. The wood seems to have been used primarily as a source of fuel, since faggots of wood had to be carried to the banks of the river Severn, loaded upon barges, carrying 17 tons at a time, and shipped downstream to the Priors Slip at Worcester. The wood was said to be very well preserved from grazing cattle, and the timber trees were described as being 'very handsome, tall and smooth'. The probate inventory of William Willmott, of Fingest, in Buckinghamshire, gent, who died in 1690, shows just how valuable this firewood could be. At the time of his death he had 1,232 loads of beechen billet wood on the wharf at Millend, on the Thames, worth £160 3s. 3d., another 1,115 loads still in his woods worth £89 3s. 9d., and a further 73 stacks of beechen stackwood in his woods worth £21 18s.

Tenants on several manors of the Duchy of Cornwall in Cornwall were expected by the terms of their leases to plant a number of trees every year, and the conditions under which woodland was let out were carefully stated. On the manor of Bonyalva, for example, in the western

45

part of St German's parish, a lease made in 1626 of an acre and a half of woodland to Thomasine Gache laid down very clearly that she was to cut the wood only once every ten years, and after every cutting 'to enclose and encoppice the same and to keep it from hurt or spoyle by beasts'. Similarly, John Cunliffe, gent, of London, had a lease in 1629 of four separate areas of woodland in Liskeard amounting to 125 acres. He also was to cut the wood only once every ten years and then 'to fence the same with mounds and hedges and to preserve the said woodes from biteings, treadings and other hurt by beasts which might hurt or hinder the groweth of the woodes.'

Woods and forests were not the only areas of Britain to have a distinctive landscape and a distinctive way of life. There were huge areas of unimproved marshland, particularly along the coasts and in the lower reaches of rivers in sixteenth- and seventeenth-century Britain. Men had long adapted themselves to living and working in this environment. In the fens of Lincolnshire and Cambridgeshire men walked upon stilts when herding their cattle, which on occasion had to be taken by boat to their grazing grounds. Cattle, sheep and horses were kept in large numbers, and they were the mainstay of the economy of the fens. The winter flooding, brought about by heavy winter rains in the surrounding uplands, caused the sluggish rivers to overflow, the flood waters bringing with them thick deposits of silt which served to enrich the meadows and pastures in the following summer, and it was rights to common of pasture over thousands of acres of lush summer grazing grounds which lay at the heart of the fenland economy. Groups of villages shared common land in the fenland pastures. The numbers of animals that individuals could have were carefully regulated, and each villager was expected to have his own distinctive brand; and these, certainly for Cottenham and Stretham in Cambridgeshire, were recorded in a book to be kept by the Town Officers who had the oversight of the regulations.

The fens also yielded fish, especially from the permanent lakes such as Whittlesey Mere, together with wildfowl, reeds, turves and sedges. Plovers, knots and godwits were fattened for the London market, where they were considered a delicacy. 'Fendowne', perhaps from the Reed Mace, provided bedding, whilst reeds were cut for thatching, and again the harvesting was carefully regulated. Hassocks, cut from great tufts of coarse grass, made kneeling on the stone floors of churches more comfortable. At the same time the rivers themselves provided a network of 'moving highways', connecting Cambridge and Thetford to the sea, and making places like King's Lynn, Spalding and Wisbech into flourishing ports, whilst villages such as Burwell, Lode, Reach and Swaffham Bulbeck became busy centres of an inland trade that developed along the drainage canals.

A similar, highly specialised, way of life had grown up in other marshlands, with local adaptations to local circumstances, in the Isle of Axholme, for example, and in the Somerset Levels.

Those who had directly to earn their livings by cultivating the soil in sixteenth and seventeenth-century Scotland had almost everywhere a more difficult task than did those in England. The climate was harsher, the topography more rugged, the soils thinner and less fertile. The system of husbandry which had developed by the middle decades of the sixteenth century was however just as subtle a response to the challenges and opportunities provided by topography as was anything to be found in contemporary England.

The basic land unit was the farm, which could vary enormously in size, from perhaps 10 or 15 acres to several thousand. The proprietor let his land out at a rent, payable at first in kind, then in a mixture of cash and kind and then on occasion entirely in cash. Payments in kind could include oats, meal, malt, hens, geese, butter, cheese, cattle, goats and fish, together with services such as ploughing, harrowing and reaping the proprietor's own crops, carrying services and peat cutting. It was a growing practice, especially in the seventeenth century, for these rents in kind to be sold, often to the tenants themselves, since the proprietor found it more convenient to have the ready cash.

Sometimes the farm was let to a single tenant, a tacksman, and often a kinsman of the proprietor. He would then either cultivate the whole of the farm himself, employing cottar labour, or else he would sublet it to other tenants. In other cases the farm was leased to joint tenants, who were then collectively responsible for paying the rent. Some of these joint tenants could, and did, then sublet their holdings. Whatever the pattern adopted in individual farms, and there could be considerable variation in the size of holding and the way in which they were set to tenants, the results were in practice often very similar.

There was first of all an almost complete absence, save in the eastern lowlands from Berwickshire to the Firth of Forth, of anything resembling the large villages of midland

England, formed round a central nucleus. Instead the cottages of individual tenants, rarely as many as a dozen, were loosely grouped into a fermtoun or clachan. Any population growth, which was likely to be slow and erratic, was accommodated by the establishment of a new fermtoun rather than by expansion of an existing one.

Secondly, although the nature of the terrain dictated that, save in the eastern lowlands, pastoral husbandry was of greater significance than arable, the actual organisation of the agricultural cycle on a farm was almost everywhere the same. Only on some large sheep farms in the southern uplands was there a complete absence of arable.

The arable of a farm was divided into two kinds: infield and outfield. The infield was cultivated every year, being sown with oats and bere, a four-row variety of barley which was better adapted to acid soils than other strains, could be sown late and yet ripened early. The cultivation of wheat was confined to the eastern lowlands, since only here was there a reasonable prospect that it would ripen. The fertility of the infield, low as it was, could be sustained only by applying to it all the available manure of the fermtoun. Cattle were stalled during the winter months and this meant a ready accumulation of animal dung. The cottages of the tenants frequently had their roofs renewed and the soot-laden turf and thatch was also spread over the infield. Finally, when the harvest was complete, livestock were turned into the stubble to graze and leave their droppings. In coastal regions sand and seaweed were added, and in many districts turf was stripped from the hillsides, again to be added to the precious infield. Even with all this effort yields were low, four-fold in a good year, six-fold in an exceptional one.

The infield itself was divided into strips, curved ridges of land sometimes twenty feet wide and as much as six feet from the crown of the ridge to the bottom of the hollow. The lands of an individual tenant 'lay in run-rig', in other words they were scattered in strips throughout the infield. (See Fig. 5.) There is some slight evidence to suggest that the strips were occasionally redistributed among the tenants, and much more to show that individual holdings were periodically re-defined or 'delt', to discourage encroachment.

The arable of the infield was supplemented by the outfield. Here the land was cultivated on a shifting system. The actual area broken up each year could vary considerably; but once it had been ploughed it was cropped continuously, without being manured, for perhaps four years, or until it was exhausted. It was then allowed to go out of cultivation and a new area of the outfield was ploughed, having the previous summer been manured to a limited extent by having livestock penned on it at night. The crop from the outfield, invariably oats, was always poor, and was used primarily to provide fodder for livestock.

Neither infield nor outfield lay in very large stretches, but instead, owing to the nature of the terrain in Scotland,

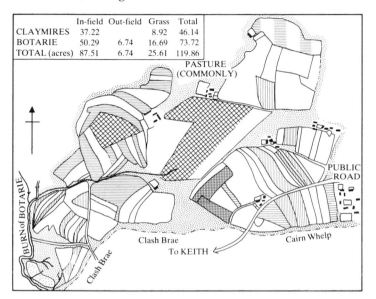

	In-field	Out-field	Grass	Total
CLAYMIRES	37.22		8.92	46.14
BOTARIE	50.29	6.74	16.69	73.72
TOTAL (acres)	87.51	6.74	25.61	119.86

5 Claymires and Botarie, in the parish of Cairnie, Banff, about 1760. Acknowledgement: G. Kay, 'The landscape of improvement, A Case Study of Agricultural Change in north-east Scotland', *Scottish Geographical Magazine*, 78, 1962, pp. 100–108. Six of the nineteen holdings have been variously shaded

in comparatively small patches, often intermingled, together with other pieces of land which were too wet or too infertile to be cultivated and which were mown for hay and were sometimes so poor and so stony as to be fit for nothing. There were, in suitable locations, yet other areas of arable. Along the banks of rivers and streams were patches of land which flooded in the winter and yet were sufficiently dry in the summer for them to be ploughed. This was haugh land. Finally, where local conditions allowed, areas of hillside were stripped of their turf and heather, the vegetation was burned and the ashes mixed in with the soil, and oats grown until the land was exhausted, when it was abandoned and another patch brought into cultivation. This was brunt land.

Both infield and outfield were enclosed within a head dyke. (See Plate 8.) This was sometimes a turf bank and ditch, sometimes a stone wall. It encircled the fermtoun and the arable. Beyond lay the common muir, an area of rough grazing and pasture running sometimes to thousands of acres. Here the livestock of the tenants were turned during the summer months to make such living as they could. The head dyke served to keep them out of the growing crops. Sometimes, especially in the Highlands, cabins were built out in these hill pastures and entire communities would migrate in the summer months to these shielings to tend the cattle and perhaps, if conditions were particularly kind, to grow some oats.

Plate 8 The village bay of St Kilda, Inverness-shire. The head dyke separating the infield and the ferm-toun from the moorland grazing is clearly visible

There was, of course, much local and regional variation in Scotland in the sixteenth and seventeenth centuries in the proportions of infield to outfield, and of both to pasture and grazing. Many farms in East Lothian were primarily arable and suffered a severe shortage of summer pastures. Other farms in the Highlands and southern uplands, the sheep runs on the Buccleuch estates in Yarrow and Ettrick for example, had no more than an acre or two of arable. There were similar variations in the proportions of single tenant as opposed to joint tenant farms, both lowland Aberdeenshire and upland Roxburghshire had more single tenants than joint tenants, for example. Nevertheless there was little significant difference between Highland and Lowland, save that settlement was even more thinly scattered in the Highlands than the Lowlands.

The rural landscape was often open and bleak. Trees were scarce, and woodland of any extent was to be found only in sheltered glens in the Highlands. Roads were very few and poorly made, and wheeled traffic almost unknown outside towns. The broad acres of undulating cornland to be found in village after village of midland England were absent from Scotland. Instead, over much of Lowland Scotland, arable, meadow, bog and stony pasture lay scattered and interspersed, reflecting in microscopic detail the underlying structures of soil and drainage, whilst in the Highlands there were vast expanses of heather, moor and upland grazing, entirely uninhabited in the winter months. The cottages of the tenants in the fermtoun were almost invariably one storey cabins with turf or thatched roofs, the ubiquitous midden outside the door, in sharp contrast to the two- or three-storeyed stone-built mansion houses of the proprietors.

There were probably more Royal Forests in Scotland than there were in England, although it is often difficult to establish their exact boundaries. However, unlike practice in England, where the highwater mark of Royal Forests was reached in the thirteenth century, the story thereafter being one of continuous shrinkage, the Scottish kings continued to create Royal Forests into the fifteenth and sixteenth centuries. The Forest of Monteith, for example, was created in 1454 and proved to be a very popular hunting ground for the Scottish court when it was in residence at Stirling Castle. Further, the Scottish Forest Laws were not nearly as savage as those in England, and hunting only became a gentleman's pastime after an Act of the Scottish Parliament, passed in 1621, forbade any man to hunt and hawk who 'has not a plough in heritage', at least the equivalent of the English forty-shilling freeholder.

One of the largest, and certainly the most famous, of the Scottish Royal Forests, was the Forest of Ettrick, known simply as The Forest. It was 27 miles long by 16 broad, and by the middle of the fourteenth century it had been divided into three wards south of the Tweed, Ettrick, Yarrow and Tweed, with Selkirk a ward north of the river. It returned to the Scottish Crown in 1455, when it was divided into holdings called 'stedes', 44½ in Ettrick, 23¾ in Yarrow and 17 in Tweed – their boundaries frequently coinciding with parish boundaries. Sheep farming became increasingly important, and the tenants of stedes paid part of their rents in lambs. Early in the sixteenth century James IV began to set The Forest to feu farm. Tenants could build a farm house, make fish ponds, build bridges and plant oak trees, and from 1509 many were being granted the right to plough in the customary places, with the implication that cultivation had already been going on, and for some time. By the end of the fifteenth century the pressure on the woodland was so great that in the Statutes of Ettrick of 1499 attempts were made, in vain as it turned out, to halt the felling of trees. By the end of the sixteenth century much of the upland areas of The Forest were given over to extensive sheep runs.

As in England, there was much destruction of woodland in Scotland in the fifteenth and sixteenth centuries as timber became more valuable than deer, and especially in the south and the east of the country as salt pans were established and coal mines opened up, with the consequent demand for timber for fuel and pit props. Acts of the Scottish Parliament going back to 1424 attempted to preserve the woodland, and an Act of 1503 claimed, with some exaggeration, that Scottish woods were 'uterlie distroyit'. An Act, passed in 1579, made it a capital offence on the third conviction for cutting green wood. Not even this savage penalty could preserve the woods for long, and when Fynes Moryson travelled through Fife in 1598 he noted that trees were very rare, apart from little groves about the dwellings of noblemen and gentlemen.

The local and regional variations compelled by topography in the rural landscape of Wales in the sixteenth and seventeenth centuries were compounded by the existence of two very different social and legal systems. Along much of the border country with England and throughout the lowlands of south Wales as far west as Pembrokeshire the English open-field system was usual. In central and northern Wales, and indeed in many of the remoter, more upland areas of south Wales, the ancient Welsh tenures were to be found.

In the valleys of the Wye, Llynfi and Usk in Breconshire, along the Monmouthshire coastlands, in the Vale of Glamorgan and the Gower Peninsula, in Pembrokeshire and in the coastal river valleys of Cardiganshire the three field system was common and widespread. The fields themselves were often smaller than their counterparts in England, and the lack of adequate documentary evidence together with early enclosure means that it is often almost impossible to establish exactly the number and size of these fields, but the legal framework within which they functioned was in all essential points very similar to that to be found in England. (See Plate 9 and Fig. 6.)

The arable was often supported by large areas of common pasture in the hills, and livestock rearing, especially of cattle, was very important. Cheese and butter were shipped in great quantities from ports such as Swansea, Oxwich and Porteynon, where a new quay had

to be built to handle the traffic, to ports along the North Devon and Somerset coasts, such as Minehead and Ilfracombe. Many of the boats engaged in this trade were owned in partnership by farmers whose cattle provided the milk that formed the basis of their prosperity.

In central and north Wales the ancient Welsh tenures still persisted. In those districts more open to English influences they were already crumbling by the end of the fifteenth century, but although the statute of 1542 brought

Plate 9 An aerial view of Rhosili, in the Gower peninsula. It should be compared with Fig. 6

53

6 The manor of Rhosili,
Glamorganshire, in 1780.
Acknowledgement: M.
Davies, 'Rhosili Open
Field and Related South
Wales Field Patterns',
*Agricultural History
Review*, 4, 1956,
pp. 80–96

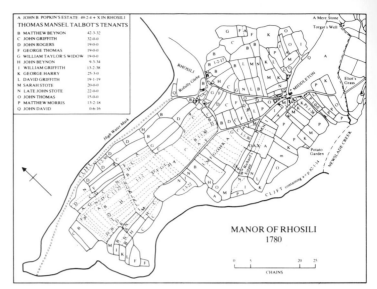

them officially to an end the change was for long widely resisted and it was the second half of the seventeenth century before it was finally accepted.

Land held by bondmen in medieval Wales was called *tir cyfrif*. It could include arable shareland cultivated in strips. It was subject to heavy rents in services and kind. By the end of the fifteenth century there were very few bondmen as such still remaining, and during the sixteenth century the services were commuted for cash rents. These often could not be paid, and so the tenants were evicted. Land held by free tenants was called *tir gwelyawg*, and again it could be cultivated in strips. This was subject to partible inheritance (*cyfran*), by which property was divided equally among all the sons of the proprietor. The consequence was the minute subdivision of property. Early in the seventeenth century it was said of the lordship of Elvell, in Radnorshire, that in three or four descents a small tenement of thirty or forty acres might be subdivided into as many parts, which greatly impoverished the inhabitants. It was possible however for the land of a group of co-heirs to remain undivided, when it was called *cytir*. This applied particularly to areas of pasture and grazing.

The disappearance of these ancient tenures, more particularly after 1542, brought considerable change into the Welsh rural landscape. At first this change was directed primarily at the legal foundations of its organisation. In due course it also affected its visual appearance. Change in the rural landscape was not however unique to Wales, but was also to be found throughout Britain. It forms the subject for the next chapter.

Rural change

The previous chapter was concerned to provide a portrait, however vague, generalized and misleading, of some of the principal man-made features of the rural landscape of sixteenth- and seventeenth-century Britain, and more especially its fields and their boundaries and the farms into which these fields were composed, its meadow and pasture, heath and moorland, its woods and marshes. These are of course by no means the only man-made elements of the rural landscape, and in later chapters we shall look at others, particularly the dwellings in which lived the men and women whose hands and minds shaped the landscape, the churches in which they worshipped, and the methods of travel which were available to them, all of which are illustrated in Plate 1 on pp. xvi–xvii.

A portrait, however, is essentially static, a moment frozen in time, whereas in fact men and women, their ideas and attitudes, change, however minutely, from day to day and from generation to generation, and it is this absence of movement through time that can make a static portrait so misleading. Change did take place in the rural landscape of sixteenth- and seventeenth-century Britain, sometimes slowly, sometimes dramatically, affecting only a field or two, or a hedgerow, in one year, an entire village in another; but the results were cumulative, so that the landscape of Britain at the end of the seventeenth century was quite unlike that at the beginning of the sixteenth.

As we have just seen, much of rural Britain in the opening decades of the sixteenth century had of necessity to be given over to arable husbandry, and crops were almost everywhere sown and reaped in fields which were cultivated in common, whether in fields subdivided to give a two- or three-course rotation, with at least part of the land lying fallow for a year, or else in an infield from which a crop was taken every year with only the winter months in which to lie fallow, supplemented by the shifting cultivation of an outfield. However, no sooner do documents begin to survive from which it is possible to reconstruct, in outline at least, the main features of this communally organised system of husbandry, namely the

55

middle and last years of the twelfth century, than it is equally clear that the system has its own history. It is not fixed and immutable, but is subject to change and one of the most significant and far-reaching factors making for change is enclosure.

Enclosure of areas of open arable land was certainly taking place in the thirteenth century. The catastrophic social, demographic and economic dislocation brought

Plate 10 The deserted village at Dunton, in Buckinghamshire. Enclosure here was a protracted affair, but was completed without a private Act of Parliament. The house platforms of the abandoned village and the medieval ridge and furrow are both clearly visible

about by the Black Death and subsequent outbreaks of the plague in the second half of the fourteenth century served to hasten the process. Labour became scarce, farms were without tenants, the arable tumbled to rough pasture. There was at the same time a rising demand in western Europe for English wool. Until the last two decades of the fifteenth century it was more profitable to rear sheep for their wool than it was to grow corn for men. Enclosure and depopulation of whole villages was the result. Men and women were turned out of their cottages which, because of their flimsy construction, quickly fell into decay and disappeared, leaving only grass-grown house platforms behind, many of which can still be seen in the landscape today. Arable fields were enclosed and divided up by hedgerows.

By the early sixteenth century so loud was the public outcry against the enclosers that the government of Henry VIII was goaded into setting up a commission of inquiry in 1517 into the extent of enclosure in some of the worst affected counties – these included Buckinghamshire, Northamptonshire, Berkshire, Oxfordshire, Leicestershire and Warwickshire. This was followed by a series of attempts to stem the tide of enclosure, with further commissions of inquiry in 1545, 1566 and 1607, the latter prompted by a serious outbreak of rioting in Northamptonshire and Leicestershire. By the early years of the seventeenth century hostility to enclosure was slowly fading, not least because its advantages were beginning to be appreciated and it was gradually becoming apparent that it need not necessarily be followed by large-scale depopulation. At the same time, more and more enclosure took place by agreement among all those concerned rather than by force or fraud. Further, rising demand for food-stuffs and industrial raw materials meant that the motives for enclosure were broadening out to encompass cattle breeding and arable husbandry, especially for specialised industrial crops, as well as sheep rearing.

By the early years of the eighteenth century the legal disadvantages of enclosure by agreement were becoming increasingly apparent and so, slowly at first – only six were passed before 1702 – recourse was had to a private Act of Parliament. By the 1760s this had become the accepted method of enclosing, although enclosure by agreement continued in isolated instances until the opening years of the nineteenth century.

The extent of parliamentary enclosure can be calculated fairly exactly. All of the Acts and almost all of the Awards survive and so the total acreage involved can be arrived at comparatively easily. For pre-parliamentary enclosure the problem is quite different. The documents are scattered and fragmentary, many of the sources, particularly those of the courts of law in which the agreements were regis-tered, are still unexplored, and certainly some enclosure took place without leaving any written record at all. Thus we can learn the extent of pre-parliamentary enclosure only in a rather negative fashion, namely by assuming that any area not enclosed by Act of Parliament must have been enclosed by some other means. Nevertheless, even this very crude approach yields a very interesting result.

Of all the English counties, only four, Cambridgeshire, Huntingdonshire, Northamptonshire and Oxfordshire, had more than half of their total acreage enclosed by Act of Parliament, and then the highest figure is only 54 per cent in Oxfordshire. This gives some measure of the impact of non-parliamentary enclosure, and it is becoming increasingly apparent that the bulk of this enclosure took place in the fifteenth, sixteenth and seventeenth centuries. In other words, the sixteenth and seventeenth centuries are one of the most formative periods in the history of the rural landscape, a period in which a pattern of comparatively small fields marked off one from the other by hedgerows, or in upland Britain by stone walls, their cultivation entirely within the discretion of a single farmer, slowly replaces an older landscape of very large fields with internal divisions marked with earthen, grass-grown balks, a landscape altogether more open, browner and very much more untidy than the one which was replacing it. Only in the years since 1945, with the rapid development of large-scale arable farming of a peculiarly rapacious kind, has this new landscape in its turn come under serious attack, and the removal of some 123,000 miles of hedgerow in the last forty years has in some parts of England produced a prairie-like landscape of dreary monotony.

Enclosure was taking place in every part of the country. A survey of the estates of the bishop of Durham made in 1647 records that at East Combe township, Robert Nicholl held the north part of a close called Westfield containing six acres and now fenced and divided from the other part of the Westfield. In the manor of Evenwood William Garth held a parcel of the moor called West Thickley containing a hundred acres of land 'as it is now divided by meetes and boundes', and in Killerby township John Hutchinson held three closes of arable land lying together called the Banckes, being 'a parcel of moor bounded in'. In Cornwall, at about the same time, the deer parks at Lanteglosse and Helsbury were described as being lately divided into closes of meadow, arable and pasture. At Hinton St George in Somerset the enclosure of the three, possibly four, common arable fields was complete by 1600, whilst at Barrington, about four miles away to the northwest, the three open arable fields continued to be cultivated in common until 1918. The common open fields at Tunstall, in Staffordshire, were enclosed by agreement in 1613, as was Stokefield in Beechingstoke, Wiltshire, in 1599. At Rousham in Oxfordshire, about 120 acres of pasture were enclosed by agreement in 1645, the open arable fields being enclosed, also by agreement, in 1775. At Woodthorpe, in Leicestershire, the tenants agreed to enclose their lands on 23 February 1663 because of the quarrels and dissensions arising among them because their arable, meadow, pasture and grass grounds lay intermixed, so that 'great waste and spoyle hath been done in their corne and grass ground'. A surveyor was to be appointed. The work was to be done with all speed. The parties were to enter upon their new plots by 17 March of that year and within two years to have them sufficiently hedged, ditched and quickset.

Again and again agreements for enclosure, when rehearsing the reasons for deciding to enclose, stress how inconvenient the open field system was. The fact that individual men's holdings lay intermixed through the arable, meadow and pasture caused interminable quarrels and complaints between neighbours, creating what at Thedingworth, in Leicestershire, in 1714, was called 'continual breach of Christian Amity and friendship'. This inconvenience must be accepted as a genuine reason for wishing to enclose, something which, for individual villagers, must have been a leap into an uncertain and perilous future from the safety of a familiar and well-tried way of life.

Other reasons and motives for enclosing are not quite so high-minded and altruistic. Tenants at Leire, in Leicestershire, stated in 1699 that because their lands lay intermixed they had not 'been able to take that improvement of their respective lands had they lain distinct and separate'. Profit was clearly more important than Christian amity. Land was also being enclosed so that it could be incorporated into the parks with which country gentlemen sought to surround their houses. By the end of the sixteenth century these parks were becoming increasingly ornamental in their purpose rather than being utilitarian deer preserves, but the impact of creating a park upon the landscape and upon the arable of the neighbouring villagers was just the same. The village of Fulbrook, in Warwickshire, was destroyed in about 1421 to make a park, renewed and extended early in the seventeenth century by Sir Thomas Lucy. It was however being divided up into farms by the end of the century and by about 1730 had disappeared altogether, save for a couple of place-names. In 1623, when the manor, town and castle of Oakham in Rutland, were surveyed, it was reported that 13 acres of the North Field had been taken in within the walls of Burghley park, although, in contrast, it was also reported that the park to Oakham castle had been divided up into four closes.

Enclosers did not, however, always have things their own way, and it was not always sweetness and light among individual villagers. By 1639 Sir Christopher Hatton had made several enclosures in Corby, in Northamptonshire. But in July of that year the constable of Corby, backed by a crowd of over sixty men and women, broke down the hedges, turned cattle into the midst of the new mown hay in the closes, and assaulted a workman employed by Hatton's bailiff. The bishop of Durham had from time to time made various attempts to improve Raley fell, a great common moor in his manor of Evenwood, but his efforts were invariably frustrated by the tenants, who had the right to turn their cattle on to the moor without stint.

Sir Matthew Sanders, 'presuming upon his own greatness being a Justice of the Peace and an eminent man in the Countrey and upon the quiett disposicons' of his tenants and neighbours, enclosed a strip of land dividing Shangton from Turlangton, in Leicestershire, probably in 1638, although there was no agreement and 'divers of the said freeholders did expressly refuse to agree or Condiscende to any such proposicons'.

Negotiations for the enclosure of Marston, in Lincolnshire, were tortuous and protracted, not least because the incumbent, Mr Nelson, raised every conceivable objection. He wanted the glebe enclosed at the cost of the two principal landowners, Sir William Thorold and Lord Brudenell. He objected to the proposed abatement of the tithes, and demanded that the bishop's approval should be sought. When pressed, he cited Deuteronomy, 'cursed is he yt removeth the old land marks', to which Lord Brudenell retorted, 'that curse in Deuteronomy no whit appals me nor doth it anny wayes belonge to the question in hand'. Only when Lord Brudenell suggested making the tenants freeholders and giving Mr Nelson the perpetual advowson did Nelson's resistance crumble.

Enclosure could transform the landscape. The vast, brown open fields, divided into furlongs and strips by balks and headlands which were often covered with coarse grass, brambles and thorn bushes, with muddy ways threading through and between the furlongs, were now laid out into small closes separated off by hedgerows and ditches. Sometimes the land was converted to pasture, sometimes it remained in cultivation, perhaps to grow wheat, or some of the new industrial crops such as woad,

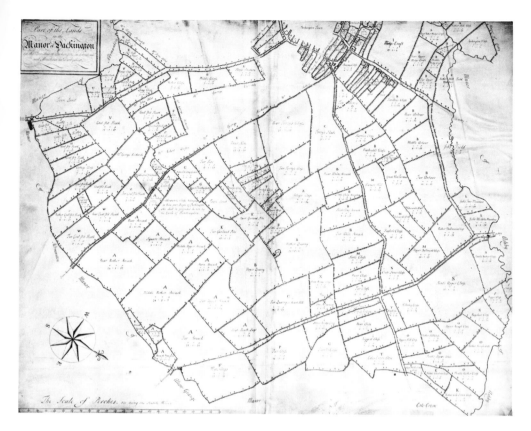

madder or rape seed. Whatever the immediate outcome, in the long term it gave men greater freedom and flexibility to cultivate their land in the way they thought best. At Fulbeck, in Lincolnshire, the low grounds from the east end of the ings, or pasture grounds, were enclosed as 'being more apt for grass than tillage', and the Heath was enclosed 'being most proper and fit for corn'.

Roads were straightened, diverted or sometimes stopped up, but they were always more clearly defined than they had been in the past. In 1607 the mayor and burgesses of Great Grimsby were said to have stopped up a highway by unlawful enclosures, and other roads said to have been stopped up or straightened by enclosure in Lincolnshire lay in Tattershall, Stallingborough, West Halton, Ashby, Crowley, Great Limber, South Elkington, Welton, and so on; the list is almost interminable. Justices on the Western Circuit Assises ordered in 1629 that all enclosures made in the previous fifty years in St Sidwells parish on roads from Exeter to London were to be pulled down, and in 1631 they ordered that the occupiers of Little Ann farm, Abbotts Ann, Hampshire, should repair at their

Plate 11 Part of an eighteenth-century map of part of the manor of Packington, in Leicestershire. Enclosure here was completed by the early years of the seventeenth century. The long, narrow closes at the top centre of the map and at the top left hand corner, together with the fairly small, squarish fields elsewhere, with their gently sinuous boundaries, are characteristic of the pattern of field boundaries established by pre-Parliamentary enclosure

61

own cost the stretch of the London to Salisbury road which they had enclosed making it almost impassable.

Farms were often engrossed as a consequence of enclosure, that is they were amalgamated so that at least one farmhouse became redundant and was allowed to fall into ruin. Again in Lincolnshire, it was reported in 1607 that in the Lindsey division alone some 290 farmhouses now stood empty because of engrossing.

Large-scale enclosure could therefore have a considerable impact upon the rural landscape, but there was also much piecemeal and small-scale enclosure, and it was also quite usual for only part of a parish or township to be enclosed at any one time, so that the whole process of enclosure could be spread over many years, sometimes a century or more. At Fulbeck, in Lincolnshire, some two thousand acres were enclosed by 1632, but a further 1300 acres still remained to be enclosed by Act of Parliament in 1803. At North Scarle, also in Lincolnshire, the North Field was enclosed in about 1677, the two other open fields being enclosed about twenty years later, the common and waste remaining open a further six years or so before they too were enclosed.

Enclosure was clearly a widespread, all-pervasive phenomenon which was changing, sometimes slowly, sometimes rapidly, the landscape of rural England in the sixteenth and seventeenth centuries, and it is probably not too much of an exaggeration to say that only a minority of villages remained entirely unaffected by it. In this respect each village has its own unique history, a history which can be encompassed only within the broadest of generalisations.

There had been much small-scale and piecemeal drainage and enclosure in the fens in the medieval centuries, but the only substantial, large-scale work was the cutting of Morton's Leam, in 1478, under the direction of John Morton, chosen Bishop of Ely in the following year. It ran from Stanground, near Peterborough, to Guyhirne, a work 12 miles long, 40 feet wide and 4 feet deep, carrying the Nene in a straight line to Wisbech. No further large-scale projects were undertaken until 1630, when the Earl of Bedford, who owned some 20,000 acres of land between Thorney and Whittlesea, agreed with a group of fenland landowners to drain that area of the southern fens which in due course became known as the Bedford Level. In 1634 the adventurers in the scheme were granted a charter of incorporation. The Earl thereupon engaged the services of the Dutchman, Cornelius Vermuyden, who was already at work on the draining of the Axholme marshes in Lincolnshire. Work began almost at once and, until the outbreak of the Civil War in 1642 brought everything to a standstill, a number of cuts, drains and associated sluices were made, some of them on a large scale. The Old Bedford River, as it came to be called, 21 miles long and 70 feet wide, from Earith to Salter's Lodge, was the principal work, but Bevill's Leam, from Whittlesey Mere to Guyhirne, 10 miles long, was also made, Morton's

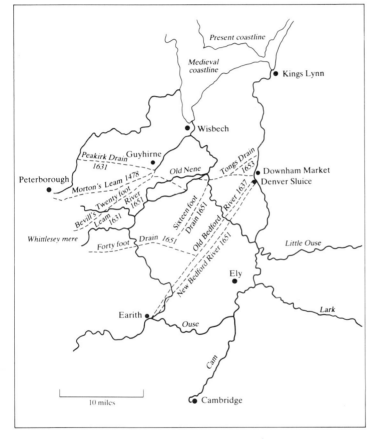

7 The southern fens. Main drainage work in the seventeenth century. The dates are those when the work was begun. The lines of the ancient waterways must be considered as only approximate. (See Plate 12.)

Leam was rebuilt, and the Peakirk Drain, 10 miles long, from Peterborough Great Fen to Guyhirne, was dug. Nevertheless, in spite of these efforts, and the expenditure of a great deal of money, the Level was still subject to winter flooding. By this time however the growing political crisis began to take precedence over everything else, and for almost ten years nothing was done. In 1649 an 'Act for the draining the Great Level of the Fens' was passed with the deliberate intention of completing the drainage so that what had hitherto been only 'summer grounds' – that is

Rural change

sufficiently free of water to allow livestock to graze in the summer – should be converted into 'winter grounds', free of flooding even in the winter, so that crops of coleseed and rapeseed could be grown, 'which is of singular use to make soap and oils within this nation', and to provide 'good pasture for feeding and breeding of cattle'. Vermuyden was appointed Director of the Works in 1650. He began with those areas which later became known as the North Level and the Middle Level. His greatest achievement here was the cutting of the New Bedford River, running more or less half a mile to the east of the Old Bedford River. (See Plate 12.) Immense banks of earth were raised, especially on the two outer banks of the New and Old Rivers, so that, together with the strip of land between the two, some 5,000 acres of grazing land deliberately designed to serve as an overflow drain in time of heavy flooding, a huge artificial water course was created, over twenty miles long and half a mile wide. In 1651 the North and Middle Levels were considered drained. Vermuyden now turned his attention to the South Level, with the actual construction work being carried out by

Plate 12 The Old and New Bedford Levels near Downham Market, looking south. The straight drain on the left is St John's Eau. This is separated from the Ouse by Denver Sluice, as rebuilt in 1959. The Ouse itself snakes across the centre of the picture and then goes off to the left. The New Bedford River on the left and the Old Bedford River on the right stretch away into the distance from their junctions with the bend of the Ouse

gangs of Scottish and Dutch prisoners of war. By 1652 the work was completed and the South Level was declared drained.

In 1663 a further Act of Parliament was passed creating a governing body for the Bedford Level. The corporation then established, the Governor, Bailiffs and Commonalty of the Company of Conservators of the Great Level of the Fens was not dissolved until 1914. Within thirty years an immense area of the southern fens, some 350,000 acres, had been drained and declared fit for cultivation. When Sir William Dugdale visited the area in 1657 he noted crops of onions, peas, hemp, flax, oats, wheat, woad and cole-seed, as well as rich meadows and pastures.

Looking back from the vantage point of the late twentieth century the draining of the Great Level seems a wholly beneficial enterprise, and the appearance of the landscape today, with its neat farms and long straight roads and ditches, appears only to confirm this impression. But in fact the whole enterprise was bitterly opposed by the fen dwellers, who found an entire way of life, based upon a highly skilled, subtle and sensitive exploitation of the opportunities offered by the fens, threatened with extinction. The fens were not a bleak, watery waste, as those who sought to drain them believed. Instead, as we saw in the previous chapter, they were a region of unusual opportunities which the inhabitants had learned over the centuries how to exploit. This traditional, delicately poised, way of life was attacked by the undertakers of the drainage schemes, and those who were threatened took appropriate measures to defend themselves. Dikes and ditches were blocked, sluices were pulled down or else kept open at flood tide and closed at the ebb. Riots and assaults upon the officers and agents of the undertakers were frequent and widespread. Games of football became suspect because they provided the pretext for the assembly of large numbers of young men who would very quickly turn their attention from the game to tearing down the banks and earthworks of the undertakers. The violence spilt over into a war of words, with the undertakers and their opponents publishing pamphlets for and against reclamation. The new crops of coleseed and rapeseed were denounced as 'but Dutch commodities and but trash and trumpery': a good fat ox was claimed to be far better than a well-grown eel, a creature which, in the traditional life of the fens, was almost a unit of currency, tithes and rents being paid in 'sticks' of eels, each 'stick' containing twenty-five eels.

Nevertheless, in spite of this opposition, the drainage of the Great Level could be declared complete in 1652. But within twenty years the disadvantages which attend every attempt on the part of men to shape their environment began to show themselves. Some areas still remained liable to flooding, and the drainage of some localities had only succeeded in making the problem worse for others. There were other natural forces at work. The Wash is an area subject to strong tides, bringing down great quantities of silt. The influence of the tide was felt as far inland as Earith on the Ouse, and almost to Peterborough on the Nene. In contrast, the rivers themselves were sluggish because the fall, or natural gradient of the land, was very slight. In consequence, heavy rainfall in the surrounding uplands combined with high tides coming up river from the sea made large-scale flooding inevitable; and the problem was compounded by the fact that all the waters of the Middle and South Levels were channelled into a single outfall, but the tides prevented the sluice gates, especially that at Denver Sluice, from opening to clear the river waters – something which also prevented the rivers from scouring their estuaries effectively.

At the same time the level of the peat fen was falling rapidly as drainage took effect. Within a short time many of the main drains across the Great Level were flowing at a higher level than their feeders, and they continued to grow above the levels of the surrounding land, which was itself shrinking as the peat dried out. Retaining banks, built out of the peat, began to crumble. Dredging channels, repairing banks and cutting weeds became increasingly important, increasingly difficult and increasingly expensive; the achievements of the 1650s were gradually disintegrating. Horse-driven pumping engines were known by 1600, and windmills were in use shortly after the Restoration; but neither of these was an unqualified success since in pumping one area clear of water they merely moved it into another, and they made the situation worse by throwing great quantities of mud into the drainage channels.

Nevertheless, in spite of these difficulties, the drainage of the Bedford Level was on the whole successful, and a considerable technical achievement. It was certainly the largest and most successful scheme of marshland drainage completed in the period covered by this book.

A number of projects to drain other areas of the fens about the Wash were launched in the early seventeenth century, with some modest success, but when times became unsettled with the outbreak of the Civil Wars, the universal hostility to the schemes on the part of the fen dwellers themselves led to much destruction of ditches, embankments and sluices. Deeping Fen, southwest of Spalding, East and West Fens, in the triangle between the River Witham and the sea, were embanked and drained in the 1630s, but riots in the 1640s destroyed the works. An Act of Parliament was obtained in 1666 for the draining of Deeping Fen, but there were further riots at the end of the century; and it was well into the eighteenth century before real progress was made.

A similar story is to be told of attempts to drain marshes in other parts of the country. Work began in Sedgemoor, in the Somerset Levels, in 1618, but almost nothing could be accomplished in the face of the bitter opposition of the commoners who, like the fen dwellers, stood to lose their livelihood if the marshes were drained. From 1627 onwards attempts were made to drain Hatfield Chase, on the borders of Yorkshire and Lincolnshire where the Trent meets the Humber. As elsewhere, Charles I took a third of the reclaimed lands, but the tenants of Epworth reacted so violently that he was compelled to add a further thousand acres to their allotment of 6,000 acres in compensation for the loss of their grazing rights. During the Civil War there was much destruction of what had been achieved, accompanied by open violence in which several men were killed. A Mr Nathaniel Reading was brave enough to take over the lease from the undertakers, and so the commoners turned their attention to him. They killed his cattle, set fire to his house and cut down his trees. Only after the commoners lost their case in the Court of Exchequer in 1719 did the violence and opposition eventually come to an end.

Attempts to enclose and drain areas of marshland where large numbers of peasant farmers had rights of common for their livestock met with almost universal opposition. The story is quite different along those coasts where land was being reclaimed from the sea. Here small proprietors were often themselves engaged in the work, and much land was successfully reclaimed, although often on a comparatively small scale. The stages in the process by which salt marsh subject to flooding by the sea was turned into fresh pasture and grazing become clear from a survey made in 1615 of Holbeach Marsh. There were at this date, it was reported, 3870 acres of 'inned' marsh which were now fresh and free from salt. A further 3,000 acres, usually flooded at high tide, were now ready to be embanked, whilst a good quantity of sands and other grounds next to the sea had not yet grown to a perfect sward. Their turn to be embanked would come. In this way, step by step, land was being reclaimed all round the coasts. It was taking place along both shores of the Thames estuary, for example, in Dartford Creek, in Swanscombe, at Barking Creek, where there was a sluice, and from the blockhouse at Tilbury as far west as Bow Creek. A similar story could be told for both shores of the Severn estuary, the Flintshire shore of the Dee estuary and along much of the Lancashire coast. In Suffolk, it was said of Havergate marsh, near Orford, in 1637, that it was not 'inned' or embanked, and yet it was not subject to flooding except in 'rageinge tydes', but there had been much embanking at Orford itself, and at Gedgrave, Sudbourne, Chillesford and Aldeburgh during the course of the previous fifty years.

Coastal reclamation of this kind was not always successful. A particularly high tide could sweep away the work of generations in the course of a single night, and men and cattle would lose their lives. Nevertheless, in spite of the dangers and setbacks, the shore-line was pushed steadily forward, successive sea-walls and embankments surviving in the landscape today to mark the stages.

Much of the forest and woodland clearing and marsh-land draining done in the first forty years of the seventeenth century was the direct consequence of the financial difficulties of James I and Charles I. Charles in particular pushed through large schemes of enclosure and drainage, and aroused a great deal of hostility that boiled over into violence on more than one occasion. James I, on the other hand, or rather his ministers, do not seem to have been quite so rapacious, and were even prepared, on occasion, to take what today would be called 'environmental factors' into account. In 1609, as part of a wide-ranging programme on the part of the Earl of Salisbury to improve James's financial position, a commission was issued to Sir Thomas Tyringham and Sir Robert Johnson to fell trees in the Royal Forest of Whittlewood, in Northamptonshire and Buckinghamshire. Only two in a hundred were to be felled, and Sir Robert Johnson was ordered to look particularly to 'What place they maie be spared without anie blemishe to the beautie of our foresaid Parkes Forests and Chaces' and he was to 'have principall care to forbeare in the felleing of anie trees or Faire tuftes soe neere the Scite or mansion howse (yf there be anie of anie note) as maie disgrace the habitacon'.

No such aesthetic niceties troubled Charles when he ordered forest clearance and enclosure. Between 1630 and 1636 the Forest of Braden, in Wiltshire, was disafforested and enclosed. Of an area of a little over four thousand acres, in which no less than fourteen villages had the right to pasture their livestock without stint, the Crown finally allotted only 390 acres as compensation for the loss of these rights of common. The Forests of Melksham, Gillingham, Pewsham and Selwood in Wiltshire, Hatfield Broadoak in

Hertfordshire, Bernwood in Buckinghamshire, Galtres in Yorkshire, and others, were all enclosed at this time, to the accompaniment of widespread disturbances and riots, very many of which were prompted by the prospects of losing valuable grazing rights, although at Dauntsey, in Wiltshire, the enclosing hedges and fences were thrown down by men working in twos in order not to constitute a riot. Many of the disturbances were led by a Henry Hoskins, known as the 'Colonel', and a mythical 'Lady Skimmington'. Soldiers sent to quell the disturbances in Wiltshire instead sided with the rioters, and there was fighting for several days at Cley Hill Farm in 1631. In fact the disturbances continued on and off for nearly twenty years, by which time a new landscape of newly built farms set in closes marked off by hedgerows had matured. Similarly, the disafforestation of the Forest of Bernwood in the 1630s was marked by violence; but by 1700 the trees had

Plate 13 The deserted village at Boarstall, in Buckinghamshire. This village was depopulated at the end of the seventeenth century. The medieval gatehouse to the manor house can be seen left of centre, and the church, rebuilt in 1817, to its right. The village lay in the field at the foot of the photograph. Ridge and furrow is just discernible in the long narrow field on the right

69

all but disappeared, one village, Boarstall, had been almost totally depopulated, and a new landscape had emerged.

Similarly, when it came to the enclosure of salt marshland, James I took only a fifth for the Crown, whereas Charles insisted upon a third. When commissioners were appointed in 1615 to survey and enclose Gedney marshes, in Lincolnshire, they allotted a fifth part, some 535 acres, to the King, marked out with stakes branded with the letter JR and the figure of the crown imperial, but they forebore to enclose and divide up the marshes at Holbeach, Tydd St Mary, Moulton and Wigtoft because they were unable to decide upon conflicting titles and claims to ownership, although they found 1268 acres of marsh at Tydd St Mary firm ground fit to be enclosed. On the other hand, when in 1636 commissioners enclosed Deeping Fen they allotted to the Crown some 2105 acres, which, they said rather obsequiously, was less than a third by over a hundred acres. At the same time they returned into the Exchequer, as they were required to do by their articles of instruction, the names of 'those that have most opposed or beene most refactory to the Agreement or Improvement', as did the commissioners who enclosed West Fen and Heath between St Ives and Somersham in Huntingdonshire.

Change in the rural landscape of England in the seventeenth century arose from a complex pattern of motives which it is almost impossible to analyse satisfactorily for the country as a whole since there are so many local and regional exceptions to any broad generalisation. Many yeomen and husbandmen welcomed enclosure: as many again were bitterly opposed to it. Many landlords were able to push through schemes of improvement in spite of the opposition of their tenants: many landlords found themselves unable to enclose and improve moorland, waste and woodland because of the opposition of their tenants.

In Scotland circumstances were quite different. Innovation came entirely from large landed proprietors. They faced greater physical difficulties than did their counterparts in England because of the nature of the terrain, but they had far fewer legal problems to overcome, and in any case were able to make effective use of the Scottish Parliament, courts and sheriffs to enable them to overcome them.

Perhaps the greatest single barrier in England to enclosure, and hence to improvement, however doubtful the actual value of this improvement may have turned out to be, was the right to common of pasture enjoyed by individual tenant farmers. In fen and woodland, where livestock husbandry was more important than arable, this right could be very valuable indeed, making all the difference between affluence and indigence, and so it was not to be given up without a struggle. In Scotland rights to common of pasture were vested in the proprietor, not the tenant, and further, it was impossible to establish a right to common by prescription, as could be done in England. There was much intercommoning over waste and moor in Scotland, but it was a matter for the proprietor, not the tenant, to guard against encroachment, and it was a matter for the proprietors alone to agree amongst themselves upon enclosure and division of the commons. Unanimity among all proprietors was necessary, but in 1647 an Act of the Scottish Parliament made the first breach in this requirement. The Act permitted a majority of the proprietors of commonties in the Lothians, Lanarkshire and Ayrshire to apply to the Court of Session for an order to divide up a common into separate blocks, the actual division being undertaken by the local Justices of the Peace and the sheriff. How far the Act was used is difficult to discover, since the 1650s were a particularly unsettled decade, and in any case it was one of those Acts repealed at the Restoration by the Act Rescissory of 1661. Nevertheless, it had set a precedent, and indicates that the Scottish landlords who dominated the Scottish Parliament were aware of the advantages of enclosure and improvement. The Act of 1647 may itself have fallen foul of the shifts in political power of the 1660s, but these could do nothing to diminish the economic attractions of enclosure. These attractions lay behind another Act of 1661 which called upon proprietors with a landed estate worth more than £1000 Scots a year to enclose at least four acres of land a year for ten years, with power to divert roads if necessary. As a further inducement such newly enclosed land was declared free of taxes for nineteen years. The Act was renewed in 1685, the exemption from taxation also being renewed for a further nineteen years. Again, it is difficult to assess the impact of this legislation, since it is clear that Scottish proprietors were enclosing land in the immediate vicinity of their country houses from at least as early as the beginning of the seventeenth century. The laying out and development of the policies to country houses and the improvement of the Mains farm went together very closely, and proved to be most influential in the diffusion of innovation by example. Only the proprietors could

71

command the resources necessary for such undertakings, and again the motives were mixed and ambivalent. Much improvement was often done because it enhanced the appearance and amenity of the house and because it was fashionable to do so, but it also had to pay for itself by increasing crop yields and improving stock strains.

Improvement of the policies – the lands in the immediate vicinity of the proprietor's mansion house – could take a number of forms. By the early seventeenth century much of Lowland Scotland was, as we have seen, almost devoid of trees, and this in spite of Acts of the Scottish Parliament forbidding the cutting of greenwood. The deliberate planting of trees, as shelter belts, in blocks for commercial purposes, or as amenity, was taking place in isolated parts of Lowland Scotland by the beginning of the seventeenth century, at Panmure House in Angus, for example, where, by the end of the century there were over 44,000 trees on 128 Scots acres, and by 1720 it was claimed that on the Yester estate in East Lothian over a million trees had been planted. Scots pine was the most commonly planted tree, but ash, elm, birch and willow were also planted in large numbers, and it seems very likely that the beech tree made its first appearance in south-eastern Scotland at this time.

At first many tenants cut down the new trees almost as soon as they were planted, not least because with an almost total absence of any other trees they were too attractive for making tools and implements. But the barony courts of the proprietors punished those who could not resist temptation, and by the end of the seventeenth century it was increasingly the practice to incorporate into written leases the requirement that the tenant should plant a stated number of trees each year. The court book of the barony of Urie, in Kincardineshire, contains numerous entries of tenants cutting trees, and in July 1682 it was noted that the laird had ordered all his tenants to plant ash trees, plane, fir, birch, rowan and wild cherry, every husbandman six a year, every cottar three, every grassman two, and to collect them at Michaelmas from the laird or his gardener.

Secondly, some enclosure was taking place to improve pasture and arable. Enclosure for pasture did enable live-stock strains to be improved, and animals were being imported from both England and Ireland for this purpose. There was at the same time mounting demand for meat and other livestock products in Scottish towns, and the fattening of cattle for driving into England and the bottom-less pit of the London food market provided the stimulus for Scottish proprietors – especially in the south-west – to enclose some large areas of pasture for cattle raising. Sir David Dunbar of Baldoon, near Wigtown, had by 1684 a cattle park large enough to winter 1,000 head of cattle, and he was sending 400–500 to England every year. He was not unique: he was merely the most successful.

In 1695 the Scottish Parliament passed three Acts designed to foster agricultural improvement: one for preserving meadow and pasture next to coastal sand dunes, one 'Anent Lands Lying in Runrig', the third to make the enclosing of commonties easier. This last Act now provided that any proprietor with rights of commonty could apply to the Court of Session to enclose commons. The consent of the other proprietors was now dispensed with. The Act 'Anent Runrig' applied only to proprietory runrig. Again any proprietor could apply to the sheriff, Justices of the Peace or lords of regality to have the lands consolidated and divided up into compact blocks. Unanimity of the proprietors concerned was now dispensed with.

The Scottish Parliament in this legislation showed a more favourable attitude towards rural change than did its contemporary in Westminster. In this it reflects the interests and wishes of the great landed proprietors who had an overwhelming influence on its actions and decisions. It is almost impossible to point to an individual field or farm and say that this is the direct consequence of this legislation, but its removal of some of the legal barriers to enclosure and improvement can only in the long term have assisted those processes of change which by the end of the seventeenth century were becoming apparent in Lowland Scotland and which would transform its rural landscape in the course of little more than a century.

Reclamation by draining was certainly taking place in Scotland in the seventeenth century but on a much smaller and more local scale than in England. There is nothing in Scotland to compare with the drainage of the Great Bedford Level in the English fens. Sir William Scott of Harden carried out some draining work at Mertoun in Berwickshire for example, and Sir William Bruce the architect did much to improve the marshy ground surrounding his house on Loch Leven. Some coastal marshes near Alloa were embanked early in the seventeenth century, although it was the end of the century before it could be said that the work was successful. Two Acts of the Scottish Parliament were passed in 1641 and in 1696 to remove some of the legal barriers in the path of schemes to drain the Pow of Inchaffray, between Crieff and Perth, but the fifty-five years between them must indicate that drainage schemes took as long in Scotland as they did in England to come to fruition.

The rural landscape of Wales was changing particularly rapidly in the sixteenth and seventeenth centuries. Much of the open field arable husbandry characteristic of the border lowlands and the coastal districts of south Wales disappeared during this period. Thus Llancadle, in Glamorgan, had, by 1622, enclosed some 85 per cent of its cultivated land into 162 small closes, and many of the boundaries thus created have remained fossilised in the landscape today. Similar relic features of enclosed strips can be seen on the slopes of Pop Hill, Dinas Powis, Glamorgan. This enclosure movement in south Wales was so widespread that it left little scope for that Parliamentary enclosure movement of the eighteenth and nineteenth centuries which affected so much of midland England. One of the consequences of this has been the widespread survival of relics and fragments from the pre-enclosure landscape. Cultivation of the arable in the common fields persisted in many districts until well into the nineteenth century – at Bronllys, in Breconshire, for example, at Caldicot in Monmouthshire, in many localities in Glamorganshire, and as far west as Llanrhystyd, in Cardiganshire. The burgesses of Laugharne, in Carmarthenshire, still own 312 acres of common fields, organised into two arable and one meadow, whilst at Rhosili, on the Gower peninsula, some areas of strip cultivation in open fields still remain (see Fig. 6 and Plate 9).

There was also much enclosure and encroachment of wood and forest, moorland waste and mountain pasture. Much was done on a very small scale indeed, an acre or two at a time, whilst on the other hand there was some large-scale enclosure, when hundreds of acres, especially of mountain grazing, was taken in. Whether in large or small pieces, the cumulative effects could mean change over a wide area. Between 1561 and 1573 encroachments in the commote of Cyfeiliog, in Montgomeryshire, amounted to over 2,000 acres. For at least one district however, this encroachment was but a return to land which had once before been cultivated but had in the intervening years been abandoned. It was said of the lordship of Kidwelly in 1609 that there had been much enclosure and encroachment on the mountain pastures, on some of which 'theare appeared divers balks and other markes whereby it seemed that parte thereof had byn before plowghed'.

Much of this enclosure and encroachment was prompted, directly or indirectly, by the legislation of 1542 which abolished partible inheritance upon the next change of inheritance. At the same time estate surveyors, whether employed by the Crown or by great landowners such as the Earl of Leicester, began to treat unenclosed land as common land and hence the property of the lord, when in fact it was frequently ancient *cytir* holdings purposely left open, unenclosed and undivided by co-heirs 'for a commoditie of more freedome and easment between them'.

Many joint tenants of *cytir* lands found the legal basis of their property rights destroyed, and so enclosure would have seemed one way round the problem. Many lords regarded this as encroachment upon common land, land which was now vested in them. As a result many tenants arrived at a composition, paying a lump sum to be free of any penalties for encroachment. This was done, for example, by the tenants of the Earl of Leicester in his lordship of Denbigh, where, as a result, enclosure seems largely to have come to an end until the outbreak of the Civil War. In other lordships however, it seems that such a composition was treated as an excuse for yet further enclosure. In the lordships of Arustley and Keveiliocke, in Montgomeryshire, it was claimed in 1609 that there had been much enclosing and fencing of wastes and commons, and many cottages erected, but the tenants stated that they had already compounded for their encroachments. Similarly, in the lordship of Dynas, in Breconshire, it was claimed early in the seventeenth century that for many years past many inhabitants had built cottages and enclosed small pieces of land from the waste, but when an attempt was made to evict them the court upheld their rights because they had made a composition with the lord which had effectively extinguished any claim that he might have had to evict them for squatting.

These developments brought great confusion and uncertainty into the ancient and long accepted structures under which men had regulated their relationships, one with another and with their environment, bringing hardship to many and opportunity to the more adventurous and unscrupulous. Those with money could buy up *tir cyfrif* holdings as ancient tenants were forced out, and pieces of *tir gwelyawg* land as subdivision made individual plots uneconomic. The result was the rapid build-up of substantial estates, accompanied by widespread enclosure, not least because, as the traditional tenures broke up and lands and estates came into new hands, the surveyors employed by the new lords to measure, map and value their new possessions, pointed again and again to the way in which enclosure could be expected to improve the value of the land, and hence the yield from rents, and with the purchase price to recoup, few could resist the temptation.

The processes, however, were not always one-sided. In the lordship of Bromfield and Yale, in Denbighshire, the ancient tenures were assumed, in the middle of the sixteenth century, to be merely tenancies at will. This caused so much consternation that it was at last agreed that the tenants, on payment of a lump sum of £800 and an additional £100 a year on their rents, should have leases for forty years. Enclosures in the lordship of Ruthin were overthrown by the tenants; and in the lordships of Kerry and Kedewen, in Montgomeryshire, where there was much intercommoning, the tenants gathered a common purse to defend their rights, and the landlord was afraid to proceed in law because he feared that he could not obtain a fair trial.

The mountainous topography of north and central Wales together with these changes combined to produce a landscape of scattered and isolated farmsteads, much small-scale and piecemeal enclosure, and vast areas of open moor and rough grazing, with squatters building their cabins in the more hospitable spots, although the widely held belief that if a cottage could be built over-night, the *tai un-nos*, then the squatter could not be evicted, had no foundation in law. Most farmers had to grow their own cereals, invariably oats, because of the difficulties of transport, but the mainstay of society was the rearing of cattle and sheep. Transhumance, or the seasonal movement of livestock, was widely practised. In the summer months cattle were driven up from the winter farm, the *hendre*, to upland pastures, to the *hafod*, or, in mid Wales the *lluest*. During the course of the sixteenth and seventeenth centuries many of these summer sites became permanent farmsteads. Many of the cattle were destined for Smithfield market, and the droving of Welsh cattle into England was already well organised and on a large scale. Two drovers, Gruffith ap David and Rees ap Meredith refused in 1605 to pay toll on the livestock they bought in Knighton market, in Radnorshire. All together they were reported to have bought 400 oxen, 200 kine, 300 beasts, 440 horses, 7000 sheep and 200 swine.

Both woodland and forest in the legal sense were wide-

spread over medieval Wales. The Great Forest of Brecknock still covered 40,000 acres in 1815, and Radnor Forest
extended over 3,000 acres in 1564. Much felling, clearing,
enclosure and disafforestation took place in the later medieval centuries and in the sixteenth and seventeenth
centuries, and there was much destruction and neglect.
Of the Forest of Coydrathe, in Pembrokeshire, it was said
early in the seventeenth century that there had been great
waste and spoil. A thousand oak trees had been felled,
and 2000 cartloads of loppings, toppings and shreddings
taken away, together with 300 loads of bark. Similarly, of
Trevlech Forest, in the lordship of Oswestry, it was said in
1602 that if it were 'inclosed and preserved from hackers,
stealers and goats there would be in short tyme good
woodes'. Wales was certainly much more heavily wooded
than it is today, but industrial and commercial demands
and the processes of enclosure and clearing already
outlined led to much permanent clearing. Timber was
being floated down the Severn in the late sixteenth
century, and down the Conwy for the shipwrights of
Liverpool in the late seventeenth, by which time the appe-
tite of the iron furnaces and forges at Pontypool and
Llanelli for charcoal had become insatiable. The result was
that many so-called forests in fact had very few trees.
Radnor Forest in 1564 had 2000 acres of waste, heath and
wild moorish ground, and a further 800 acres of low
shrubs, hazel and thorn much eaten by goats out of its
total area of 3000 acres. A survey of the Forest of Elinco-
thie, in Carmarthenshire, made in 1584, revealed 1765
acres of arable, 361 acres of moor and mead, 104 acres
of rough heath and moor, and only 287 acres of wood
ground.

The rural landscape of Wales was changing particularly
rapidly in the sixteenth and seventeenth centuries. Many
miles of new boundaries, whether quickset hedges or
stone walls, appeared, and many new farmhouses and
cottages. In this Wales did not differ very markedly from
England, where as we have just seen, there was also much
enclosing, clearing and felling of trees, laying out of new
roads, fields and farms. Where the Welsh experience does
differ from that of England in the two centuries covered
by this book is that in Wales the legal structures which
governed the relationships between the parts of the landscape changed more profoundly than they did in England.
In Wales a unique medieval social and legal structure disin-
tegrated in the course of these two centuries to be replaced
by a totally alien one. Some of the most profoundly perma-

Rural change   nent and deeply conservative areas of the social organisation of any society, namely the laws of inheritance and
the forms of land tenure, were changed in Wales, and
with them the perceived relationships between man and
his environment. The changes brought widespread and
protracted resistance. They also brought ample opportunities for social and economic betterment on the part of those
who had the initiative, the means and the ability to exploit
them, comments which could equally well apply, not only
to Wales, but also to the whole of Britain in the sixteenth
and seventeenth centuries.

Mines and mills, forges and furnaces

We have spent two long chapters describing and analysing the rural landscape of Britain in the sixteenth and seventeenth centuries. This is only right and proper. The majority of the population even at the end of the seventeenth century relied directly upon the cultivation of the soil, whether as landlords, owner-occupiers, tenants or labourers, for their livelihood. Indeed, it is not until the census of 1851 that at last more people lived in towns than in the countryside although, as we shall see in Chapter 6, the problem of drawing a clear and consistent line between town and country is a vexed one, to which answers can vary over time.

Nevertheless, agriculture by this time was well beyond subsistence level save perhaps in the remotest parts of Highland Britain, and the surpluses produced for market supported tradesmen and craftsmen, shopkeepers, booksellers, clergymen, carriers and bargemasters, lawyers, excisemen, soldiers and sailors, who in their turn provided goods and services of every kind. There was, however, no clear or sharp division between agriculture on the one hand and commerce and manufacture on the other, not least because the occupational specialisation which is so characteristic a feature of industrialised society was only in the first stages of its development at this time. Much industry was domestic in its organisation, including almost every branch of the textile industry. Many farmers also made nails, stockings or earthenware pots, and many shopkeepers kept pigs and grew wheat and oats.

The sixteenth and seventeenth centuries saw important changes in most branches of mining and manufacturing, whether purely technical, such as the steady replacement of the iron bloomery by the blast furnace, or a change in direction, such as the proliferation of new kinds of woollen textiles under the broad heading of the new draperies. There was also a growth in the scale of many mining and manufacturing enterprises. Thus although statistics from the period are notoriously unreliable it seems very likely that coal production, for example, grew from about 200,000 tons a year in the 1550s to about 3 million tons a year in the 1690s.

However, in spite of this growth, which is quite unmistakeable if one compares almost every aspect of manufacture in 1550 with those in 1700, it still gives a more accurate impression to talk of manufacture, in the sense of things being made by hand, even in 1700, than it does to talk of industry, with its twentieth-century overtones of large factories and mechanised mass-production. Everything was still carried out on a very small scale: a dozen men

8 A section through an iron blast furnace in the Forest of Dean, published in 1677 by Henry Powle. The building was 24 feet square, nearly 30 feet high, and built of brick or stone.
Acknowledgement: H. Powle, 'An Account of the Iron Works in the Forest of Dean', *Philosophical Transactions of the Royal Society*, 12, 1677–78, p. 925

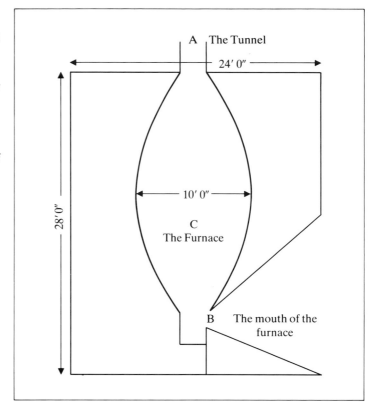

could keep a blast furnace going quite satisfactorily , and a similar number could man a coal pit. The largest single industrial enterprise by far in seventeenth-century Britain was the naval dockyard at Chatham, which, in the 1690s, was employing 1500 men. Further, it must be appreciated that manufacture was much more widespread than it is today. Iron furnaces and forges were to be found in the Lake District, the Sussex Weald and in Radnorshire and Montgomeryshire (see Fig. 9). Coal was mined in Anglesey, pottery made in Prestonpans, and an iron bloomery was established at Letterewe, Wester Ross, in 1607. Finally, it is even more important to appreciate just how close was the interdependence of agriculture and manufacture. Much of the raw materials for manufacture came from the land: wool, dyes, leather, wheat for bread and barley for beer, whilst the dependence of furnaces of every kind upon wood for fuel meant that coppicing was an important form of land use. At the same time much of the capital investment required for manufacturing enterprises was drawn directly from agricultural profits, whether by a Burslem potter or by William Paget for his iron furnaces on Cannock Chase.

Unfortunately, the very nature of mining and manufacturing enterprises means the almost total destruction of the visual evidence of the earliest stages of their development. The result is that although the sites of many iron works, furnaces of every kind, quarries and mines, are known, very little survives above ground which is earlier than the eighteenth century, and because of the domestic nature of many other manufactures such as nailing and textiles, nothing visual survives at all, and so we have to rely entirely upon documentary evidence for the reconstruction of this aspect of the landscape of the sixteenth and seventeenth centuries.

Britain is fortunate in having a wide range of mineral resources: iron, coal, lead, tin, copper, stone, sand and clay. These have all been mined and quarried since prehistoric times, and in the sixteenth and seventeenth centuries their exploitation expanded rapidly.

Coal was to be found at or near the surface in many parts of Britain: in the west Midlands, Somerset, Leicestershire, Nottinghamshire, Yorkshire and Lanarkshire, north and south Wales, Northumberland and Durham, and on both sides of the Firth of Forth. Much of this surface coal could be obtained from open pits, or by digging into the hillside. Many pits were bell-shaped, that is to say a wide shaft was dug, perhaps twenty feet deep, and then the coal was removed in every direction for as far as the miners dared to go without bringing on a collapse of the roof, whereupon they would dig another similar shallow pit near by. Such mining was little better than pillage in its wasteful and haphazard nature, and succeeded in turning the Black Country of south Staffordshire into what has been called a 'water logged rabbit warren', a desert of water filled pits and smouldering waste heaps.

By the middle years of the sixteenth century deeper shafts were being sunk. These were perhaps 7 to 10 feet square, lined with timber, sometimes as much as 100 feet deep, and as the coal itself was removed when tunnels were driven into the seams, so the roof was supported with timbers. Both men and coal were brought to the surface by a rope or chain worked by a windlass turned by two, three or four men, or, by the beginning of the seventeenth century, a horse. The pit shaft often also had a ladder against one side. The work was hard and dangerous. Ropes and ladder rungs broke, and men missed their footing in the dark.

The deeper the shaft the more acute became the problems of ventilation and drainage. In some pits a separate ventilation shaft was dug and a fire lit at the bottom to

Plate 14 Mining in the sixteenth century. This engraving, taken from *De Re Metallica*, by Agricola, published in 1556, illustrates German practice, but mines in England were not substantially different, with manually operated winding gear, timber lined shafts and tunnels, and, on the left hand side, a ladder up one side of the shaft

provide an updraught of hot air. This however merely served to increase the risks of explosion from fire damp, or methane. One such explosion in the Mostyn collieries in Flintshire in 1675 carried a man's body up the shaft and over some trees which grew near the pit head, together with much of the winding gear, and the noise of the explosion was heard fifteen miles away. The problems and danger caused by fire damp and by choke damp – a mixture of carbon dioxide and nitrogen – were neither properly understood nor overcome in this period, and they gave rise to endless legends and superstitions as, in an unscientific age, men sought to explain the inexplicable.

Drainage was just as big a problem. As pit shafts were sunk ever deeper so they broke through the water table and flooding became ever more dangerous. Where conditions allowed, it was sometimes possible to drive an adit or horizontal passage from the lowest part of the mine to an outfall lower down a hill side so that the water would drain away by the force of gravity. In many pits however there was no option but to devise some kind of pump. Early in the sixteenth century men were hauling buckets of water to the surface by hand at the coal mine at Ewloe, in Flintshire. By the end of the century Sir George Bruce of Carnock had his 'Egyptian wheel' at work on the seashore at Culross to drain his coal mines, which had first been worked by the monks of the abbey and were now extending out under the sea. It consisted of a horizontal wheel turned by horses. This in its turn was geared to a vertical wheel which raised an endless chain of buckets so positioned that they filled automatically in the drainage sump at the foot of the shaft, and then emptied automatically on reaching the surface. This horse dredge was certainly the first to be built in Scotland, and may well have been the first built in Britain. Thereafter similar devices were to be found in mines the length and breadth of Britain, and in due course, again where conditions were suitable, the wheel was powered by water, as at the Mostyn pits in Flintshire in 1684, for example.

But such machinery was expensive to maintain and very inefficient, and so the search for some practical alternative went on for much of the seventeenth century. In the 1650s the Marquis of Worcester was experimenting, unsuccessfully as it turned out, with using a steam-powered engine to raise flood water from his mines at Raglan, but it was not until the very end of the seventeenth century that the combined efforts of Savery and Newcomen overcame many of the initial problems involved in the harnessing of steam power. The first steam-powered engine built anywhere in the world was at work pumping out a coal mine near Dudley, in Worcestershire, by 1712.

The other problem facing coal mine owners was that of transport. The costs of land transport could double the price of coal over ten miles and so the most profitable mines were those near to navigable water. Few could have solved the problem more neatly than did that Sir George Bruce of Carnock already mentioned. As his coal mines reached out under the sea, so he hit upon an ingenious solution to his transport problems. In about 1590 he sank a vertical pit from the foreshore to the mine below. In effect he had to build an artificial island, some 50 feet in diameter and 20 feet high, complete with a quay to which boats could be moored at high tide and loaded with coal. Unfortunately the works were destroyed in a great storm in 1625, but sufficient still remains on the foreshore at Culross to show where this island once stood.

Another solution, and this time of more general application, was also found at the end of the sixteenth century, based very probably, as were so many technical improvements in mining generally at this time, upon German example. This was the use of a railway, with wagons running upon it. The first rails were of wood, and the earliest recorded instance in Britain is the wagon way laid down by Sir Francis Willoughby from his coal mines at Wollaton to a wharf on the Trent, in use by 1598. Shortly afterwards a similar wagon way was working at Broseley, down to the Severn in Shropshire, and they were being employed along the Tyne by about the same date. At the very end of the seventeenth century Sir Humphrey Mackworth laid wooden rails at his pits at Neath. These carried wagons underground right up to the coal face. When they were loaded they ran downhill to the wharf at Neath Bank, and it took great courage and skill on the part of the men who worked them to keep them on the rails. When they were empty they were pulled back up to the coal face by horses.

The demand for coal as a fuel was growing rapidly in the last half of the sixteenth century, and production grew to meet the demand. The greatest single market was London, and coal was carried by ship from Newcastle to the Thames in ever increasing quantities. Nearly 33,000 tons was shipped from the Tyne to London in 1563–4. In 1658–9 the figure was nearly 530,000 tons. It was used wherever and whenever it could be obtained, whether as a domestic fuel or for industrial purposes. George Owen, writing of Pembrokeshire very early in the seventeenth century, noted how the coal, which outcropped at the surface in a narrow belt in the south of the county, was widely used as a domestic fuel and had replaced the peat which had to be used in the less fortunately endowed northern part of the county. As a fuel for industrial purposes it was increasingly used, in salt and sugar boiling, in starch making, brewing, brick, tile and pottery making, for dyeing and for glass making. There was, for example, an important salt works at Portsea, in Hampshire, by the end of the sixteenth century, producing 30 ways of salt a week, at 40 bushels to the way, but it took 200 ways of coal to boil the salt. Similar salt works were to be found along the north-east coast, and on the shores of the Firth of Forth, where the ever thrifty Sir George Bruce used the sea water pumped out of his coal mines to make salt. By the Restoration, many of these coal-burning industries were to be found in London, together with tens of thousands of hearths in private houses. Foreigners and natives alike complained bitterly of the choking fogs and soot-laden atmosphere of London, and John Evelyn, in his *Fumifugium*, published in 1661, likened the city to the scene at the sack of Troy.

Details recorded of the manor of Whickham, about two miles from Newcastle upon Tyne, in a survey of the estates of the bishop of Durham, made in 1647, reveal vividly the impact that coal mining could have, however small individual pits may have been, and also the money to be made from it. The commons of the manor, 'with Cole Carriages and other Carriages are totally spoyled with great beaten and worne ways', and there were also numerous houses and cottages on the waste occupied by miners, in addition to the houses of the staithemen at the staithes where the coal was loaded into barges or keels, to travel down the Tyne to the waiting ships. There were fifteen coal pits working in the manor, and although the seams then being mined were nearly exhausted there was another beneath, already being worked nearer the Tyne, so that the pits were worth £2500 to the owner over and above the rent reserved on the whole manor.

Coal mining was probably the single most important extractive industry in seventeenth-century Britain, both in terms of its contribution to the economy and in terms of its visual impact. By the end of the century it was being used in a widening range of industries where heat was essential at some stage in the manufacturing process. Many of these coal-fired industries drew their raw materials from mines and quarries – bricks, pottery and tiles, glass making, copper and lead smelting – others from raw materials produced from the land – dyeing and brewing – whilst the smallest group drew its raw materials from overseas – sugar boiling. The one industry where, in spite of desperate attempts to overcome the technical problems involved, coal could not be used was in the iron industry.

We are accustomed, at the end of the twentieth century, to see industries such as brick making, brewing and glass making concentrated in large factories employing hundreds of men and found only in two or three centres over the country, often with catastrophic environmental consequences. The structure of industry in the sixteenth and seventeenth centuries was quite unlike this. Industrial plant was small. A building over 25 feet high was almost unheard of, and even in iron furnaces and forges they were often built of timber and thatch. Further, many industries, glass making for example, were semi-nomadic, and so a kiln or a furnace would be worked for perhaps five or ten years before being abandoned in favour of another site. Nevertheless, in spite of their small size, such industrial plants could have a disastrous impact upon the environment. Towns along the coast of Sussex and Kent complained bitterly of the devastation caused in the woods of the Weald by the insatiable demand for charcoal by the iron furnaces, and Leland, writing in the 1530s, noted that lead smelting had destroyed the woods in the Ystwyth valley, about Clawdd Mwyn.

Clays suitable for making bricks and tiles are widely distributed over Britain (see Plate 18), but the adoption of bricks for building purposes after the departure of the Romans was a long, slow process and was by no means complete by the end of the seventeenth century. As a very crude generalisation it may be stated that brick making developed first in the south and east of England and then spread very slowly north and west. Brick was used at Little Wenham Hall, in Suffolk, at the end of the thirteenth century, in the undercroft to the Merchant Venturers Hall in York in the middle of the fourteenth and in one of the town gates at Beverley early in the fifteenth. Over 2½ million bricks were used in the building of Eton College in the last half of the fifteenth century, many being made nearby in Slough. These buildings however are exceptions, and it is the end of the sixteenth century before brick making becomes at all widespread and it is from probate inventories that we can catch a glimpse of the way in which this trade was organised. Henry Wiseman, brick striker, of Ipswich, died in 1589, leaving personal possessions worth £55 12s. 6d., but of this total only £2 10s. was for burnt bricks and £3 10s. for unburnt bricks. Much more important to him were his sheep and cattle, worth £25, nearly half the total. There was as yet no clear-cut distinction between agriculture and industry. Slough continued to be important for brick making. When John Hewes, brickmaker, of Slough, died in 1684 he left in all £154 3s. 6d. in personal possessions. He had three old clay carts, thirteen old barrows 'for the use of a brick makers trade', and two moulding tables for bricks, together with 50,000 burned bricks, 120,000 raw bricks, and at Cowley in Middlesex he had about 8,000 burned bricks, 30,000 raw bricks and about 60,000 burning in the clamp at the time of his death. He also had £8 5s. in sea coal. A brick maker like John Hewes must have been working for the general market, and it may be that many of the bricks he was making went towards the rebuilding of London after the Great Fire. There must have been many more like him by the end of the seventeenth century as the presence of so many quiet, unpretentious brick houses in towns and villages the length of the country testifies. He also had an acre and a half of oats growing, perhaps as fodder for his three old nags which he may have used to pull his three old clay carts. Otherwise, the link between agriculture and industry has by now been severed.

Brick kilns were often tunnel shaped, and were themselves lined with bricks. One at Runsell Green, Danbury, in Essex, was about 12 feet long by 16 feet wide. There was an important brick making industry here for much of the sixteenth and seventeenth centuries. It was also usual for bricks to be made on site, especially when a country house was to be built. When Ven House, Milborne Port, in Somerset, was being built between 1698 and 1700, over half a million bricks were made from clays dug on the site, the resulting pits then being filled with water and incorporated as long straight canals into the gardens, a very neat solution to a difficult problem.

Brick making is not the only industry to make use of clay. Tiles and domestic pottery of every kind, including clay smoking pipes, were made in kilns all over the country. No less than forty-six tile kilns were recorded in Essex in 1595 for example, and it is clear that there were very many more pottery kilns at work in the sixteenth and seventeenth centuries than figure in the standard histories of English pottery. Burslem, before the end of the seventeenth century, was scarcely known outside its own region, and then principally as a supplier of pottery butter pots to the market at Uttoxeter. Gilbert Wedgwood was making pottery at Overhouse, Burslem, by 1612 and it was his son Thomas, the grandfather of the great Josiah, who built the Churchyard works in 1679, complete with a horse-driven mill.

The Overhouse pottery in 1667 was a building of two bays, a pot oven and a smoke house. By about 1710 there were thirty-five pot works in Burslem, but many potters remained as part-time farmers, although the involvement in agriculture declined noticeably in the early eighteenth century as potters themselves became more specialised and more skilled. Only from this period does Burslem begin to assume a national importance.

The pottery works at Ticknall and at Wrotham were probably just as important as those at Burslem in the seventeenth century as regional suppliers of cheap domestic wares, and pottery kilns in north Devon, Cornwall and south Wales made large earthenware pots for preserving pilchards. A pottery site at Cove, in Hampshire, is entirely unrecorded in the literature on English pottery, and no kiln was found when the site was excavated, and yet enormous quantities of wasters, broken and discarded fragments of every kind, were uncovered, revealing just how diverse a range of domestic pottery was made in the seventeenth century, and also how skilfully it was thrown. There is evidence of plates and platters, porringers, skillets, cups, mugs, pipkins, dripping pans, butter pots, chafing dishes, condiment dishes and candle-sticks, as well as the ubiquitous chamberpots and money boxes.

Pottery works were becoming increasingly more sophis-ticated during the course of the seventeenth century. A domed, round single flue kiln had been in use for centuries, perhaps six feet in diameter and about eight feet high, lagged with turf. They were frequently built of stones bonded with clay. They could take a week to fill, fire, cool and empty, and needed frequent rebuilding. The site needed sheds in which to stack clay and fuel, and to dry the unfired and store the finished wares. One sixteenth-century pottery site at Bourne in Lincolnshire also had a house for the potter, and in this it was probably not unique. From the second half of the seventeenth century the kiln was itself being housed in a permanent brick or stone bottle-shaped structure, and coal was used as the fuel wherever possible. These bottle kilns became ever larger and more numerous so that by the beginning of the nineteenth century they dominated the skyline of the Staffordshire pottery towns. The new, however, rarely totally replaces the old, and a single flue updraught kiln continued in use at Verwood, in Wiltshire, until the 1950s.

The clay had at first to be prepared by hand, but a horse gin had been adapted to the process in Burslem by 1678, and by the end of the century water-powered corn mills were being converted for this purpose, with a number

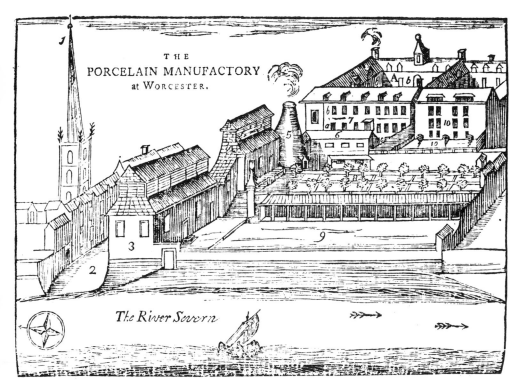

along the Scotch brook, between Moddershall and Stone, within convenient distance of Burslem.

The second half of the sixteenth century saw important technical developments taking place in the English pottery industry, many of them originating from the continent, especially from Germany and the Low Countries. Two potters from Antwerp settled in Norwich in 1567 before moving to London. They were probably the first to make delftware in England by adding tin oxide to the glaze. By mid-seventeenth century delftware was being made in Aldgate, Southwark and Lambeth as well as in Bristol.

By the end of the fifteenth century German potters had learned to make stoneware by firing certain clays to very

Plate 15 The porcelain manufactory at Worcester in 1752. Building No. 3 is the biscuit kiln, No. 5 is the great kiln, No. 6 the pressing and modelling gallery, No. 7 the rooms for throwing, turning and stove drying the wares No. 10 is Mr Evett's house and garden: he was landlord of the premises. No. 9 is the yard for coal, conveniently situated on the banks of the River Severn

high temperatures. In 1626 a patent was granted to Thomas Rous and Abraham Cullyn of London to make stoneware in England. Rous had been born in Holland, whilst Cullyn was born in Norwich the son of a Dutch refugee. Whether in fact they actually made any stonewares is uncertain, but John Dwight, granted a similar patent in 1671, certainly did at his factory in Fulham. By the end of the century stoneware was being made in Staffordshire, in York, Nottingham and Southampton.

Glass making was another industry which by the end of the seventeenth century was widely distributed over Britain, owed a great deal to immigrant craftsmen and has also left very little above ground today. Glass was being made in Chiddingfold, in Surrey, from the fourteenth century, and the parish, together with the neighbouring ones of Kirdford and Wisborough, continued to be an important centre of the industry until early in the seventeenth century. In 1567 Jean Carré, from Arras, built two glasshouses at Fernfold, in Sussex, including a furnace sixteen feet long by seven feet wide. Another glass furnace, at Vann Farm, near Chiddingfold, was about twelve feet by five feet six, with projecting wings at each corner. Glass needs to be heated three times during its manufacture and it seems very likely that all three processes could be carried out in the one furnace. Another winged furnace, dating from the last quarter of the sixteenth century, is known at Rosedale, Lastingham, in Yorkshire.

Carré died in 1572, by which time he had also established a glasshouse in London to make crystal glass, in which he was helped by a Venetian, Giacomo Verzelini. By the end of the sixteenth century glass making had spread into Staffordshire: there are fifteen known glass furnace sites in Bagots Park alone, to Newent and Woodchester in Gloucestershire, to St Weonards in Herefordshire, and to the Stour valley. Many of these glasshouses were operated by immigrant craftsmen from Normandy and from Lorraine, and some families, the Tyzacks, for example, moved on from Sussex into Staffordshire, where they were making glass at Eccleshall in 1585, and then to the Stour valley, where Paul Tyzack was at work by 1612.

Glass making was one of the earlier industries to use coal to fire its furnace, and a patent of monopoly for this purpose was granted in 1611. In 1615 Sir Robert Mansell purchased the patent, and established glasshouses using coal in London, the Isle of Purbeck, Milford Haven and Swansea, all to no avail. Not until he built a glasshouse at Newcastle upon Tyne did he start to make money from the venture, and success came only when he employed immigrant craftsmen. His monopoly was probably helped by a royal proclamation, also issued in 1615, forbidding the use of wood as fuel in glass furnaces. The use of coal meant covering the pot in which the glass was being heated, since sulphur compounds given off from the coal would combine with any lead present to form lead sulphide, which makes the glass black. In 1673 George Ravenscroft succeeded in making lead crystal glass, and by 1700 the process was common knowledge among English glass makers. By this time also the usual timber, barn-like structure which made up the glasshouse, often with a louvred lantern over the furnace itself, was being replaced by the cone-shaped building of brick which became typical of English glasshouses in the eighteenth century.

It is once again the invaluable probate inventories which enable us to glimpse something of the humanity behind the generalisations. Thomas Gibbons, late of Bedminster, in Somerset, glass maker, died in 1698. His personal estate totalled £279 19s. 10d., including the tools and raw materials in his glasshouse. He had a ladle, ten pairs of pipes and seven moulds with which he would actually have shaped the molten glass. He had a beam and weights to weigh out the raw materials, which included a hundredweight of red lead, over 50 quarters of sand, and 3 tons of kelp. Kelp, obtained from seaweed, was an important source of the sodium which is an essential ingredient in glass making. He had four covered pots, in which the glass would actually have been melted, and a hundredweight of peat, which he probably used for fuel, whilst the furnace was said to be worth £3. He had £24 12s. 6d. in glass of all sorts, twenty pair of crates and two new boxes for packing. He clearly had an extensive trade, since among the debts owed to him at the time of his death was the sum of £3 3s. 4d. for goods sent to New England.

Brick and tile making, pottery manufacture and glass making were clearly widespread over Britain, certainly in the seventeenth century, and their demand for wood as fuel could devastate timber resources over a wide area. Henry Percy, ninth Earl of Northumberland, lived to regret allowing a glasshouse to be established in the park at Petworth because of the destruction caused in the woodlands. These industries also contributed the basic raw materials to the waves of new building that swept over Britain in the seventeenth century, bringing about a marked improvement in standards of cleanliness, warmth

91

and privacy, and London was rebuilt in brick, tiled and glazed after the Great Fire without sucking in vast quantities of foreign materials.

All three industries were certainly more important in this period than many historians would allow, but it is very likely that the iron industry was more significant than all three put together. Again, like the industries just described, it was widely dispersed, migratory and intermittent in its operations. Its basic fuel, until well past the period covered by this book, was charcoal, which it is almost impossible to transport satisfactorily in quantity, so that furnaces and forges had often to be built in comparatively isolated locations as they sought out the woods to supply their ever-growing demands for charcoal. In 1704 it was estimated that the furnaces and forges at Pontypool and Llanelli needed an annual cut over 320 acres of coppice to make a total of 700 tons of cast iron and 410 tons of bar iron. The coppice was cut when sixteen years old. This meant a total working area of woodland of 5120 acres, just eight square miles of land devoted entirely to woodland to supply just one industry.

All medieval iron was produced by the direct or bloomery method. Iron ore was smelted using charcoal in a shallow bowl-shaped pit, lined with clay or stone, and surrounded with a platform of stones upon which the smelters stood to do their work. The actual pit might be up to two feet six inches deep and perhaps two feet in diameter, housed in a furnace house built of wood and with a thatched roof. After perhaps twelve hours of constant and careful attention a bloomery might yield a crude bloom of iron weighing about a hundredweight. Before it could be used it had to be consolidated by repeated hammering and reheating up to white heat, about 1400° Centigrade. This might be done in the same hearth, or in another nearby, called a string hearth. Both hearths were provided with bellows, always the most expensive item of equipment in a bloomery, and often operated by water power from the thirteenth century onwards.

Bloomeries were slow and inefficient. They might extract perhaps 12 per cent of the iron from the ore. But they were comparatively cheap to build and to operate, and they continued to be used until well beyond the end of the seventeenth century. There was for example one at Muncaster Head Farm in Eskdale and another at Garstang, between Preston and Lancaster, in operation at the end of the seventeenth century.

The first blast furnace built in Britain was erected in

1496 at Newbridge in Sussex. It marked one of the most important technological developments ever to take place in the iron industry. The blast furnace (see Fig. 8) was essentially a tall square structure of masonry, by 1600 about 18 feet high, whilst the Gloucester furnace, in Kent, was, at the end of the seventeenth century, 28 feet high and said to be the highest in Britain. Although the furnace itself was built of masonry, the ancillary buildings, including that over the casting floor, were usually of timber and thatch. The furnace itself was fed with charcoal and iron ore at the top, usually by men wheeling barrows up an inclined slope. As the fuel was consumed and the iron melted so the top load moved slowly down the shaft of the furnace to meet the blast of heat from the hearth at the bottom. Once charged and in operation a furnace could run for many weeks, such a 'campaign' usually taking place during the winter months. The furnace was tapped at the bottom from time to time and could produce as much as a ton of iron a day. By the middle of the seventeenth century this had risen to as much as three tons.

The iron thus produced was cast iron, with anything up to 5 per cent of carbon, making it very brittle. This meant that it had to go through further refining processes to convert it into wrought iron. The refining consisted of heating and reheating the iron whilst it was being hammered to remove the excess carbon and other impurities left behind from the furnace. This was done in the forge, which could be close to the furnace, or an altogether separate establishment. Furnace and forge were, almost from their introduction into Britain, water powered in that a water wheel was used to drive the bellows which provided the blast both for the furnace and the forge, as well as the power to move the heavy tilt hammer in the forge. As in the bloomery, it was the bellows which were always the most expensive items to maintain. Since the operations in furnace and forge were quite distinct at least two water wheels were required, and it was this that encouraged the separation of furnace and forge as they sought out a constant and steady source of power.

Their other prerequisite was a supply of fuel. This had to be charcoal since, in spite of much effort and experiment from the end of the sixteenth century onwards the problems inherent in the use of coal in the blast furnace were not overcome until 1709. Sources of timber for conversion to charcoal together with water power for the bellows and hammer were much more important determinants of the location of furnaces and forges than was the supply of iron ore. If either failed, then the furnace or forge had to be abandoned. An account of the iron works of Sir Fulke Greville on Cannock Chase, in Staffordshire, made in 1611, described how the dams and pools for the water wheels had been broken down by sudden floods, and noted that the cottages erected for the workmen were covered with clods or turves and were of little worth and that the iron-stone which had been used had to come from Walsall, some five or six miles distant. But the reason why the iron works had to close was because the woods lately growing on Cannock were now 'spent and gone and so none to maintain the said iron works'.

The earliest furnaces and forges were in the Weald, where timber and water were both plentiful. There were nine furnaces here by 1542. In 1543 the casting of guns in iron began at Buxted, and the demand for guns provided an enormous stimulus for the expansion of the iron industry in the Weald, so that over the next five years eleven new furnaces were built. A survey made in 1574 lists forty-nine furnaces and fifty-eight forges, of which only seven furnaces were outside the Weald. In the last half of the sixteenth century iron making spread rapidly. There was a blast furnace on Cannock Chase by 1561, and the first furnace was established in Glamorganshire shortly afterwards, an offshoot of the Sidney iron works at Robertsbridge and Panningridge in the Sussex Weald, established early in 1541. One was built near West Bromwich in about 1590, another near Dudley about five years later, by which time there were two at Sheffield, and one had been built at Rievaulx in 1576. By 1610 there was one on the shores of Lochmaree, in the Highlands of Scotland.

A detailed list, compiled in 1717, names 176 iron works in England and Wales, comprising 60 furnaces and 116 forges. There were in addition an unknown number of the by now old-fashioned bloomery iron works in Lancashire. It is possible to compile a map from this list, and it shows the distribution of the iron industry in England and Wales as it was at the close of the period covered by this book. This enormous industrial enterprise must, by this time, have been worth several million pounds. A great deal of documentary evidence relating to it still survives, much of it unpublished, and there are, certainly for the eighteenth century, many drawings and paintings which give a vivid impression of what a blast furnace must have looked like, and at the same time convey something of what it must have been like to have worked in a furnace or forge.

But almost nothing now survives above ground. Documents relating to the forge on Thursley Heath, in Surrey, give some idea of its appearance. There was, in 1623, a forge, hammer and beam, bellows, several houses for workmen, a water course with ponds, sluices and floodgates. In 1666 there were said to be a pair of furnace bellows, five wheelbarrows, twelve coal baskets for carrying charcoal, separate bellows for both the finery and the chafery, hammers, tongs, an anvil, an iron house, a hammerhouse, a tool house, a peat house and dwelling

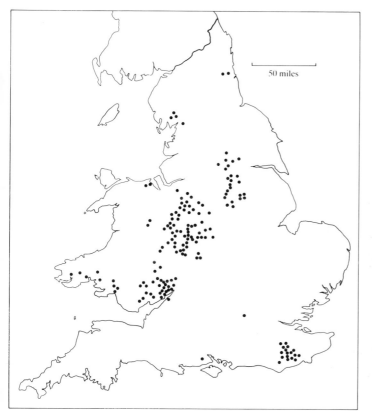

9 Iron furnaces and forges in England and Wales in 1717

50 miles

houses for the workmen. Many of the sites of such furnaces and forges are known precisely, and a number have been excavated. They are marked today by mounds of slag, the footings of the furnace and perhaps a little of the stonework, as at Upper Soudley, in the Forest of Dean, by the post holes of the workmens' houses and the store sheds, by silted up and overgrown watercourses, and above all, and especially in the Weald, by quiet treeshaded pools made by damming a small stream in order to create

Mines and mills, forges and furnaces

a store of power to drive bellows and hammers. It is difficult now, standing beside them of a summer's afternoon, to imagine the noise and heat of the furnace or forge which once they served.

The mining of non-ferrous metals, especially tin, lead, zinc and copper, was widespread in many districts of the Highland Zone of Britain during the sixteenth and seventeenth centuries, although the story is a very confused one, not least because veins of these metals are very erratic

Plate 16 The hammer pond at Hawkins Pond, Mannings Heath, Sussex

in their occurrence. Many were opened up during this period and as quickly abandoned in the face of flooding, exhaustion of the veins or lack of money and technical knowledge. Many of the sites have since been worked over and, as with coal and iron workings, it is almost impossible to detect surviving features that are certainly of this period.

The Company of Mines Royal was founded in 1568 by royal charter with the object of exploiting gold, silver and copper mines in the north of England and in Wales, its monopoly based on the royal claim to all mines in which any metals used for coinage were to be found. It relied heavily upon German investment at first, and also upon German technical knowledge. A large community of German miners, many from the Tyrol, was established near Keswick to mine and smelt the copper which had been discovered nearby. A smelting house was built, and wood cutters and charcoal burners brought from Cannock Chase and Shropshire to manufacture the necessary fuel. At the same time a search was made for coal, and a reasonable supply was found at Bolton, some twelve miles to the north of Keswick. A great deal of money was spent, but with little return on the investment. A survey made in 1600 gives some of the reasons for the lack of success. The commissioners visited the mines in the February, and found the frost so great that the water wheels to the smelting house could not work. About eight years ago the great charcoal barn had been burned down because some of the charcoal had not been sufficiently quenched, a loss of £66 13s. 4d. In the previous two and a half years it had cost £4 7s. 8d. to produce every quintal, about 100 lbs, of copper, and yet it could be sold for only £4 2s. 6d., all carriage charges allowed. The God's Gift mine, about three miles from Keswick, had only three pickmen and two labourers at work at this date, and its pumping engine would cost £153 6s. 8d. and take nine months to put into working order. In the face of these and other difficulties the company found it prudent to lease the mines to the German family Hechstetter, and their lease was renewed in 1601. All the mine buildings and equipment were destroyed by Parliamentary soldiers in 1651 and within twenty years even the location of the mines had been forgotten.

A rather similar company, the Society of Mineral and Battery Works, was also established by royal charter in 1568 with the object of introducing into England the making of brass and the manufacture of iron plates by means of hammers, the true meaning of 'battery work'. It could also search and mine copper and zinc outside the areas reserved for the Company of Mines Royal. Calamine, from which zinc, an important constituent of brass, can be extracted, was found at Worley Hill, in Somerset, and the Company began to search for a suitable spot, combining water power and ample supplies of wood for charcoal, on which to begin its work. Eventually it was decided to set up a works at Tintern, using a tributary of the Wye, the Angevy, as the source of power. Here a building some fifty feet long by thirty feet wide was built, with four water wheels, two furnaces and two forges, for the making and drawing of wire. The brass making activities were leased out in 1582, and were promptly moved to Isleworth and two years later also to Rotherhithe, where for a number of years they were very successful. The wire works at Tintern encountered a great deal of difficulty at first, and had to rely for long upon German craftsmen, whilst competition from continental wire was always a problem. However by the end of the sixteenth century the works were in a flourishing state, and said to be employing about 120 people. Wire was used to make pins, fish-hooks, needles of every kind from sewing needles to fearsome implements for sewing sails, bird cages, spurs, bridles, hooks and eyes, mouse traps, dog chains, curtain rings and buckles, but above all for the wool cards used in preparing wool for the spinners.

In spite of its success at the turn of the century, the fortunes of the Tintern wire works fluctuated considerably during the course of the seventeenth century. In 1646 Thomas Foley took over the management, and in about 1672 he set up a furnace and two forges to provide the raw materials for the wire works, with the Upper Forge also on the Angevy brook, a little above the wire works. The works were again prospering by the end of the seventeenth century, and indeed did not finally close until the end of the nineteenth century.

Mines of lead, copper and silver were eagerly sought in Cornwall and in Wales throughout this period, either under licence from the two companies, or licence from the Crown or without the consent of either. In about 1584 a copper smelting works had been established at Aberdulais, near Neath, using ores from both Cornwall and Cardiganshire, but it seems to have closed by about 1600. In the early decades of the seventeenth century lead and silver mining in Cardiganshire were so successful that in 1638 a mint was opened at Aberystwyth to make the silver then being mined into coins. It was captured by Parliamentary forces in 1646 and operations came to an end. The 1690s saw a renewal of activity in the mining and smelting of lead and copper, and a number of new companies were formed, including the London Lead Company with mines in Flintshire and a smelting plant at Gadlys. At the same time Sir Humphrey Mackworth built a copper smelting plant at Melin Cryddan, near his coal mines at Neath, which supplied the fuel. By 1690 Sir Carbery Pryse had opened up a lead and silver mine at Bwlch yr Esgairhir which was considered to be so rich that it was called the Welsh Potosi. The mine was claimed by Anthony

Shepherd as lessee under the Company of Mines Royal of its monopoly of silver and lead workings. The case, in fact there were two, was heard in the Court of Exchequer, during the course of which the Crown ceased to defend the monopoly. The situation was clarified by an Act of Parliament of 1693 under which the Crown gave up all claim to a monopoly of mineral rights unless the mines were of pure gold and silver.

Both companies were seriously affected by the loss of their monopoly rights, and eventually in 1710 they agreed upon a merger. In 1718 a controlling interest in their shares was obtained by an insurance group, with the intention of using the Company as a basis for developing marine insurance. This caused a great deal of opposition and so a grant of incorporation was sought and obtained. In 1720 the Company emerged under the title of the Royal Exchange Assurance.

Not all non-ferrous mining was in the hands of these two companies, in spite of their monopolies. Lead mining along much of the Pennine chain, for example, was carried on by small-scale miners who were often farmers as well. Thus the Earl of Cumberland leased out his lead mines on Grassington Low Moor in the 1620s to miners of this kind, he providing the smelt mill, and by 1630s a second. Further south, in the Derbyshire Hundred of the High Peak and the manor of Wirksworth, the miners themselves were closely regulated under their own ancient customs. Individual miners were free to search for lead where they wished. When a vein was found it was registered with the Barmaster, and all disputes were settled in the Barmoot court. The smelting was done in a simple hearth or 'bole', a hollow in the ground covered with turf and facing into the wind. The lead when it melted ran out into moulds to solidify into leaden pigs. The miner then paid a thirteenth part of his production as a royalty to the Lord of the Field, who was the monarch until Elizabeth disposed of her rights. Exploration for lead was certainly encouraged under this organisation, and large areas of the Derbyshire moors, around Winster, Bonsall, Sheldon, Bradwell and Castleton, for example, are littered with pits and spoil heaps which show vividly how miners followed the veins or 'rakes' across the landscape, sometimes for miles.

Lead mining in the Mendips was organised in a rather similar way, the Lords Royal of Mendip taking ten per cent of production, and disputes being settled in a special mining court. Again, especially around Charterhouse and Priddy the landscape is scarred by the lead miners.

Mines and mills, forges and furnaces

The tin miners of Devon and Cornwall were governed by their own Stannary parliaments and courts, in which laws were passed and transgressors punished. Tinners could search freely for tin over unenclosed land, divert streams where necessary and cut timber for the fuel they required. By the end of the fifteenth century tin was being mined by means of shafts, which as they went ever deeper became increasingly difficult to keep free from flood water. Tin lodes could also be located by cutting a trench across

Plate 17 The long lines of shallow pits made by miners as they followed the veins of lead across the countryside are clearly visible on this aerial photograph of the landscape near Wardlow, in Derbyshire

likely ground and then diverting a stream into it. This would quickly remove unwanted material and expose the tin. In this way the landscape was permanently gashed and scored by the tinners' workings.

We have seen earlier in this chapter how coal replaced wood as a source of heat in an increasingly wide range of manufactures. There were however many problems to be overcome before coal could be used satisfactorily. Malt dried with raw coal made an undrinkable beer, and so by about 1603 attempts were being made to dry malt with coal which had itself been roasted to drive off the impurities. Success was a long time coming and it seems to have been the 1640s before coke was being used successfully to dry malt from which a palatable beer could be brewed. It continued to be impossible to use coal in blast furnaces however and it was not until 1709 that Abraham Darby made iron successfully using coke at his Coalbrookdale ironworks, and even then the technique spread only very slowly and it was the second half of the eighteenth century before it began to be adopted on any scale.

Coal was used for heating, boiling, drying and roasting. Its energy was not yet harnessed to provide any motive power, and it was not until 1712 that a coal-fired steam engine was built near Dudley to pump water from a coal mine. Only then was the first tentative step taken down the road that was to revolutionise man's command over energy and power. Before this, and indeed for long after, he had to rely upon his own muscular strength, or that of animals, especially horses, or else upon the intermittent and capricious power of wind and water.

Animals provided a great deal of the energy needs of pre-industrial Britain. Horses and oxen pulled ploughs, harrows, carts and wagons. A horse, plodding patiently in a circle, provided the energy to wind up baskets containing both coal and miners. Horses pulled barges upstream against the current, and wagons uphill against the force of gravity. Messages, however urgent, could go no faster than relays of horses could gallop. The whole complex industrial empire of Sir Ambrose Crowley, by the end of the seventeenth century the wealthiest ironmaster in Britain, relied upon the post boy and his horse, since he rarely went outside London and conducted his business almost entirely by post from his house and warehouse at Greenwich. Clay for making pottery had to be carefully prepared. It was weathered, sometimes for as much as two years before being steeped in water, 'blunged', that is beaten with a spatula, and kneaded to remove air pockets, stones and gravel. This work, hard, laborious and dirty, had to be done by hand, but by 1678 Thomas Wedgwood was using a horse gin for the purpose, and by the early eighteenth century potters had learned how to adapt water corn mills to this end.

The energy of water had been harnessed to drive water mills since Roman times, and they were very widely distributed throughout Britain in the sixteenth and seven- teenth centuries. They were used at first to grind grain

101

into flour, but by the middle of the sixteenth century they had been adapted, and would continue to be adapted, to a wide range of other industrial purposes. One of the most important processes in the manufacture of woollen cloth is fulling, when the cloth is washed in fuller's earth in order to shrink and felt it. This was done at first by hand, or at least by foot, because men would walk up and down barefooted in the troughs in which the cloth was soaking. In the thirteenth century the water mill was adapted to this process, replacing human effort. Heavy wooden hammers were moved up and down by means of cams on the driving shaft. From its first introduction the blast furnace in the iron industry depended upon bellows powered by water wheels, and the separate forges in which the iron pigs were refined also had furnaces requiring water-powered bellows and water-powered tilt hammers.

Windmills make their first appearance in England in the middle years of the twelfth century and they too become very common and, like water mills, they could be fairly easily adapted from their original purpose of grinding grain to carrying out many other functions, including pumping.

Mills of every kind, whether horse, water or wind powered, were very common indeed throughout pre-industrial Britain. Very few parishes were without at least one, most had several, and of each kind, and it is abundantly clear from the documentary evidence that they could be converted comparatively easily from one purpose to another. It is clear, too, that it required only a small stream to turn a water wheel. What was more important than volume of water was that the flow should be steady and regular. The stream issuing from Cheddar gorge was described by Michael Drayton in *Poly-Olbion* as being very forcible, driving twelve mills within a mile's quarter of its head, and in the sixteenth century Trill Mill stream, running along the south walls of Oxford, had several mills on it.

Many people still found themselves obliged to grind their corn at the manorial mill, a monopoly exploited by manorial lord and miller alike. Most Scottish tenants were 'thirled to the mill', although the practice was dying out rapidly in England, especially after the Restoration. In Manchester there were, for example, three corn mills and one fulling mill on the river Irk in the sixteenth century. All the inhabitants had to grind their corn in these manorial mills, the profits from which were granted to maintain the Grammar School in 1525. There were burgh

Plate 18 The seventeenth-century windmill at Brill, in Buckinghamshire. The disused clay pits produced by the now defunct Brill brick, tile and pottery industry can be seen to the right of the mill

mills in Stirling in the sixteenth century, and in 1654 it was clearly and forcefully stated that the whole neighbourhood was thirled to the Bridge and Borrow mills, which were to be leased out yearly with the rest of the common good of the town. All common bakers and freemen of Oxford owed suit to the castle mills, as the town council was at pains to point out until 1678, and the inhabitants of Newcastle under Lyme were similarly expected to grind their corn at the castle mills until the end of the seventeenth century.

Yet other tenants found themselves obliged to contribute to the repair of the mills. It was said, for example, early in the seventeenth century that the customary tenants in the lordship of Brecon owed suit and service to the King's Mills in Dyvinuck Laywell by the service of carrying wood, timber and stone for the repair of the mill and grinding all their grain there, for which, of course, they had to pay the customary tolls. Similarly, and at about the same time, the water corn mill called Melin Rhud Owen, Llandisselt, in Cardiganshire, was repaired by the tenants, each tenement having to perform a customary portion of the work, including thatching the mill and scouring the pond. Rather similar terms were exacted from the tenants of the barony of Uric, in Kincardineshire. Here every thirteenth peck of meal ground at the mill went to the miller, and tenants were expected to keep the mill in repair and the mill race free from weeds; they could be compelled on twelve hours' notice to go to work to repair the embankment of the race, and every plough had to send two men and two horses for 'home-draweing off the milne stones off the milne of Cowie'. In contrast, in a survey of the lordship of Oswestry made in 1602 it was said that the lord's customary mill was now so decayed that the place where once it stood was almost forgotten, and so the tenants pretended a freedom to grind their corn where they would.

There is documentary evidence in abundance to suggest how widespread water and windmills were in this period, and how diverse their functions could be. In 1647 there was a lead smelting mill in Wolsingham, county Durham, which had formerly been a fulling mill and was now let for a rent of £6 13s. 4d., but in the same survey the water corn mill at Whickham was said to be now quite decayed and fallen to the ground. There was at the same period both a water corn mill and a windmill at Gateshead, and at Houghton le Spring there were two water corn mills and three windmills. For Bishop Middleham it was said that the water corn mill at Sedgefield was in great decay and that the copy and leaseholders ought to repair it and were bound to grind their corn at it. There was also a windmill on the glebe land. There were two water mills in Ayr, to which the burgesses were thirled. A survey of Duchy of Cornwall lands in Cornwall made in 1647 reveals several tin smelting houses in which the bellows were water powered: at Calstock, for example, and there were several blowing and stamping mills in the manor of Helston. A blowing mill was used for smelting the tin ore, and a stamping mill was used for crushing it. By 1670 windmills were being used in the Bedford Level in the fens to pump water up into the water-courses as drainage problems became increasingly acute as the peat began to shrink, leaving the water-course embankments above the level of the surrounding countryside. Ogilby's road maps, published in 1675, mark a paper mill near Rugeley, powder mills and saw mills near Hounslow, and three windmills just to the east of Brighton.

There is one manufacture which remains to be discussed, and this is the textile industry. The manufacture of woollen cloth of a great variety of shades, textures and finishes was carried on almost everywhere in Britain and during the seventeenth century silk, linen and cotton were added. Woollen cloth dominated the export trade and, as we shall see in Chapter 9, much of inland carrying as well. But it was very much a domestic manufacture, with spinning, weaving, dyeing and finishing carried out in the yards and outhouses attached to private dwelling houses as well as indoors. Further, very many households of any size would expect to be self-supporting in the spinning and weaving of woollen and linen cloth for everyday use, and housewives, their daughters and servants would make it up into clothes. The only part of the manufacturing process calling for special premises was fulling, done in water-powered mills at least from the thirteenth century. These differ only in their internal machinery from other water-powered mills, and in any case, as we have seen, the functions of water mills could change easily and frequently, so that it is very difficult to attribute any surviving building today solely to the textile industry. Thus one of the most important manufactures of Tudor and Stuart Britain has left almost no direct visual evidence at all behind it, and indeed its very presence in the land-scape at the time would have been difficult to detect. Indirectly however it lies behind many Cotswold towns and villages and the churches of East Anglian towns such as Lavenham and Long Melford since they were built with money which in the end came from the backs of sheep.

At Arlington Mill, near Bibury, in Gloucestershire, the mill itself seems to have been rebuilt in the seventeenth century and used both as a corn mill and a fulling mill, and at Arlington Row there is a row of small cottages dating from the same period built to house the weavers who made the cloth fulled in Arlington Mill. At Boyndie, in Banffshire, there is a seventeenth-century lint mill, in which flax was scutched, that is the soaked flax stems were beaten to separate out the fibres, but, as in England, buildings which can be certainly attributed to any branch of the textile industry in Scotland are almost invariably eighteenth century in date.

The first textile factory was a water-powered mill built in Derby in 1702 by Thomas Cotchett for the throwing of silk, but it was not a success, and the next one was Thomas Lombe's mill, also in Derby and also for silk-throwing, built in 1717. It is only from this time that purpose-built weavers' cottages and textile mills begin to survive.

Manufacture and mining develop enormously during the course of the sixteenth and seventeenth centuries, in spite of many technical difficulties, much wasted money and effort and numerous short-term fluctuations in production. In the nature of things manufacturing and mining destroy almost all of the evidence of their past, and this chapter can be illustrated only by the broken and

Mines and mills, forges and furnaces

Plate 19 The row of cottages built early in the seventeenth century to house workers at Arlington Mill, near Bibury, in Gloucestershire

scattered remnants that the transformation of industry in the nineteenth century has left behind. It is also the only chapter of this book that cannot be easily illustrated from Plate 1 apart from the windmill on the skyline; unless one looks closely at the clothes of the men and women working in the fields, the sickles and other implements which they are using, and the harness of their horses, in other words the products of the mines, mills and forges which have formed the theme of this chapter.

Building

The houses in which men, their wives, children, servants and apprentices lived and worked in the first decades of the sixteenth century were essentially medieval. By the end of the seventeenth century many men and women lived in houses which were essentially modern. The intervening years brought marked and sometimes dramatic changes in what men expected in the way of comfort, amenity, privacy, warmth and cleanliness in their homes. Brick replaced timber and wattle and daub. Glass for windows became cheap. Chimneys and fireplaces replaced the open fire in the centre of the principal room in the house, with the result that upstairs rooms could now be heated and people no longer had to endure the smarting eyes and sore throats brought on by smoke from the central hearth swirling round a room in its vain search for a way out through a hole in the roof.

These two centuries brought great changes in the design and layout of houses, in their methods and materials of construction and in their external appearance. But the processes of change were slow and uneven. The housing stock of medieval Britain was not swept away overnight. Houses continued to be built to traditional designs long after the seventeenth century had come to an end, and it is important to appreciate that the survival rate, both of medieval and of early modern houses, has been very uneven, both geographically and socially, so that generalisations based solely on surviving examples in the landscape today are likely to be misleading. Further, in the adoption and adaptation of new ideas the North and West of Britain could be as much as a hundred years behind the South and the East.

Many of the new ideas came ultimately from Renaissance Italy, although frequently through the filter of France and the Low Countries rather than directly from Italy itself. The rate at which these ideas diffused over the country was slow, uneven, patchy and as much a matter of fashion and personal connection as anything else. At the same time the traditional vernacular building styles were themselves undergoing change: the great medieval hall, open to the roof, was ceiled over; staircases and chimneys were inserted. Thus change came from two directions: first of all from within the vernacular tradition itself, and secondly from Italy. By the end of the seventeenth century the two had fused, with one or the other more or less dominant according to region and type of building; but it was the early nineteenth century before vernacular building styles ceased to be a living tradition, by which time the themes from Renaissance Italy had themselves been transformed, superseded and replaced by the often indiscriminate eclecticism of Victorian architecture.

The starting point for our exploration of these processes of change must be the medieval house. This was invariably a rectangular building open to the roof. It could vary considerably in size and could be timber-framed in its construction, or else built of stone, turf or chalk, depending upon the wealth of its owner and the availability of local building materials. It was almost invariably thatched. At first it contained only one room, the hall. This was heated from a central hearth, the smoke from which, it was hoped, would find its way out through a hole in the roof. By the fourteenth century this simple structure was showing signs of change. The hall was being divided up, in the interest of greater privacy. (See Fig. 10.) There could, of course, be numerous ways in which this subdivision was arranged, and the names and purposes of the rooms could also vary. The ground floor chamber was called the parlour by the end of the fourteenth century and was – and will remain in some parts of the country until the end of the seventeenth century – primarily a sleeping room. Frequently the blocks at either end of the house had a first floor room over them, with access by means of a ladder or staircase. The central hall however still remained open to the roof, so that there was no intercommunication between the rooms on the first floor.

By the early years of the sixteenth century the open hall was diminishing in its importance as the central room in the house, and during the course of the century important structural changes were made in existing houses to reflect this shift in social habits, whilst newly built houses included them from the first. The central hall was ceiled over by having a first floor inserted. The earliest conversion of this kind which can be dated was made at Hookwood Manor, Charlwood, Surrey, in 1571. A more drastic alteration was made at Trout's Farm, Ockley, also in Surrey, some ten years later, when the hall was demolished and a two storey block erected in its place. By this time open halls had ceased to be built in new buildings over much of southern England. Lower down the social scale however, two- and three-room one storey cottages continued to be built. Old Farmhouse, Assington, and Thatch Cottage, Chilton by Sudbury, Suffolk, are surviving examples of buildings of this kind, and several also remain in the Fylde, in Lancashire.

If the hall is to be ceiled over, then something must be

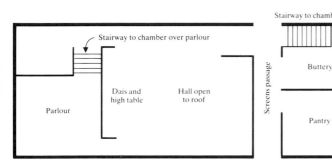

10 A late medieval open-hall house plan, based upon Old Bell Farm, Harrietsham, Kent

done about the central fire. The commonest solution was to build a chimney stack backing on to the through passage. This meant that at least the hall could still be heated, and so also in due course, could the room directly over it. The ceiling over the hall also meant that decoration of the roof timbers became a waste of time, and as a consequence elaborately carved crown and king posts supporting a central collar purlin disappear and much more simple side purlins are used instead.

At about the same time that the open hall was disappearing so too was the through passage. Entrance to the house was now by means of a small lobby, the rest of the space where the through passage once lay being taken up with a central chimney stack which would heat two rooms because it incorporated two back-to-back fireplaces. Beyond the chimney stack was a staircase, giving easy and convenient access to the first floor rooms. By the early seventeenth century three-celled houses of this kind were common all over south-eastern England, although the earliest known example of a lobby entrance house of this kind is Old Hall Farm, Kneesall, Nottinghamshire, dating from before 1536. (See Fig. 11 and Plate 20.)

In this way, the vernacular tradition, by responding to new social pressures and demands, during the course of less than a hundred years brought quite astonishing changes into the layout of hundreds of cottages and farmhouses, producing houses that were cleaner, more convenient and certainly very much more private than anything hitherto. This had all been done without recourse to Italian models, French designs or Flemish decoration, and it was still incorporated within traditional building techniques of timber-framed construction, panelling and close-studding, with walls infilled with wattle and daub. New materials were incorporated when they had proved their worth and had become sufficiently cheap: glass for windows passed these tests by the end of the sixteenth

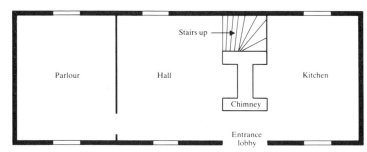

11 The ground-floor plan of a late sixteenth-century three-cell lobby entrance house

Plate 20 Old Hall Farm, Kneesall, Nottinghamshire, built, perhaps as a hunting lodge, in about 1536 for Sir John Hussey. It is the earliest known example of the three-cell lobby entrance house, with an axial chimney stack heating two rooms, and a door opposite opening into a small lobby. It is built of brick with terracotta decorations (see also Fig. 11)

century, but brick was used at first only for the new chimney stacks. It does not appear as a walling material in small houses before the second and third decades of the seventeenth century.

However, any impression these paragraphs may have given that the vernacular tradition produced a uniform house plan the length and breadth of Britain is far from the truth. The vernacular tradition was deeply embedded in local and regional variations of occupation, farming practices, inheritance laws, climate, altitude and geology, and these variations are reflected in local and regional building practices and house forms.

Open hall houses were often built with side aisles in the medieval centuries. By the fifteenth century these aisles were disappearing over much of southern England. They

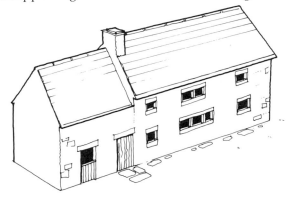

12 A Lakeland long house in the early eighteenth century

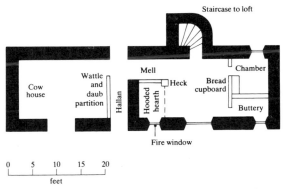

persisted well into the sixteenth century on the eastern slopes of the Pennines, especially in the huge parish of Halifax, often with only one aisle rather than two, and when change did come they were faced with stone and altered and adapted rather than being demolished, and only the most careful study of internal structural details can reveal the medieval heart behind a late seventeenth-century façade.

The rooms beyond the through passage of the late medieval hall house were not always service rooms. They could instead serve as a byre in which cattle were housed, especially in the winter months. This long house was once

111

Plate 21 The long house at Spout House, Bilsdale Midcable, Yorkshire. It is a cruck-built house with late seventeenth-century stone walls. The door at the east end leads into a wide passage, suggesting that the room at the end on the right may once have been a byre, but it has been altered and the windows are modern. The view is from the south-west

widespread over much of Britain, but by the early sixteenth century it was largely confined to the north and east, and in Devonshire and the Lake District substantial and well-built long houses were occupied by prosperous farmers until well into the eighteenth century; and even then they were not abandoned. Instead new byres were built for the livestock and the old ones were converted into accommodation for human beings.

Timber frame construction was widely used wherever supplies of timber were to be found, and in some parts of Britain it was used for decorative purposes where other building materials were more plentiful and used in traditional buildings. Thus in Burford, in the Cotswolds, timber framing was used to decorate the street fronts of houses otherwise built of stone, and in Wales, where stone was the normal building material, timber framed houses were built in the towns, such as Caernarvon, Conway, Beaumaris, Brecon, Wrexham and Llanidloes. Timber framed houses could achieve a rich variety of decoration, a dignity and a sense of organic unity in districts as far apart as Kent and Suffolk, Shropshire and Montgomeryshire, quite the equal of anything to be found in any Italianate country house.

But timber framing is only one technique employing wood to be used in houses built in the vernacular tradition. Cruck construction, a method in which curved blades of timber erected in pairs are used to bear the main weight of

the roof, is another. Substantial cruck-built houses, using timbers of good scantling, date from the fourteenth century, and it is clear too that it is a construction technique that was once widespread over much of Britain. By the early years of the sixteenth century the use of crucks is declining, and when still used later in the century they are found usually only in cottages and using poor quality timbers. Crucks were still used over much of Scotland until well into the eighteenth century, whilst in Wales they were superseded by timber framed construction in the north-east during the sixteenth century, save that scarfed crucks continued in use in Carmarthenshire and Cardiganshire.

Wood, whether employed in timber framing or in cruck construction, is not, however, the only building material employed in the vernacular tradition. Stone, including flint, and unbaked earths were also extensively used, again depending upon the availability of local supplies. It is this use of local materials of every kind that gives to so much vernacular building that sense of organic unity with its environment. After all, so much of it has, literally, been hewn from the ground on which it stands.

Plate 22 An aerial view of Little Moreton Hall, Cheshire, a conservative, essentially medieval, timber-framed country house built and added to from the end of the fifteenth century to the end of the sixteenth. It is the country version of the house illustrated in Plate 43

Running from south-west to north-east in a great band from Dorset to East Yorkshire is the English limestone belt. Here are to be found a wide variety of building stones, some of first class quality, some rather poor stuff that was used simply because it was locally available and cheap to obtain. Here are to be found some of the quarries that have yielded some of the finest English building stones: Taynton, mentioned in Domesday Book, Painswick, Barnack, Ancaster, Clipsham, Ketton, Collyweston and Ham Hill. These quarries, and many more, provided the raw materials for the stone houses and cottages of the Cotswolds, north Oxfordshire, Northamptonshire and Lincolnshire. It is however characteristic of the vernacular tradition that, even when it is using a widespread raw material, local and regional variations should develop. In the Cotswolds, for example, where so much of the building is seventeenth rather than sixteenth century, it is common to find the entrance to a farmhouse or cottage in the gable end, next to the chimney. When first floor accommodation was first provided it was usual to light these rooms by means of low, long dormer windows that, under the thatched roof, look like eyes under thick

eyebrows. Later in the seventeenth century, when it became usual to build in upstairs rooms from the first, the windows were set into gables, giving to Cotswold houses of every kind their distinctive and characteristic appearance. In the stone belt villages of north Somerset house plans were very conservative throughout the seventeenth century, but local masons moved from using hollow chamfers to the stone mullions of windows in the last two decades of the sixteenth century to ovolo in the second decade of the seventeenth and back again to chamfers in the last decade of the century. Similarly, over much of Devon and Cornwall, chimneys were very frequently built at the front of the house (see Plate 59) rather than in the interior or at one end. It is these local, subtle variations that give to the vernacular tradition of building in the sixteenth and seventeenth centuries its endless fascination.

To the south-east of the limestone belt lies a great arc of chalkland. Chalk itself can be used as a building material but it is not particularly durable. The important building material of the chalklands is not the chalk itself, but the flint, which occurs naturally in the chalk beds. Flint makes a hard, durable building material and, when it is broken open to reveal the black glassy interior, it can also make a very attractive one. Flint, because of its hardness and the fact that it occurs in irregularly shaped nodules, can be very difficult to use successfully, and so, when it is

115

used as a building material, it is broken up into small, fairly regular pieces. Even then it has to be contained within brick or stone quoins or window dressings, since it is so difficult to handle at corners. This is why so many Norfolk churches, built of flint, have round towers. It can also be used set in square panels alternating with brick or stone. The overall effect can provide surface patterns of great variety and subtlety of texture. (See Plate 3.)

The use of unbaked earths for building purposes is widespread over Britain. (See Plate 59.) When mixed with water, stones and chopped straw, provided with a sound plinth and a good roof and then rendered with whitewash or plaster, these unbaked earths, known as cob, wichert, or clay lump, can provide remarkably durable building materials. Many houses and cottages, built of wichert, in Haddenham in Buckinghamshire still survive today to give to this Buckinghamshire town its unique atmosphere. Devonshire has more clay houses surviving than any other English county. Large numbers have been recorded in Northamptonshire. Leicestershire and Warwickshire, and over a hundred are known in the Solway Firth area of Cumberland. Nor are these invariably the cottages of the poor. Sir Walter Raleigh was born in 1552 in a fine E plan house, Hayes Barton, near East Budleigh, a house with walls of cob.

The vernacular tradition, in which masons and carpenters, using local material, built houses and cottages of every size in accordance with local and regional needs, was to be found the length and breadth of Britain. It is as much a part of the landscape of Wales and Scotland as it is of England, with the same local and regional variations and the same subtle and complex interaction between geology, climate and society.

The lands to the east of the central mountain chain in Wales are in many respects extensions of the English lowlands. They have the same fertile soils, the same climate, and are also accessible to the same range of ideas that informed the vernacular tradition of Cheshire, Shropshire and Herefordshire. The consequence is a strong tradition of fine timber framed building in the eastern half of Denbighshire, over much of Montgomeryshire and Radnorshire and into Monmouthshire, a tradition that persists until the middle years of the eighteenth century. This is a region in which timber framing by and large supersedes cruck construction during the course of the sixteenth century, but the vernacular tradition, as elsewhere in Britain, can produce its own local patterns and styles. In Montgomeryshire, for example, many of the floors in some of the larger timber framed houses, instead of being of earth or even stone flags, are made of river pebbles set in elaborate decorative patterns.

Over the rest of Wales, save in the towns, building was in stone. Many parts of the country were remote, isolated and poor. New ideas spread only very slowly, and it is the end of the sixteenth century before the developments in house plan to be found in south-east England at the end of the fifteenth century begin to find their way into Carmarthenshire or Caernarvonshire. At the same time it is clear that in Wales people from the gentry and yeoman strata of society were living in houses much smaller and much less sophisticated than those occupied by men from similar ranks in English society, although this is not to deny that there are fine vernacular houses, whether in timber, as at Penarth, Newtown, Montgomeryshire, or stone, as at Pentrehobyn, Mold, in Flintshire, houses that English gentry or yeomen would have been proud to live in.

Vernacular houses in Wales were frequently built into the slope of a hillside. The simplest had only one room, and were built of clay and turf and thatched with rushes, and had neither windows nor chimneys. Such cabins are described by travellers in Wales as late as the end of the eighteenth century. Small single-storeyed cottages are still a very common feature of the landscape in districts such as Snowdonia, but they are all very much better constructed than those described by travellers would appear to have been, and so it would seem very likely that those which are to be seen today are little more than a hundred and fifty years old. They are in any case very difficult to date, and even so crude an example as Hendy in Waunfawr, Caernarvonshire, is probably no older than the eighteenth century.

An example of a better quality house, still built entirely

Plate 26 Hendy, Waunfawr, Caernarvonshire, a single-storey cottage probably built in the eighteenth century. Earlier ones were less substantial than this, being built of clay and turf, and so they have not survived

within a local tradition, is Ystradfaelog, Llanwnnog, Montgomeryshire. This was built at the end of the sixteenth century as a single-storey open hearth hall house within the regional vernacular tradition. Its parlour, chimney, hall and service rooms ascend slightly up the slope. It is timber framed, erected upon a low masonry plinth. The timber framing is in large squares or panels, again a feature that is characteristic of the regional vernacular tradition. Somewhere about the middle of the seventeenth century it was 'modernised' by the insertion of a floor over the open hall and the building of the internal hearth and chimney stack.

Houses of this kind illustrate the subtle regional variations to be found within the vernacular tradition and also the ability of that tradition to absorb and adopt new ideas, whether inspired by the need for greater comfort and privacy, or more purely materialistic in their origins, since it has been suggested that the many fine timber framed buildings dating from the second half of the seventeenth century to be found in north-east and eastern Wales are a reflection of the prosperity brought to the region by the development of the woollen textile industry there over the previous century. Similarly, the substantial quality of the houses in Halifax parish has been associated with the textile trade there, and the wealth of Lavenham in the sixteenth century is self-evident. Burwell, in Cambridge-

Plate 27 Ystradfaelog, Llanwnnog, Montgomeryshire, a timber framed house built at the end of the sixteenth century (see Fig. 13)

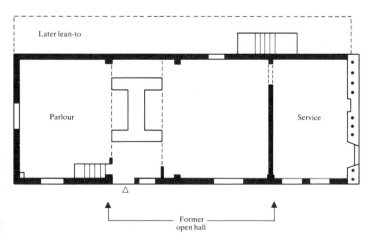

Later lean-to

Parlour

Service

Former open hall

13 Plan of Ystradfaelog, Llanwnnog, Montgomeryshire (see Plate 27). Acknowledgement: P. Smith and C. E. V. Owen, 'A Short Architectural Note on Ystradfaelog, The Bryn and Lower Gwestydd', *Montgomeryshire Collections*, 59, 1965–6, pp. 102–11.

shire, also has many fine late sixteenth- and seventeenth-century houses, perhaps the consequence of the extensive waterborne trade of the time.

Vernacular building can also reflect patterns of family relationships. One of the most interesting examples of this may be seen in the 'unit' houses to be found in many parts of Wales as well as in Herefordshire, Lancashire and Cheshire. In this 'unit' system the domestic accommodation of a sometimes quite substantial house is duplicated

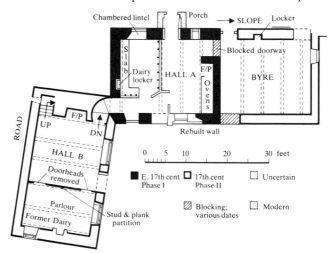

14 Plan of the 'unit' houses at Llanddegyman, Llanfihangel Cwm Du, Breconshire. Acknowledgement: S. R. Jones and J. T. Smith, 'The Houses of Breconshire, Part IV', *Brycheiniog*, 12, 1966–7, pp. 1–92

in another range of buildings, sometimes facing the first house across a yard, sometimes joined on at one corner but often with no internal communication between the two blocks. At Llanddegyman-fawr, Llanfihangel Cwm Du, in Breconshire, a long house, incorporating a byre, hall and service rooms, with men and animals sharing the same cross-passage entrance, was built early in the seventeenth century. A generation or so later a second block was added at right angles, containing hall, parlour and service room with a communicating doorway. At Plasnewydd, Llanfrothen, there are three houses.

Similar buildings are not unknown in England. At Chorley Hall, Wilmslow, a medieval hall had in about 1560 a timber framed addition built on to project at right angles from one corner. Rufford Old Hall was originally an open hall with two-storeyed ends. In 1662 a second block was added, built at right angles and probably just touching at the corner. Houses of this kind are to be found in eastern Lancashire and the adjoining parts of Cheshire, but there is a marked tendency in the later seventeenth century for additional building to obscure the dual nature of the domestic arrangements. Another example can be found at

Lamonby Farm, Cumberland. This has two dwellings and a byre in the same block of building. Similarly, Thickbigging Farm, Mainland, Orkney was originally three houses lying one behind the other with very narrow gaps between the walls. These have been filled in and the walls opened to make interconnecting passageways.

It has been suggested that houses of this kind represent one solution to the problems caused by laws of partible inheritance, under which property is subdivided among all the sons. It is not impossible to imagine two closely related families deciding to manage a farm in common rather than to subdivide it still further. A second house, built close to the first, would enable this to be done without the two families being compelled actually to live together.

That sons and daughters did live in close proximity to their parents after marriage is evident from a survey made in 1611 of the Forest of Macclesfield. At Rainow, in Cheshire and within the bounds of the forest, lived Thomas Clarke. He occupied a dwelling house of three bays. He also had a barn of four bays and a turf house of one bay. In addition there was one other little house of two bays 'wherein his sone dwelleth being sometime the kitchen to the said messuage', and there was also another little house of one bay newly erected in the occupation of Francis Clarke. However, too much must not be read into this, since it was not uncommon to find outbuildings converted into dwellings. At Fossdale in Wensleydale, for example, there was in 1614 a dwelling house with a yard and two garden plots and a turf house converted into a dwelling house, and at Simonstone a dwelling house with a detached kitchen had been made into two several dwellings which appear to have shared a barn, a turf house, gardens and garths.

Vernacular building in Scotland shows the same kind of organic unity with society and with topography as that to be found in either Wales or England. Unfortunately, as in Wales, there are very few cottages and small farmhouses surviving which are more than 150 years old, and so reconstruction of the housing of the great bulk of the Scottish people in the sixteenth and seventeenth centuries has to rely upon the comments of travellers and upon analogy with buildings which seem to have been built as recently as the end of the eighteenth century.

The cottages which made up a Scottish fermtoun were invariably, at least until the end of the seventeenth century, of a single storey only. The walls were built of locally available materials – stone, alternate layers of stones and turf, clay and wickerwork. Stones were often only roughly dressed, and to use them in conjunction with alternate layers of turf meant that in fact the stones were bedded in the turf, which served in the place of mortar. Both cottages and farmhouses were built in this way, and at least one church, that at Ach-na-h'uaidh, in Sutherland. If the stones were not bound with turf, but were used dry, then the interior walls were frequently plastered in clay. Stone-built dwellings in the Highlands and Islands very often had immensely thick walls, sometimes up to 8 feet in thickness. These were made of two layers or skins of stone, the core being filled with clay. It was not uncommon for there to be space for a bed within the thickness of the walls. The rafters of the roof rested on the inner wall, so that rain ran off the roof and into the central core, serving to compact the clay. Walls of this nature were often so thick that they were grassed over and sheep could graze on them.

Clay was also widely used as a walling material, and houses and cottages built of this material still survive in Banffshire and Aberdeenshire even today. Town houses in Errol were also built of the same material, and, again, at least one church, that at Aberlady, East Lothian.

Clay and turf dwellings frequently had their internal walls supported on a wickerwork frame. In barns the gablets were often built only of wickerwork, to give good ventilation for drying the grain and hay stored inside, and in long houses the partition separating the household from its livestock was also often made of nothing more substantial than wickerwork. Such 'creel houses' as they were called once were very common over Ross and Cromarty and the Hebrides. Dr Johnson stayed in one at Anoch, Glenmoriston, during his journey through the Highlands in 1773.

The poorest cottages had one room only. Larger houses were infrequently of the 'but and ben' type: a kitchen/living room and a bedroom, the partition between the two often being no more than the box beds which were almost universal throughout Scotland. The oval or circular huts built on the summer shielings sometimes had two interconnecting rooms built within the massive thickness of the walls, whilst in the Hebrides a larger rectangular structure might have several interconnecting rooms, including a byre, lying more or less parallel, for all the world like a row of sausages. Any inner rooms were entirely without windows. Animals were walled into the byre at the beginning of winter, and those that survived had to be carried out in the spring. Byre and 'fireroom' were often separated by no more than a step. Living conditions for both men and animals must have been appalling, probably among the worst anywhere in Britain at this time.

The roof itself could be thatched with straw, turf or heather. It often needed to be secured with ropes and weights to prevent it blowing off in the winter gales. In any case the actual roof itself was frequently renewed, sometimes as often as every year, the rotted and soot-laden old covering then being spread as manure over the infield.

Cottages and houses of this kind, long and low and of massive construction, often hug the contours of the land and can bend in plan in order to follow natural features. Here, the relationship between man and a hostile environment was peculiarly close and can have left very little room for any kind of social refinement.

The distinction between tenant farmer and the proprietor was particularly sharp in Scotland in the sixteenth and seventeenth centuries, and was marked by equally distinctive differences in housing. The distinction is further pointed by the unsettled nature of Scottish society and the ever-present danger of an English attack, whether by border raiders or a full-scale military invasion. The need for defence was overwhelming. The result was the tower house. This consisted essentially of a square block, sometimes four storeys high, with the main accommodation on the first floor, the ground floor being a barrel-vaulted room of massive construction used for storage purposes. The tower itself was set inside a barmkin, a walled enclosure, often used also for herding cattle. The staircase was frequently built in the thickness of the walls, although there was occasionally a projecting staircase wing or turret, as at Darnick Tower, Roxburghshire, for example.

Gradually, and more especially from the middle years of the sixteenth century onwards, the needs of defence became less pressing. Windows became larger, and instead of a single monolithic block, some lateral expansion became possible, as for example at Melgund Castle, Angus, a four-storey tower house with a two-storey domestic range added. An L-shaped plan emerged during the seventeenth century, with the staircase in an external tower in the re-entrant angle between the main block and the wing. There were some modest concessions to comfort, privacy and even beauty: there is for example

123

some fine panelling and plaster work in the upper rooms at Pilmuir, East Lothian, built in 1624, and a slow awareness of external appearance, the horizontal string courses to Innes House, Morayshire, built 1640–1653, being some slight genuflexion in this direction. But rooms still opened directly off one another, the principal rooms were still to be found on the first floor, the ground floor rooms remaining as storage and service rooms. Only at the very end of the seventeenth century does the stern vernacular

Plate 28 Darnick Tower, Roxburghshire, a three-storey sixteenth-century tower house, with the staircase in the projecting wing. A number of carved stones taken from Melrose Abbey were used in its construction

tradition of the Scottish tower house begin to unbend.

The vernacular tradition has its roots deep in the structure of the society for which it builds: its patterns of family life and social structure, its economic framework, its topographical setting. As we have seen, this tradition was itself a living, growing tradition, reflecting within itself changes within its society. However by the fourth and fifth decades of the sixteenth century the first signs can be detected in building done, either for the royal court or in the private mansions of men closely connected with the court, in both England and Scotland, of new themes and patterns in building coming from Renaissance Italy, themes and patterns that would come in only fitfully at first but which would be widely accepted over almost the whole of Britain by the last years of the seventeenth century. These themes meant the slow death of the vernacular tradition.

Perhaps the first herald of the Renaissance in English building is to be seen at Hampton Court, the palace begun by Cardinal Wolsey in 1515. Here are a series of medallion portrait busts of the Roman emperors adorning an otherwise entirely medieval building. At the same time the Cardinal began work on York Place in London. In 1525 he found it expedient to 'give' Hampton Court to Henry VIII, and in October 1529 York Place was declared forfeit to the Crown following Wolsey's indictment in King's Bench under the Statute of Praemunire. Henry continued building at both Hampton Court and York Place, which became the Palace of Whitehall. Here a gatehouse, demolished in 1723, had both Doric and Ionic pilasters.

There were at the same time a small group of Italian craftsmen at work in England, of whom the most important by far was Pietro Torrigiano. In 1511 he built the tomb of Margaret Beaufort, Henry VIII's grandmother, and from 1512 he was working upon the splendid tomb of Henry VII in Westminster Abbey. The equal to anything that Torrigiano did is to be found in the screen erected between 1532 and 1536 in the chapel of King's College Cambridge, a masterpiece of Renaissance craftsmanship, although those responsible for its construction remain unknown. In 1538 Henry VIII began the Palace of Nonsuch, his most extravagant and most splendid building enterprise, prompted by jealousy of Francis I of France, who was at work upon the Château de Chambord at this time. Again, as at Hampton Court, the overall spirit of the building was medieval, but foreign craftsmen carried out much of the decorative work and at least one, Nicholas Bellin of Modena, actually left Fontainebleau to come to work at Nonsuch, admittedly to avoid a charge of fraud. The palace was unfinished at the time of Henry's death in 1547, and was demolished in 1687.

In this way the first seeds of the Renaissance were sown in England. Confined at first to court circles and to applied decoration, and with no real concept of the true spirit of classical architecture, the thread is from now on never really lost, in spite of English hostility to foreign craftsmen, compounded by the fact that so many were Italian Roman Catholics. The new ideas spread only slowly from court circles. In 1540 Sir William Sharington acquired Lacock Abbey, in Wiltshire. For the next ten years he carried out a great deal of rebuilding, and although it does not all survive what there is shows a remarkable feeling for the detail of classical architecture. He employed an English mason, John Chapman. Sharington's patron was Lord Seymour of Sudeley, the brother of the Duke of Somerset. Sharington was one of the most rapacious and unpleasant of those who clustered about the court of the boy king, Edward VI, first of all under the Duke of Somerset and then, after his execution in 1552, the Duke of Northumberland. The Duke of Northumberland in 1550 sent John Shute to Italy to study classical architecture at first hand, although it was long before this particular seed bore fruit. It was only in 1563 that he published his *First and Chief Groundes of Architecture*, the first appearance in England of descriptions and engravings of the orders of classical architecture.

Somerset himself began to build his great house along the banks of the Thames in 1547. In due course it became known as Somerset House. In charge of the actual buildings operations was his steward, Sir John Thynne, who was already rebuilding his own property, Longleat, and at the same time Somerset's private secretary was William Cecil. There was a great fire at Longleat in 1567 and Sir John Thynne had to start again. The house which finally emerged, some dozen or so years later, is one of the most splendid of sixteenth-century great houses, an outwards-looking house of stately symmetry.

Cecil succeeded to the family property at Burghley in 1553 and almost at once began to rebuild the modest manor house that he found there, and on an increasingly lavish scale. In 1564 he bought the manor of Theobalds, in Hertfordshire, and began to build there as well. Expenditure rose dramatically, and in 1571–1572 it topped £2,700 in the one year at Theobalds alone, an immense sum of money. Theobalds was a prodigy house upon a prodigious scale. There were five courtyards, of which the inner, or Fountain Court, was 84 feet square. He built a Great Gallery that was 123 feet long by 21 feet wide. When Cecil died, in 1598, Burghley House passed to his eldest son, and Theobalds to his younger son, Robert, who became Earl of Salisbury and principal minister to James I. In 1607 Salisbury was persuaded by James to exchange Theobalds for Hatfield. Theobalds then became one of James' favourite residences, not least because the hunting in the park was so good, and he died there in 1625. In 1650 it was sold by order of Parliament and the huge house largely dismantled.

Sir John Thynne and Sir William Cecil had at least one characteristic in common. They both took an intense and detailed interest in every stage of the building of their great houses. They were in effect their own architects and their own contractors, buying materials and hiring craftsmen and labourers, checking accounts and providing drawings and plans at every stage, and this in addition to leading extremely busy lives as men of affairs. In this they were not unique, and it is the nineteenth century before a professional architect takes over the functions once performed almost as a matter of course by anyone wishing to build or rebuild his house. Skilled craftsmen, and the great majority were always Englishmen, were in great demand, travelling the length and breadth of the country from one great house to the next upon the recommendation or at the request of some landlord anxious to outdo his neighbours in the splendour and extravagance of his building. Thus the mason Robert Smythson worked for a long time at Longleat before going on to execute much of the carved stonework and masonry at Wollaton, in Nottinghamshire, completed in 1588 for Sir Francis Willoughby and perhaps the most ostentatious and exuberant prodigy house in an age of exuberance.

By this time the new themes and ideas from Renaissance Italy were in full flood in England, but in reaching this country they suffered a sea change. Direct links with Italy were few and uncertain, not least because the religious controversies of the time could make too long a stay in Italy politically dangerous. Instead the fountain head as far as England was concerned was Flanders, and especially Antwerp. Books of every kind, including illustrated ones on architecture, poured from the Antwerp printing presses, and many made the short journey across the North Sea. The outbreak of the wars of religion in northern Europe and the revolt of the Netherlands brought refugees as well as books, and so, for a variety of reasons, religious and political, Englishmen saw the Renaissance through Flemish eyes in the last decades of the sixteenth century. Two of the most important Flemish pattern books were *Architecture*, published in 1563, the work of Vredeman de Vries, and the *Architectura* of Wendel Dietterlin, published in 1598. In books such as these the clarity and balance of classical architecture are almost submerged in an extravagant delight in convoluted linear decoration, the sources of the strap-work patterns that so intrigued Elizabethan builders, and an interest in grotesque human forms that is at once macabre and erotic. These were often toned

down when actually incorporated in English building, so that it is almost impossible to find direct imitations of Flemish models, although their sources as the inspiration for the decoration at Wollaton, for example, or at Charlton House, Greenwich, is obvious. It is reinforced by the use of materials imported direct from Flanders, and the continuing employment of Flemish craftsmen. Thus the stone gallery to the great hall at Theobalds was made in Flanders, and erected in 1569–1570. The slates to the turrets were also probably imported from Flanders. Flemish craftsmen worked at Burghley. When Lord Salisbury began to build the great house at Hatfield he imported marble from Carrera and stone from Caen, and employed one of the most distinguished craftsmen of the day, Maximilian Colt, from Arras. Colt had already designed the monument to Queen Elizabeth in Westminster Abbey, and that to Sir Christopher Hatton in old St Paul's, destroyed in the Great Fire. When Lord Salisbury died in 1612 Colt designed the monument to him at Hatfield.

It was the same court circles that led to the introduction of Renaissance themes into Wales. Sir Richard Clough, a merchant of proverbial wealth who had made the dangerous pilgrimage to Jerusalem and acted as factor at Antwerp between 1552 and 1569 for Sir Thomas Gresham, married in 1567 the wealthiest heiress in Denbighshire, Catherine of Berain. He then built two houses. Plas Clough was a straightforward, rather traditional building, although built of brick, something very unusual for north Wales at the time. His second house, Bachegraig, came as a total stranger into the Welsh countryside. It was a regular cube block built after the latest Flemish models, and for long the only house in Wales to express Renaissance ideals in their entirety. It was a complete break with the past, and entirely out of its time. Its like is not seen again in Wales until another court official, Sir John Trevor, Surveyor of the Queen's Ships, built Plas-teg at Hope in Flintshire, in about 1610 – a square house with extruded corner towers rising a storey above the main line of the roof.

In Scotland there was an outburst of building in the Renaissance style that was even more premature than that in Wales. There was a great deal of building carried out under the personal direction of James VI, who died in 1542 – especially at Linlithgow, Falkland and Stirling. French masons were employed about the building at Falkland Palace and at Stirling Castle, and their influence is still apparent in the surviving buildings today. This spread no further, however, and there are only very isolated examples of Renaissance-inspired ornament, at Crichton Castle, for example, before the end of the sixteenth century, and even in the first half of the seventeenth century the new ideas spread only very slowly. Some decorative stone work that draws its inspiration from Anglo-Flemish models is to be found at Pinkie, Midlothian, built for the Earl of Dunfermline from 1613 onwards, and most obviously at Heriot's Hospital, Edinburgh, begun in 1628, a symmetrical block with mock castellated corner towers. It is only at the very end of the seventeenth century that the new ideas become at all firmly established in Scotland.

By the second decade of the seventeenth century a peculiarly English version of Renaissance principles of architecture, and more especially of decoration, was firmly established in England; and it was much copied in the uppermost levels of society in the building of those great prodigy houses in which they gave physical expression to their rivalry and to their obligation to provide an appropriate setting for a royal visit, something which could make them politically but break them financially. But also by the

Plate 30 Heriot's Hospital, Edinburgh, founded under the will of George Heriot, who died in 1624, for the education of orphaned boys. The building was largely designed by William Wallace in a strange blend of old and new styles

second decade of the seventeenth century the man who, by returning to the fountain head of classical architecture was to introduce into England buildings of the purest classical form was at the height of his powers. This man was Inigo Jones. He had long been employed at court as a designer for the stage settings for masques, and had only just returned from an extended tour of Italy in the train of the Earl of Arundel when in 1615 he succeeded to the office of Surveyor of the King's Works. In the following year he designed the Queen's House at Greenwich (see Plate 60), although it was 1635 before it was finally finished, after a long gap between 1618 and 1629 when no building work at all was carried out. In 1619 a fire in the Palace of Whitehall destroyed the old Banqueting House, and Jones was called upon to design a new one. This was finished by the March of 1620 and as such is the first absolutely classical building completed in Britain. In concept and spirit it draws its inspiration directly from Palladio. Jones had read and re-read Palladio's *I Quattro Libri dell'Architettura*, had taken a copy with him on his Italian visit, had studied at first hand the same classical buildings that Palladio had described, and he continued

to annotate Palladio's text throughout his life. His copy still survives, and is preserved at Worcester College, Oxford, along with many of his drawings. It is clear that Jones absorbed, not only the superficialities of Renaissance architectural decoration, but also the basic principles which informed the work of Palladio and the classical architecture from which he, in his turn, drew his inspiration. For Palladio architecture was an expression of the divine harmony that lay behind the external world, a harmony both mathematical and musical, and to be found in the subtle proportions of each part of a building: plan and elevation, interior and exterior, room and room, combine to give an integrated, harmonious, three-dimensional whole. It is this concept of a building as a whole that Inigo Jones was the first to grasp in England, since building hitherto had been a matter of addition rather than integration, and so it is not too much of an exaggeration to say that in comparing Plates 22 and 31 one is comparing two quite different mental world pictures, and that in order to explain fully their differences and intentions it is necessary to explore much of the history of the western world. It is in this way that the landscape acquires its

Plate 31 The Banqueting House, Whitehall, designed by Inigo Jones and completed in 1622. It was almost entirely refaced by Sir John Soane in 1829

131

extraordinarily rich historical depth and its endless fascination for those who would share in this wealth.

Inigo Jones may be safely associated with some twenty buildings, of which eight survive at least in part, and another four remain more or less as he left them. From 1625 he was connected with the Commission of Works, through which Charles I made half-hearted attempts to control both the physical spread of London and the haphazard nature of its growth. In this way Inigo Jones was concerned with the layout of Lincoln's Inn Fields and of Covent Garden, where the church of St Paul still stands as a monument to his genius. (See Plate 47.) Nevertheless even here his work must be seen as part of the interests of an intellectual coterie about the court, and as the personal rule of Charles I became increasingly unpopular so those who were associated in any way with it became increasingly isolated. Thus it is only in the years after the Restoration that the example of Jones finds any real following.

Even whilst Jones was at work much building was going on which was an extension of and a development from the exuberant Anglo-Flemish style of the second half of the sixteenth century. This new trend has been called 'artisan mannerism' since it was the product of masons and bricklayers, carpenters and joiners who had absorbed much of Flemish mannerism but knew almost nothing of the classical principles of balance and proportion which lay at several removes behind it. Dutch and Flemish influences continued to be important, although less flamboyant, and increasing use was made of brick as a building material. The Dutch House at Kew, built in 1631 for Samuel Fortrey, a London merchant of Dutch origin, is a splendid example of this development, whilst Raynham Hall, in Norfolk, being built for Sir Roger Townshend at almost exactly the same time, is a curious blend of old and new. It has a great hall and screens passage. It is built of brick. It has curved Dutch gables. It also has a classical portico to the centre of the garden front. Such conservative houses continue to be built into the last quarter of the seventeenth century, and they look increasingly old-fashioned. Sudbury Hall, in Derbyshire, was being built in the 1660s and 1670s according to the designs and interests of its owner, George Vernon. It has the hipped roof and tall, monumental chimney stacks characteristic of more consciously fashionable houses of the time, but its diaper brickwork, its oversize windows, the two-storeyed entrance porch and the long gallery are all reminiscent of an earlier age.

But neither Inigo Jones nor the often almost unknown practical masons and carpenters of the artisan mannerist style were responsible for the design of Coleshill, in Berkshire, a house which served for almost 150 years as the model for the ideal English country house. Such a house, in its idyllic parkland setting, seems, even today, to occupy the central place in an idealised landscape, one which is all the more poignant because the values which lay behind it have now passed away. Coleshill was built in about 1650 to designs by Sir Roger Pratt. The outbreak of the Civil War had compelled him to leave England, and between 1643 and 1649 he travelled extensively in the Low Countries, France and Italy. On his return he designed the house for his cousin, Sir George Pratt. It shows the influence of his travels, and of his acquaintance with Inigo Jones, and yet it is dominated by neither. It is very much in his own style, and contains a number of features which are not perhaps in themselves entirely new, but are brought together in one house for the first time. He gave Coleshill a hipped roof, with balustrade and cupola and dormer windows. Two principal floors are of almost equal importance. Tall chimney stacks are given great prominence. In the interior plan the hall finally becomes an entrance vestibule, and the main staircase, a double flight meeting on a first floor gallery, rises out of it. Even more important is the fact that the interior is divided into two halves by a corridor running down its length, with rooms

Plate 32 Coleshill House, Berkshire, designed by Sir Roger Pratt in the 1650s

opening off. This meant an enormous increase in privacy since people could now move from one room to another by means of the corridor and no longer had to pass through any intermediate rooms as had hitherto to be done, with the likelihood of catching the occupants doing – literally – anything. Sadly this house was demolished after a fire in 1952.

Sir Roger Pratt then went on to build a town residence in Piccadilly for the Earl of Clarendon, and although this survived for no more than sixteen years, being demolished in 1683, it was probably more widely imitated than Coleshill. Nothing is known of its plan but a fine engraving of the front exists, showing a house with two projecting wings and many of the architectural features to be found at Coleshill. Clarendon House and Coleshill set the pattern for the English country house for the rest of the century. Only in the very last years is a new note struck, by William Talman in his designs for the south front at Chatsworth, building from 1686 onwards, with a grave, almost Baroque, monumentality emphasised by giant pilasters, large keystones over the windows and the absence of a visible roof, concealed behind a balustrade surmounted with urns. In 1702 Talman was forced to resign from the post of Comptroller of the Royal Works, and the office was given to Sir John Vanbrugh, already working on the designs for Castle Howard. A new phase in the history of the English house was about to begin.

By the end of the seventeenth century the new Renaissance and classical themes were also to be found in Wales and in Scotland. Double-pile houses were being built in Wales before the end of the sixteenth century, as at Newton, St David's Without, Breconshire, of about 1582, and Treowen, Wonastow, Monmouthshire of 1627, although neither has the connecting internal corridor which is the chief innovation of the double-pile plan at Coleshill, and traditional elements still remain very strong. In several seventeenth-century houses the hall had been transformed from being the principal room in the house to being only an entrance vestibule, as at Plas Berw, Llanidan, Anglesey, for example, of 1615, or Trosymarian, Llangoed, also in Anglesey, of about 1678, but in neither of these does the staircase rise out of the hall as it does at Coleshill. At the same time houses which were built as new were reorientated so that they lay across the slope rather than downhill, and this meant that the front of the house now become more important than the rear. The façade could now be made symmetrical and decoration could be concentrated on it.

Classical architecture came even later to Scotland, and although William Wallace, appointed King's Master Mason in 1617, added some Anglo-Flemish decoration to Linlithgow Palace in about 1620 and built Heriot's Hospital in Edinburgh from 1628, his example had little effect, and it is only with the appointment of Sir William Bruce as Surveyor-General for Scotland in 1671 that classical architecture began to take root. His alterations and extensions

to Holyroodhouse show a competent handling of the classical orders in a French fashion, but his best piece of work is his own house, Kinross House, built between 1686 and 1693; here Coleshill, suitably modified, with a double cube saloon on the second floor, comes to Scotland.

Plate 33 Kinross House, Kinross-shire, built by Sir William Bruce in 1685 for his own use

It is only appropriate to end this chapter with Sir John Vanbrugh and Sir William Bruce, since it is through the medium of the semi-professional designer from the middle and upper ranks of society working for a wealthy clientèle who shared his values, education and cultural interests that further development and innovation will appear in British building styles. The vernacular traditions are by now in full retreat almost everywhere as local masons and bricklayers adopt the new fashions as best they can. The story of the displacement of the vernacular tradition, the acceptance of the principles of classical architecture, and in due course their rejection, is written particularly clearly across the landscape; fortunately much of this story is still legible today.

135

Chapter six

Towns

Historians and geographers use words like village, town and city with an easy familiarity that serves to conceal the fact that there is no break in the continuum of human settlement that stretches from an isolated farmstead to megalopolis, and that these words both lack precision and change their meaning over time. It is almost impossible, even today, to draw satisfactory and consistent dividing lines between town and village. The task is made even more difficult for the sixteenth and seventeenth centuries since so much of the information upon which we have to base our classification of human settlement in these two centuries is fragmented, unreliable, misleading or simply does not exist. In addition we must also appreciate that the word 'town' was then applied to any human settlement, however small and even, in Scotland, to a single building. The problem of definition is compounded because it is clear from the evidence that the distinction between rural and urban, town and country was, in these two centuries, blurred and indistinct. (See Plates 1 and 69.) Indeed it has been seriously suggested, following Leander Albertus (as quoted in Robert Burton's *Anatomy of Melancholy*), that the only true urban settlement in seventeenth-century Britain was London, and even here streets and houses still had spread no very great distance from the walls of the medieval city.

Nevertheless the division between town and village is important, since towns have a distinctive role to play in human society. A significant proportion of townsmen, no longer dependent entirely upon their own efforts for the provision of their basic needs, find themselves able to provide goods and services which are 'exported', sometimes no further than to neighbouring farms and villages, sometimes over immense distances by land and sea. Countrymen pay for these goods and services by the sale of their surplus agricultural produce in urban markets and fairs, which is where townsmen buy the foodstuffs which release them from the burden and the necessity of growing their own, thus making towns as much consumers as they are points of exchange.

This is of course a very crude and grossly over-simplified account of the difference between town and village but it does nonetheless point to a more satisfactory ground for distinguishing between them, namely that of function, than others which have been used, principally size as represented by numbers of inhabitants, and legal status as incorporated boroughs, neither of which is really very satisfactory.

Towns and cities in Britain in the sixteenth and seventeenth centuries were, by the standards of the late twentieth century, very small indeed, and to make such a comparison across two or more centuries serves only to illustrate the way in which the word 'town' itself has changed its meaning. Norwich, even at the end of the seventeenth century, had fewer than 30,000 inhabitants, and yet was the second largest town in England after London, whilst Birmingham had perhaps 10,000 inhabitants and Manchester perhaps the same. Glasgow in 1610 may have had a population of 7,600, and Southampton, which probably had 4,200 inhabitants in 1596 was reduced to 2,900 in 1696. Both Brecon and Carmarthen, with about 2,200 inhabitants in about 1670, had more people living in them than either Swansea or Cardiff, and about the same number lived in Paisley and in Kendal.

It was because towns were so small that the rural/urban dichotomy was so blurred as to be almost non-existent during the sixteenth and seventeenth centuries. Very many towns consisted of no more than a handful of streets – there were only eight in Glasgow before 1667 – back lanes and alleys where buildings had by no means blotted out gardens, closes and orchards. Almost everyone kept pigs and chickens, and those who could afford to do so kept horses, since they provided the only means of transport apart from walking. This meant that the sights, sounds and smells which the late twentieth-century city dweller associates with the countryside, and hence with holidays and outdoor leisure pursuits rather than with everyday life, were in this period the normal experience of almost everyone, whether it was the scent of new-mown hay or the stench from a farm-yard midden, the lowing of cattle, the stamp of a horse in its stable and the rattle of its harness.

This intimate association of town and country was reinforced by the fact that most small towns and many large ones were still surrounded by their open fields, so that it was an accepted way of life for townsmen to combine some trade or manufacture with the cultivation of their strips in the common fields in just the same fashion as any husbandman in a conventional three-field village. William Smyth, yeoman, of Newport Pagnell, dealt in bone lace; he had £84 17s. 8d. worth of it at the time of his death in 1682. But he also had 24 acres in the tilth field, 19¾ in the breach field and 23 in the fallow field. Leicester and Cambridge (see Plate 1) retained their open fields until the eighteenth century was almost over, and those of Stamford were not finally enclosed until the last quarter of the nineteenth century. In Scotland however burghal common lands, in which strips rotated in succession among the burgesses, were falling into private ownership by the sixteenth century, so that, for example, the Burrowfield of Ayr was almost entirely privately owned by the end of the century. Towns in the sixteenth and seventeenth centuries were deeply rooted in a rural environment, so that town administration could be as much concerned with fields, crops and animals as with more obviously urban matters such as shops and markets. Thus the common warder appointed in 1635 in Newcastle under Lyme to keep the streets clean was also expected to oversee the town fields and hedges; and two years earlier a town shepherd was appointed. In the Scottish burgh of Kirkintilloch the bailies in August of 1671 ordered the weeding of the gool, or wild chrysanthemum and a notorious weed, from the town fields.

Thus mere size is less than satisfactory as a guide to the differences between town and village in this period, and to attempt to use it to point these differences serves only to sever the complex and intimate linkages between town and country. Indeed for many Welsh towns these linkages were if anything becoming stronger in this period as their military functions declined and they ceased to be regarded as alien intruders in a hostile environment.

Relics of these urban/rural links have not all entirely disappeared. Even today about 210 freemen of the City of Oxford have registered grazing rights over Port Meadow, an area of common pasture immediately to the north-west of the town where their ancestors have enjoyed similar rights since the time of Domesday Book.

Some towns may be marked off from others by the grant of the legal status of being a borough or, in Scotland, a burgh. In England by the opening years of the sixteenth century this legal status was granted by means of a charter from the Crown. During the two hundred years covered by this book a number of towns were incorporated for the first time in this way, Chipping Norton in 1607, for example, Penzance in 1615 and Camelford in 1669, but the initiative for the granting of the charter came invariably from the town itself, although Queen Mary granted charters in 1554 to a number of towns, including Banbury, Buckingham and Aylesbury, as a reward for their loyalty in the face of the attempt of the Duke of Northumberland to put Lady Jane Grey on the throne after the death of Edward VI. There was no question of any kind of government policy for the incorporation of large, populous or wealthy towns, and so the way in which these charters of incorporation were distributed bears no relationship at all to size, importance or prosperity. Thus neither Manchester, Sheffield nor Birmingham acquired a charter before the nineteenth century, whilst South Molton, Marazion and Langport Eastover did. This may be contrasted with the scene in Scotland where an Act of the Scottish Parliament passed in 1597 called for the planting of burghs in Kintyre, Lochaber and Lewis, and this was eventually translated into action. Stornoway was founded in 1607, Gordonsburgh, the basis for Fort William, was established in 1618, and Lochhead, which eventually became Campbeltown, was established in about 1618, became a burgh of barony in 1667 and a royal burgh in 1700.

In Wales the situation was slightly different in that local magnates continued to grant charters to towns long after the Crown had assumed this right in England. The last seigneurial charter granted to a Welsh town seems to have been that which the Earl of Worcester granted to his borough of Chepstow in 1524. After the Act of Union of 1536 Welsh towns were incorporated only by the Crown and on the same principles as those in England. Thus Carmarthen received a charter in 1546, Brecon in 1556 and New Radnor in 1562.

In Scotland on the other hand, burghs could be incorporated by means of a charter from the Crown, when it was known as a royal burgh, or by way of a charter from the lord of the barony in which it lay, when it was known as a burgh of barony, and the erection of a burgh of barony in this way was considered to be no more than an amplification of the rights of the baron. Between 1561 and 1707 no less than 235 burghs of barony were created in Scotland, although only 115 of these eventually became viable, the remainder failing to acquire any recognisable urban characteristics and becoming instead merely 'parchment burghs'. It was not unusual for a Scottish burgh to progress from being a burgh of barony to being a royal burgh. This happened at Glasgow, a burgh of barony by the end of the twelfth century, but made a royal burgh only in 1611.

Thus the mere grant of incorporation as a borough was no indicator of truly urban status, provided no guarantee that the settlement so marked out would develop into a town, and certainly its absence was no hindrance to the growth of urban functions. As the great Jacobean lawyer Sir Edward Coke wrote, 'a towne is the genus, and a Borough is the species, for . . . every Borough is a Towne, but every Towne is not a Borough'.

Neither size nor legal status are very satisfactory indicators of towns, since the word town could be, and was, applied to places that were very small indeed, and a number of important towns during these two centuries were never incorporated as boroughs. This is why, when searching for any significant distinction between a village and a town, we are compelled to look to function as providing the surest guide. A village will become a town when a significant proportion of its inhabitants, perhaps as many as a third, are engaged in non-agricultural occupations, more especially when they are producing goods and services for the use of people living outside the immediate confines of the town, so that it acts as a focal point for the surrounding district, however small. In 1599 there were in Manchester no less than fifty butchers' stalls which, given the population of the town at the time, would have meant about ten households for each stall, something which scarcely makes economic sense. Instead it seems very likely that people were coming from a wide area around the town in order to buy their meat. In this way, in spite of its small size and lack of formal incorporation, Manchester at the end of the sixteenth century was fulfilling a distinctly urban function.

The concept of a town and its existence in the landscape presupposes a certain density of population, although as we have seen this was on a very small scale when compared to the numbers to be found in towns today. This density of population is reflected in the pattern of streets and buildings that make up the physical environment of a town. Urban buildings have changed and changed again in many towns in Britain since the end of the seventeenth century, and changed not only in their form but also in their function. The town plan itself however, the pattern of streets and blocks of buildings, has proved to be remarkably durable, and in many towns today the length and breadth of Britain it is still possible to trace at least the outline of a pattern of streets that

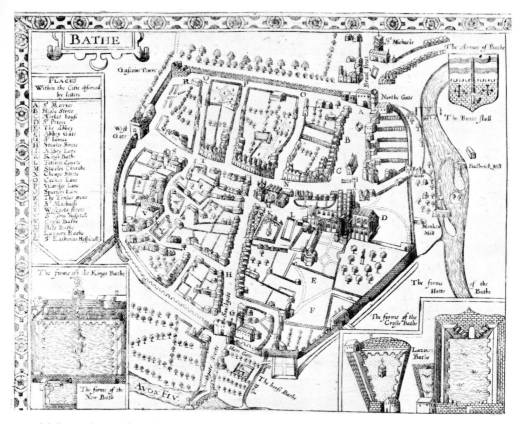

The following labels appear on the map:

BATHE

PLACES
Within the Citie observed
by letters

- A: St Marys
- B: High Street
- C: Market house
- D: St Peters
- E: The Abbey
- F: Abbey Gate
- G: St James
- H: Staules Strete
- I: Abbey Lane
- K: Kings Bath
- L: Tennis Courte
- M: Stanles Churche
- N: Cheape Strete
- O: Cookes Lane
- P: Vicaridge Lane
- Q: Spartles Lane
- R: The Timber grene
- S: St Michaels
- T: Westgate Strete
- V: St James Hospitall
- W: Crosse Bathe
- X: Hote Bathe
- Y: Lazars Bathe
- Z: St Katherins Hospitall

Gascoins Toure · West Gate · North Gate · St Michaels · Broad Streate · The Armes of Bathe · The Boxie stall · Balbrock Mill · Monkes Mill · Tennis Yerde · The forme of the Kings Bathe · The forme of the Hotte Bathe · The forme of the Crosse Bathe · Lazours Bathe · The forme of the New Bath · AVON FLV · Southgate · Hote Gate · The house Bathe · Via The house Bathe

would have been familiar to sixteenth- and seventeenth-century townsmen, although those of today are very much cleaner and sweeter smelling and have also frequently changed their names. We are fortunate in having plans for many towns dating from the early years of the seventeenth century. Those published by John Speed in his *Theatre of Great Britain* in 1611 are diagrammatic bird's eye views rather than plans and their detail cannot be relied on, but for many towns they are the earliest plans that we have. By the end of the seventeenth century some remarkably accurate town plans were being made, that of John Ogilby of Ipswich, for example or Loggan's plan of Cambridge, made in 1688. These plans provide the basic framework with which we can begin to reconstruct the topography of towns in early modern Britain.

The plans of towns in the sixteenth and seventeenth centuries were of course inherited from their medieval ancestors, and it is important to appreciate that very many towns were deliberately laid out in the medieval centuries. In England and Wales the great age for the planting of new towns was over by 1350. Falmouth, founded in 1613,

Plate 34 John Speed's plan of Bath, published in 1611. The medieval walls and gates are clearly shown. There are still plenty of open spaces within the walls, and extra-mural building is almost non-existent. The Bath of John Wood, father and son, will be built beyond the North Gate. The Market House lies in the open space between the North Gate and the abbey, together with the stocks and pillory

141

is the only new town established during the sixteenth and seventeenth centuries but its street pattern shows no evidence of conscious urban planning. In Scotland, however, new burghs continue to be established throughout the period.

The plans adopted for the layout of the streets of a newly established town show considerable variation, and it is clear that they were often profoundly influenced by the topography of the chosen sites, as at Pembroke for example, or at Alnwick. It seems that regular gridiron plans were used in only a minority of towns. This pattern may be more or less intact today, as at Stratford-upon-Avon for example, where in 1196 the bishop of Worcester laid out a new town of three streets running parallel and three at right angles to the river Avon as an appendage to the already existing village, or at Flint, where in 1277 Edward I ordered the building of an entirely new town and castle of four principal streets and a central market place surrounded by a bank and ditch, at a total cost over four and a half years of some £7,000. In other towns the original regularity of a planned town has been almost entirely obscured by later developments, as at Ipswich, where a rectangular pattern of streets that probably dates from Middle Saxon times has been all but obscured by later building.

Although very many of the towns of Roman Britain were laid out upon a regular gridiron pattern, this has been lost almost everywhere, and the street plans of Roman towns make no real contribution to the street plans of their medieval successors and hence to sixteenth- and seventeenth-century towns. It seems to be no more than coincidence if a medieval street follows a Roman one for a short distance. This applies even in London, where the pattern of Roman streets is all but lost, the most important survival being the length of Westcheap and Eastcheap.

Much more influential upon the topography of sixteenth- and seventeenth-century towns than any survival of street patterns from Roman times has been the survival of Roman town walls. At York and Chester, London and Chichester, Colchester and Lincoln, where a Roman gate still stands, the Roman walls have been of profound significance in shaping the pattern of intra-mural streets, even though the walls have themselves been rebuilt during the course of the medieval centuries. Very many other towns were fortified from the tenth century onwards, and their town walls proved to be of similar significance. A number of towns had substantial masonry walls with towers, battlements and moats, as at Oxford, Southampton, New-castle upon Tyne and Great Yarmouth, whilst others, Ipswich and Cambridge, for example, had only a ditch and earthen embankment. Both could be equally influential in dictating intra-mural street patterns. In several towns the line of the medieval walls has long been obscured by later building, and it is only in the pattern of the streets that were compelled to follow the walls that their line can still be discerned. This has happened at Bristol, for example, where St Leonard's Lane, Bell Lane and Tower Lane mark out between them almost half of the medieval wall.

Many medieval town corporations were intensely proud of their walls, and spent a great deal of money on building and repair work. By the opening years of the sixteenth century however the need had all but disappeared save for a few towns of strategic military importance, such as Portsmouth, Hull and Berwick-upon-Tweed, where considerable additions to the fortifications were made. During the sixteenth century municipal pride slowly evaporated under the burden of the immense costs of maintaining the walls. Town walls fell slowly into decay. Many were hastily refurbished at the time of the Civil Wars in the 1640s, once more to be neglected in the years after the Restoration, although those of Newcastle upon Tyne were once more repaired at the time of the Napoleonic Wars. Part of Oxford's city wall was demolished to make way for the Sheldonian Theatre, built to designs by Sir Christopher Wren from 1664 onwards, but it was not until 1700 that a gate was opened in the wall lying immediately to the north of New College. Nevertheless, in spite of the perils which town walls have had to face through the centuries much still remains. At Chester and at York they survive all but complete, and there are still fairly long stretches at Newcastle upon Tyne, Norwich and Great Yarmouth, although much is obscured by later building.

Far fewer Scottish towns acquired walls than in either England or Wales. Edinburgh was walled in the opening years of the fifteenth century. Other towns were first fortified later than English or Welsh ones, under the threat of invasion from England. Thus Selkirk was given the right to town walls in 1540, and the walls of Stirling date from 1547, whilst those for Peebles were built between 1570 and 1574 and were maintained well into the eighteenth century.

Town walls, ditches and gates, by drawing clear, firm lines between town and country (see Plate 34), undoubtedly served to enhance a sense of separateness among townsmen, and it was long before this barrier, at once physical and mental, was breached. At the same time they were frequently a source of civic pride. Town gates were often of more use as collecting points for tolls demanded of those who wished to enter the town to buy and sell in the markets than for any defensive purposes. Several towns with no more than ditches had substantial gates which could only have been used in this way. At Beverley there were four main gates, or bars, and several minor

Plate 35 Peebles town wall and bastion, built 1570–4

ones, but no evidence of town walls. Nevertheless North Bar was rebuilt in local brick between 1409 and 1410, and the wide street of North Bar Without seems to have served as an assembly point for those waiting to enter the town. Town gates were also often used as gaols, as at York, Chester and Oxford, where the North Gate was progressively enlarged to accommodate the prison until, by the time of its demolition in 1771, it was an immense vaulted tunnel seventy feet long and about twelve feet wide. A number of other towns lost their gates only at the end of the eighteenth century, and several still survive today, as at Rye and Sandwich, Southampton where the Bargate, still standing, had the Guildhall on the upper floor, Beverley, Tenby and St Andrews.

The morphology of sixteenth- and seventeenth-century towns owes very little to any Roman predecessor, much more to any defences, Roman or medieval, and most of all to the pattern of streets laid out when the town was first planned. Even in Manchester, one of the towns most profoundly affected by industrialisation in the eighteenth and nineteenth centuries, the street plan marked out on a map of 1650 is still recognisable today. Only the rebuilding consequent upon the bombing of the Second World War,

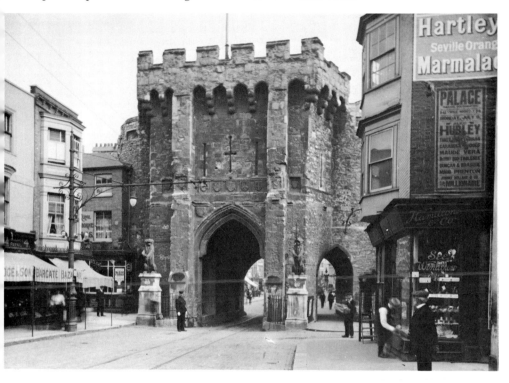

by combining the bulldozer and compulsory purchase, has been able to bring about any large-scale changes in town plans.

Many town street plans reached the limit of their pre-industrial extent by the end of the thirteenth century, and saw little further change on any scale until the eighteenth century. There are of course individual exceptions to such a sweeping generalisation, especially London, but for many towns – Norwich, Ipswich, Gloucester, Nottingham – the sixteenth and seventeenth centuries saw little addition to their medieval street plans. In Glasgow the eight principal streets of the medieval town saw no addition until Candleriggs was laid out in 1662, and the next street to be planned was King Street in the 1720s. At

Plate 36 Bargate, Southampton, a photograph taken in 1906. Second World War bombing and subsequent demolition has sadly emasculated this splendid medieval gateway

145

Bristol, suburban development did not really begin until the years after the Restoration. By way of contrast, in Cambridge the medieval street plan was particularly affected in the fifteenth and sixteenth centuries by the building of the colleges of the University. These gradually came to monopolise the area between the river and Trumpington Street, so that the town became cut off from its river, a number of streets, lanes and riverside hythes were closed, and the town lost much of its importance as a river port. The purchase of land by Henry VI for the site of his new college of King's during the 1440s was particularly important in this respect, leading to the closing of part of Milne Street, the whole of Schools Lane, King's Childer Lane, the loss of the Salt Hythe and the demolition of the church and vicarage of St John Zachary. King's College Chapel is clearly visible in Plate 1.

The pattern of streets is of course only one part of the topography of a town. The streets themselves serve to enclose and mark off plots of land, and at the same time they may also open out to provide public open spaces. The blocks of land enclosed within the network of streets may in turn be subdivided, and, as with the streets, the property boundaries within these blocks have also proved to be one of the most permanent features of a townscape. When a town was being laid out it was usual to provide its new inhabitants with a plot of land, very frequently rectangular, with the short side facing on to the street. Such burgage plots as they were called could vary considerably in size from one town to another. Those in Glasgow, for example, measure 220 yards long by 5½ yards wide, whilst those in New Salisbury, established in 1217, measured 38½ yards long by 16½ yards wide; those on the south side of Edinburgh High Street were 25 feet wide and 450 feet long. Once laid out, perhaps early in the thirteenth century, this initial regularity of burgage plots could be gradually eroded, either by amalgamation or else by subdivision, but such changes took place on a piecemeal scale and over a long period of time, so that it is not uncommon for these medieval burgage plots to remain recognisable – at least in their main outlines – even today.

One of the most important spaces provided in the street pattern of any town was that occupied by the market. Such open spaces could be rectangular, triangular, or else formed by the gradual divergence of the building lines in a street to provide an approximately oval space, sometimes of immense size. One of the largest market places in England is that at Marlborough, in Wiltshire, formed in just this way. Yet other markets were held at the crossing formed by the intersection of principal streets in a town meeting together at right angles at some focal point. The Carfax in Oxford served as the town's chief market place until 1774, with stalls extending far down all the streets leading off. Penniless Bench, an open arcaded structure built against the east end of St Martin's church and rebuilt in stone in 1667, served on market days as a place for the sale of butter.

Plate 37 The long broad market place at Marlborough, Wiltshire

Some market places were formed at the gates of the abbey or of the castle which formed the point of growth for the urban community. The great rectangular market place at Bury St Edmunds was laid out immediately outside the north gate of the abbey, probably in the middle years of the eleventh century, whilst at Caernarvon there were two market places. One lay in Market Street, one of the regular pattern of streets laid out within the walled town attached to the castle built by Edward I, and the second lay on the Green, Y Maes Glas, immediately outside the town walls. This latter developed because Caernarvon, like the other plantations of Edward I in Wales, was an English enclave set among a hostile native population, and Welshmen were for long forbidden to enter within the walls (see Plate 42).

By the middle years of the sixteenth century it was usual in many towns to find a number of specialised marketing areas, whether for fish, butter, cheese, hay, corn, sheep or horses. In Banbury there were separate corn and pig markets, as well as areas set aside for cow, sheep and horse fairs. Reading had a Butter Market lying off the south-west corner of the main Market Place, whilst in Leicester in the sixteenth and seventeenth centuries there were separate areas for the sale of meat, wood, horses, sheep, hay and grain. Markets had to be regulated in the interests of good order and honesty, and this regulation was undertaken by the corporation of the town. As the bailiff of Winslow remarked, 'if there were not someone to regulate the Markett, the Markett would come to confusion'. The corporation rented out stalls, supervised the quality of goods, especially foodstuffs, exposed for sale, and the accuracy of the weights and measures used. During much of the sixteenth and seventeenth centuries these duties were taken seriously and the mayor would frequently make a solemn visitation of the market before ordering a bell to be rung so that trading could begin. The stalls should have been taken down at the end of each market, but in spite of all that the officers of the corporation could do, some were left standing from one market day to the next, and in due course they became permanent buildings, so that market places in many towns today are often smaller than they were even in the sixteenth century, since it is clear that encroachment of this kind began within a few years of the original market place being laid out. Such encroachments are often distinguishable on modern town maps by the narrow lanes and alleys that intersect them, as at Bury St Edmunds, where the narrow Skinner Street threads the length of a block of buildings that is clearly an encroachment in the Buttermarket. In other towns the market itself has shifted, the consequence of a variety of economic and social pressures: at Glasgow, for example, the original market place lay immediately to the south of the cathedral and the archbishop's palace. By the beginning of the sixteenth century it had been largely built over, and so the market was moved to the new centre of commercial activity, the cross-road formed where the High Street, Trongate, Saltmarket Street and Westgallowgate meet.

The market place was often marked by a cross, and some towns had more than one. In Devizes the cheese, butter and yarn markets were marked by crosses, although the yarn cross was replaced by a yarn hall in 1575. Of the four market crosses in Salisbury the Poultry Cross, a hexagonal fifteenth-century structure, still stands, but the four once to be found in Shaftesbury have all been demolished, the last in 1827. The market cross was sometimes a single column, such as that built at Carlisle in 1682, an unfluted Ionic column on a square base, or that at Kilwinning which still retains a wooden cross-head, perhaps a relic from the time when all market crosses were of wood.

Plate 38 The medieval market cross at Salisbury, Wiltshire

It could also be a much more elaborate structure, such as that at Chichester, built in 1501, an octagonal open-sided building with ribs running up the centre to form a central open crown. A rather similar octagonal building with flying buttresses was built at Malmesbury in about 1500 and a splendid mercat cross was built in Aberdeen in 1686 to designs by John Montgomerie. It was 21 feet in diameter and had stalls and booths under the arched encircling wall. The finest market cross still standing in Scotland, that at Prestonpans, built early in the seventeenth century, has a circular base divided into eight compartments, two of which have doors. One door gives access to an internal chamber, whilst the second leads by way of a narrow stair to a platform on the roof, on which is erected a column surmounted by a heraldic beast.

Instead of, and sometimes in addition to, the market cross, the market also had a market house, and in Scotland the tolbooth often combined the two, with the mercat cross on the landing of the external staircase to the tolbooth. The market house frequently had two storeys, the ground floor being open whilst the first floor was supported upon arcaded pillars. The first floor served sometimes as a council chamber and occasionally as a school room. Market houses and town halls – the two share very similar functions in the sixteenth and seventeenth centuries – became a centre of civic pride at this time and were frequently built or rebuilt upon a grand scale and with lavish ornament. A particularly fine example survived in Hereford until its demolition in 1862. That at Leominster, built in 1633 by John Abel, the King's Carpenter, still stands. That so distinguished a craftsman could be employed is a mark of the importance attached to this symbol of municipal pride and dignity. The cost of such ostentation was frequently met by a country gentleman of the neighbourhood, anxious to extend and cement his patronage in the town. Thus the town hall at Alcester was paid for by Sir Fulke Greville, that at Amersham by Sir Marmaduke Drake and that at Watlington by Thomas Stonor.

In due course those artistic influences which transformed the country house also affected the town hall and although the traditional form persisted it was now clothed in classical columns, pilasters and cupolas. The earliest example of this new style of town or market house must be that at Rothwell, in Northamptonshire, built in 1578 at the expense of Sir Thomas Tresham, whose motives of self-advertisement are ingenuously denied in the inscription. Later examples include that at Bungay and the one at Morpeth, built in 1714 to designs by Sir John Vanbrugh, but the most splendid of all seventeenth-century town halls must surely be that at Abingdon, built by Christopher Kempster between 1678 and 1680.

The Scottish equivalent of the town hall is the tolbooth, and there is a similar story of increasing sophistication of traditional forms. Medieval ones were generally of stone, although that at Elgin seems to have been of timber and thatch. At first they were essentially towers, perhaps intended for defensive purposes, but by the opening years of the sixteenth century the tower had become the burgh prison, and had acquired the belfry to house the bell required in all burghs by Act of the Scottish Parliament to be rung to summon the burgh councillors to meetings. By the end of the century they were complex structures combining bell tower, council chamber, court room and

prison. The council chamber and court room were usually on the first floor, as in the massive three-storey building at Musselburgh, built in about 1590, and approached by an external flight of stairs, sometimes double, and, as at Sanquhar, with a cross on the landing. At Dingwall the ground floor contained a series of storage chambers and a prison, whilst at Glasgow the ground floor was divided up into stalls and booths, the rents from which went towards the cost of the upkeep of the building, something which could be a serious drain on burgh finances. At Ayr, for example, in 1615–16 £100 Scots was spent to build the bell-house on the tolbooth, £4 10s. for bringing the bell

Plate 39 The Town Hall, Hereford, demolished in 1862. This print is probably a proposed reconstruction of what was then a derelict building, but it almost certainly represents it as it was in its heyday

Plate 40 The Town Hall, Abingdon, Berkshire, built to designs by Christopher Kempster between 1678 and 1680

Plate 41 A late nineteenth-century photograph of the Tolbooth, Musselburgh, Midlothian, built in 1590, with additions in 1762

from Irvine, and another £9 2s. on rebuilding part of the tolbooth stair, 'blawin doun by storme of weddir'.

Another building type that could have a profound and dramatic impact upon a town plan was a castle. William the Conqueror built a number of castles in English towns in the years after 1066, often destroying a great deal of urban property in the process. At Stamford only five houses were demolished to make way for the castle, and only eight at Wallingford, but in Norwich ninety-eight were destroyed, and in Lincoln 166, whilst in York, where there were seven wards or shires, one was laid waste for the building of the castle.

These early castles were at first invariably of earthen bank and ditch with wooden palisade and keep. The remains of the castle mound in Cambridge can be seen in Plate 1. In some towns these were in due course replaced by masonry structures, whilst in others they have disappeared so completely that their site is uncertain, as at Ipswich, or their very existence doubtful, as at Aylesbury, where only the street name Castle Fee survives to hint at what might have been. A number of towns still retain their medieval stone castles more or less intact, and one of the most splendid examples must be that at Ludlow. Others were more or less in ruins by the opening years of the sixteenth century. That at Wallingford for example was stripped of much of its materials in 1550 to repair Windsor castle. It was hastily refurbished during the Civil War, and finally demolished in 1652–3. At Nottingham the castle was slighted in 1651. The site was acquired by the Duke of Newcastle in 1675 and he proceeded to build a large house on the site of the keep. The castle at Buckingham was almost certainly never rebuilt in stone, and in 1670 the motte was levelled to make a bowling green, and the parish church was rebuilt on it between 1777 and 1781.

In England only a very few towns owe their origins directly to the building of a castle. Devizes grew up in the early twelfth century in the space between the inner and outer ditch of the castle, and the town which grew up between the castle wall and the river at Windsor in the years after the Norman Conquest quickly attracted to itself the life and commerce from Old Windsor, where the Anglo-Saxon kings had a palace. In Wales however the castle is the dominant factor in the founding of towns. At Caernarvon, for example, castle, town and quay were planned and built all of a piece between 1283 and 1292. It was only during the course of the sixteenth century that Welsh towns outgrew their military origins to become centres of urban life rather than military outposts. Denbigh provides the best example of this process. The castle stands on a steep hill, a splendid defensive site but too cramped for urban life. By the early fourteenth century there were more burgesses living outside the town walls than inside as the town migrated downhill to a more level site where a market could be held. The castle ceased to play a vital role in town life, and by the end of the sixteenth

153

Plate 42 An aerial view of Caernarvon. The borough founded by Edward I in 1284 at the foot of the castle and surrounded by wall and towers is in the bottom right-hand corner of the picture. The three parallel streets of the medieval town plan are clearly visible. The length nearest the camera of the middle one is Market Street and used as a market by the English townsmen. The triangular market place, Y Maes Glas, outside the town walls to the left, would have been used by Welshmen

century was almost derelict.

Walls and castles, town halls and market places, however important in themselves and however significant their role in shaping the morphology of a town, are of less importance in its overall topography than are the houses of the men and women who live and work in it, not least because very few towns in Britain had a full complement of these buildings and many functioned perfectly satisfactorily as towns with only one or two.

Houses provide shelter for human beings and at the same time reinforce the role of the family and household as the basic unit of social organisation by providing facilities for family life beyond the view of strangers. We have already looked in Chapter 1 at something of the role of the family and household in pre-industrial society and we have seen that its functions were wider than those of the family today. These wider functions are reflected in the physical format of the house itself. Houses today are primarily residential locations for a nuclear family. Houses in pre-industrial society were also workshops, places of manufacture, offices, warehouses and retail shops. This is because almost the whole of trade, commerce and manufacture was small-scale and domestic, with a very important consequence: the journey to work, so common a feature of everyday life at the end of the twentieth century, was at the end of the sixteenth century confined to a very few occupations, such as mining, fishing and ship-building, in which it was impossible to avoid it. Houses in the sixteenth and seventeenth centuries were both places of residence and places of work, and this dual function is reflected both in their layout and in the social topography of the town. These two factors were intimately linked in their operation and together moulded the topography of the town in a fashion which was broken only with the coming of industrialisation.

Houses, in towns as in the countryside, can range in size from a one-roomed cabin to a mansion of twenty or thirty rooms or more, the size reflecting the wealth and social standing of the head of the household that occupied it. Houses in towns were however subject to a number of pressures and constraints which were largely absent from the countryside. Towns by their nature are comparatively densely inhabited. This means that building sites are much sought after, and the most valuable part of the site is its frontage to the street, and certainly in the centres of towns it is the street frontage which gives access to the markets where, in the end, the money is to be made. As a consequence house plots tended to be long and narrow and, as we have seen, were deliberately laid out in this way when the town was first planned, so that houses frequently occupied the full width of the plot, abutting directly on to the walls of neighbouring properties on either side. Expansion could take place either upwards, or back into the length of the plot, or else both, with the result that houses in towns in the sixteenth and seventeenth centuries were often two, three or four storeys high, with gables facing on to the street, and a conglomeration of buildings, warehouses and stables stretching back some distance, frequently surrounding an inner courtyard. Admission to the buildings was either by means of an entry from the street at ground floor level through an arch under one of the gables, with first and second floor rooms over, or else by means of a gate from a back lane running at the rear of the property. Sometimes it was by both, the back lane in suitable locations in towns like Ipswich, Kings Lynn and Hull being replaced by a private quay giving access to the river, so that a merchant could unload his goods straight into his warehouses at the rear of his house and sell them in the shop at the front, any processing necessary taking place in the intermediate buildings. Domestic accommodation lay behind and over the shop, although it is only very gradually and during the course of the seventeenth century that rooms became dedicated to a special function instead of being miscellaneous store rooms. Buildings to the rear could be stables, barns, workshops, warehouses, brewhouses, even privies, whilst the yard which allowed access to these buildings was often given over to manufacturing processes, middens, pigs and chickens. Thus Henry Piper, a canvas weaver of Ipswich, who died in 1615, had, according to his probate inventory, two workhouses with looms and spinning wheels in them, and a brewhouse, whilst in his yard were poles with yarn upon them, and finished pieces of canvas were stored in a little room next to his parlour, with more yarn stored in a chamber over the shop, together with a bedstead, a saddle and stirrups, a saw, a birdcage and a pitchfork. Alexander White, a plumber of Eton, in Buckinghamshire,

Plate 43 Ireland's Mansion, Shrewsbury, a late nineteenth-century photograph. This splendid timber-framed town house was built in about 1575 for Robert Ireland, a wealthy wool merchant. It is the town version of Plate 22, and should also be compared with Plate 45

had, according to his probate inventory, a kitchen and scullery, hall, parlour, dining room, bed chambers over, rooms for men servants and maid servants, a larder, four garrets, a 'Yellow roome up one paire of Staires', a room within that, a grey room, two yards, a wash house, a stable with a room behind, a coal house, as well as two more kitchens in the lower house and a 'Plumbery' in which he had lead worth £40. Such rambling agglomerations of rooms and yards and outbuildings had their own organic unity. Behind an often imposing façade they lined the main streets of most towns in pre-industrial Britain.

However not all town houses were large, with numerous rooms, warehouses and workshops. One or two-room cottages were just as plentiful, cottages in which living conditions must have been as crowded and wretched as those in twenty-roomed houses were expansive and comfortable. There is evidence to show that rows of small cottages were being built as speculative ventures by the sixteenth-century equivalent of today's property developers. Half Moon Street, Sherborne, has a row of small tenements, built of stone in about 1532–4 and added to in the late sixteenth century. Abbey Cottages, in Church Street, Tewkesbury, comprises a row of at least 23 two ground-floor, one first-floor-roomed cottages built early in

Plate 44 Nos 34–40, Church Street, Tewkesbury, Gloucestershire. A row of cottages, probably late fifteenth century in date and now restored, built as a speculative development by the monks of the abbey

the sixteenth century, and seventeenth-century cottages, of two storeys although with only one room on each and linked with a spiral staircase, still survive in Bridge Street, All Saints Street and Friar Street in King's Lynn.

Houses in towns in the beginning of the sixteenth century were almost invariably built of timber, with the walls infilled with wattle and daub, and with thatched roofs. Stone was used only where local supplies were

Plate 45 Sparrowe's House, Ipswich, Suffolk. This is an essentially medieval town house, altered and added to in the seventeenth century, especially in about 1670, when it was decorated with some splendidly exuberant plaster pargetting

plentiful, as at Burford, for example, where it seems that timber framing was used in the sixteenth and seventeenth centuries for purely decorative purposes on houses basically of stone construction.

Many of the larger houses in principal streets were often lavishly decorated with elaborate carving to their timbers or else with plaster pargetting. Brick was still uncommon, although it was being used in the middle years of the fourteenth century in Norwich, Beverley and York, where the undercroft to the Merchant Venturers Hall was built of brick in 1358. One of the most difficult mental reconstructions that the landscape historian has to do is to appreciate that towns like Manchester, Sheffield, London and Liverpool were all built of timber and thatched houses at this time, and that the faces that these towns present today are essentially of the nineteenth and twentieth centuries.

The almost universal presence of timber and thatch, combined with the use of fire for domestic purposes and industrial processes such as malting and dyeing, meant that fires were very common. Very few towns wholly escaped fire on a large scale in the sixteenth and seventeenth centuries, the Great Fire of London being merely the most famous and the most destructive. Stratford upon Avon, for example, was devastated by fire in 1594, 1595, 1614 and 1641, Warwick in 1694, Marlborough in 1653, Bungay in 1688, Glasgow in 1652, Oxford in 1644, 1657 and 1671, Kelso in 1684 and Edinburgh in 1701. One consequence of these fires has been to rob very many towns of sixteenth- and seventeenth-century buildings, whilst urban renewal in later centuries has removed many more. This means that many towns have only isolated surviving examples, such as Staples Inn in Holborn in London, now heavily restored, whilst any extensive survivals are to be found either in small towns such as Ludlow or Lavenham, or else in towns such as Shrewsbury, York and Ipswich, towns which were not in the forefront of industrialisation in the nineteenth century.

Many towns experienced a major rebuilding of their houses from the middle years of the sixteenth century onwards, although much of this was alteration and adaptation of existing medieval houses in the interests of greater comfort and privacy. Chimneys and staircases were inserted as the hall, the central room in medieval houses, was ceiled over and other rooms developed more specialised functions. In most towns except London there was, however, very little expansion of the built-up area before the second half of the seventeenth century and newcomers into towns were usually accommodated, either by the subdivision of larger houses or else by the building of cottages in back yards and gardens. In Worcester for example, a survey of 1649 reveals that such subdivision was common. A house in the cathedral cemetery was described as being divided into two tenements, one of two rooms and a shop on the ground floor with two rooms over, and the other of two rooms with two over, whilst another house in the same cemetery, formerly a stable, had been subdivided into three tenements, each of one up and one down. Almost every municipal corporation in

Britain seems to have legislated at some time or other against this subdivision and the subletting of accommodation to newcomers, described graphically by the town council of Stirling in 1615 as 'sindrie unlauchfull persones, unfremen, vagabundis and idyll levaris', but the frequency with which such orders were issued and repeated can only point to widespread evasion.

Town houses in Scotland developed along rather similar principles to those in England and Wales but with a number of structural differences. There seems to have been a surge of urban rebuilding and renewal in many Scottish towns in the sixteenth and seventeenth centuries, during the course of which medieval timber houses were replaced with stone ones, many of those being rebuilt in the main streets of Edinburgh being to designs by Robert Mylne of Balforgie, the king's Master Mason. However the rate and pace of change varied considerably from one town to another: Glasgow, for example, had only a few stone buildings before the end of the seventeenth century.

Access to Scottish town houses was often by means of a passageway under the front tenement leading into a wynd, close or narrow lane with a staircase leading off, occasionally, as in Haddington, with a round tower for the stairs in the re-entry angle of an L-shaped block. The staircase then led up three, four, sometimes eight or nine in Edinburgh, storeys, with a separate dwelling on each floor. Since the staircase was common it was very rarely cleaned and became the repository for filth and rubbish of every imaginable kind. These stone houses often had open wooden galleries at the front, with stalls and booths on the ground floor at street level. In time these wooden galleries were boarded up and converted into rooms. Gables were often crow-stepped. The lane or close often gave further access to a tangle of stables, barns, cellars, bakehouses and taverns occupying the rear portions of the building lots.

The houses we have described so far, whether large or small, opulent or poverty-stricken, were essentially vernacular in their design, methods of building and materials used. The vernacular tradition was by no means static, but change came slowly and was accommodated within a local, conservative tradition. Even when brick was adopted as a building material it was common for it to be used as a replacement for the wattle and daub infilling between the studding of traditional timber-framed houses and it was well into the seventeenth century before house carpenters and bricklayers felt able to abandon the crutch of timber-framing and build solely in brick, something which was happening in York and King's Lynn from the middle of the seventeenth century. Similarly the actual techniques of building remained unchanged, with the work being done by masons, carpenters and bricklayers without any supervision from anyone remotely approaching a modern architect. Thus when the manse at Anstruther was rebuilt in 1590 the minister did all the organising, buying stone, lime and other materials and paying the workmen.

Nevertheless the dissolution of the vernacular tradition in towns was under way by the second and third decades of the seventeenth century, and from the same solvents that were attacking the vernacular tradition in country houses, namely themes, ideas and patterns from Renaissance Italy, either direct or else via France and the Low Countries.

The new ideas manifested themselves in a search for regularity and symmetry of façade, in the adoption of ornament that is ultimately classical in its inspiration and in the use of brick as a building material. Some entirely new houses were built in the new fashion, more were built on the foundations of a demolished one, and yet others were merely altered and adapted with a new façade to conceal a medieval timber-framed house. Such themes and patterns were not of course confined to dwelling houses. Town halls and market houses, schools and churches show the same elements, and all show them being incorporated in the same way: the adoption of ornament in a rather superficial and clumsy way is followed by a more radical incorporation of more fundamental elements as builders became more familiar with the spirit of the new ideas and acquired greater skill in handling them. The town hall at Alcester, built in 1618, follows the traditional pattern of having the ground floor open on arcades, but the columns to the arcades are Tuscan, and there is a similar feature to the Old Market House in Shrewsbury, built in 1596. Peacock's School, in Rye, built of brick in 1636, has giant pilasters and Dutch gables, and must be one of the first half-dozen buildings in England to use these features. The Civil War brought much destruction to towns like Worcester, and at the same time brought almost to a halt any normal processes of building and rebuilding in most other towns, so that it is only in the years after the Restoration that the new themes and styles spread at all rapidly. Nevertheless, whatever the rate of diffusion in individual towns, the results in England were

almost everywhere the same. By the end of the seventeenth century there were few towns without at least some town houses incorporating these new Renaissance themes, whether in new façades to old houses or else entirely new ones; and in some towns such houses were numerous, as in Bradford upon Avon for example, or Stamford.

The decline of the vernacular tradition in town houses took place in Scotland very much more slowly than it did in England, although it would appear that the processes were very similar. The first traces of the new themes are to be found in an increasing regularity of façade and decoration as timber houses were gradually rebuilt in stone, but where these features are to be found in English town building in the first decades of the seventeenth century it is the last decade of the century before they appear in Scotland, and again through the same channels of communication, namely the publication of pattern books and the slow accumulation of practical experience acquired by working on country houses by local master-masons, men like Tobias Bauchop of Alloa, who worked with Sir William Bruce in the last decades of the century.

The interaction between urban house design and the nature of industrial and commercial activity in pre-industrial society gave towns a social topography which was quite unlike that of towns today. Because the journey to work was uncommon this made street frontages valuable and the nearer the centre of a town the more valuable they were, so that only those who could afford them lived there. This meant that wealthy and prosperous merchants, shopkeepers and tradesmen lived in the centres of towns with a tendency for poorer people to congregate in the suburbs, giving rise to ribbon developments of poorer and smaller houses such as occurred in Frankwell, in Shrewsbury. Nevertheless there were smaller houses in the centres of towns, frequently occupying awkwardly shaped plots of land or infilling the backyards and gardens of larger properties. This gave to the centres of towns a social topography quite unlike that of today: as much residential as commercial with large houses lining the main streets.

At the same time there was a marked tendency, especially in medieval towns, for practitioners of the same trades to congregate together in the same streets. This occupational segregation was breaking down rapidly from the middle years of the sixteenth century, but it has left its mark in the large numbers of streets bearing occupational names. Street names have changed as rapidly and as extensively as other placenames, but where the topography of medieval towns has been studied in detail then very many names of these occupational streets have been recovered. St Aldate's, Oxford, was once called Fish Street, whilst to the west of Cornmarket lay Drapery Lane and Shoe Lane. Cambridge once had Broiderers Lane, Goldsmiths Row and Braziers Lane, whilst Petty Cury, a name meaning 'little kitchen', was in the sixteenth century lined with cook shops. London still has Fish Street, Pudding Lane and Milk Street, Cornhill, Poultry and Ironmonger Lane. Broad Street in Stirling was once called Market Place, and Flece Market lay parallel and to the south. Queens Street in Windsor was once called Butchers Row, and in Shrewsbury Butcher Row, Fish Street and Milk Street still survive.

It is clear that the second half of the sixteenth and much of the seventeenth centuries saw a great deal of building in towns, although much of this was in fact rebuilding on long-occupied sites, and much more was alteration and refacing. But when this rebuilding did take place the buildings themselves were poured into the traditional pattern of streets and property boundaries. Even if the new houses followed the new Renaissance-inspired styles no attempt was made to import another Renaissance theme, the concept of the planned, ideal city. This concept finds its origins in the fifteenth-century writings on architecture of the Italians Leon Alberti and Filarete. Their works were widely distributed, both in print and in manuscript, and their ideas were taken up and developed, first of all in Italy and then, in the seventeenth century, in France, Germany and the Low Countries. The ideal city was given a gridiron pattern of streets, with open squares and long straight vistas, although much theoretical speculation was concerned with the problems of adapting such plans to the new style of fortification imposed by the development of artillery. In practice, only very few entirely new towns were laid out in western Europe, and the majority of these were planned as fortresses, as at Palmanova, begun in 1593, or Naarden, near Amsterdam, or Philipville and Charleville along the eastern frontiers of France. Yet other new towns were laid out as adjuncts to the country palaces of the great. The two most obvious examples are Richelieu, begun in 1631 at the gates of the cardinal's immense château, now demolished, and Versailles.

Theoretical speculation about the layout of the ideal city was much more influential when it was applied to the large-scale rebuilding of existing towns. A succession of popes throughout the sixteenth century, from Julius II to Sixtus V, began the rebuilding of Rome on the grand scale, inspired by the desire to make the city the symbol of the power and dignity of the church, to provide adequate processional ways for pilgrims, and to improve drainage and sanitation. Immense vistas were opened up, with three great streets focusing on what is now the Piazza de Popolo, and the rebuilding of St Peter's was begun. It was the nineteenth century before the work was finally completed but the sheer scale and magnificence of the whole concept dazzled contemporaries. Only a ruler of the authority, vision and resources of Sixtus V – he is said to have spent over a million ducats on building alone during his short reign, 1585–1590 – could plan on this scale.

Less grandiose, and probably more influential in England, were the building schemes going on in Paris at the beginning of the seventeenth century. The Place Dauphine, on the Ile de la Cité, was laid out as a triangular open space with houses of uniform design in 1607, and the Place Royale (now the Place des Vosges) was the first example of an enclosed residential square with arcaded houses of uniform elevation built anywhere in Europe. It was completed in 1612, and Inigo Jones was in Paris in 1609.

The concept of the planned town returned only very slowly to England after the hiatus of the later medieval centuries and then only to small-scale building developments in existing towns. Inigo Jones was associated with two of the earliest schemes, and the influence of his continental models is obvious.

Between 1541 and 1552 an area of land bounded by Drury Lane, the Strand, St Martin's Lane and Long Acre, formerly the property of the Convent of St Peter, Westminster, was granted to John Russell, the first Earl of Bedford. It was still largely pasture, and there were a number of elm trees growing on it. In 1615 a central close was marked off with a brick wall, and Long Acre was laid out as a street and partially built up. In February 1631 Francis, the fourth Earl, received a licence to build in Covent Garden 'houses fitt for the habitation of gentlemen'. The scheme was fitted within the walled area, the piazza was the central part of this area, and the church of St Paul's, at the western end of the piazza, was the focal point of the entire project. The houses on the north and west sides were four storeys high, the top two storeys extending out over arcaded ground floor walks. They were all required to be built to the same uniform façade. Both church and houses were built to designs of Inigo Jones, who, whether drawing his inspiration from the Place Royale in Paris, or, as John Evelyn thought, from the Piazza d'Arme in Leghorn, or from Palladio, or from the well of his own genius, composed what has been called 'the first and finest of London's long sequence of residential squares'. Building went on rapidly, and almost all of the houses were occupied by 1639. Sadly however, it is now all but impossible to recapture anything of the splendour and nobility of Jones's original scheme. A market was already in existence in 1654, and one was formally established in 1670, by which time the piazza was rapidly losing its social exclusiveness. Market stalls began to appear and in due course became permanent, the present market buildings, completed in 1830, replacing the previous huddle of buildings. Some rebuilding of the original houses was already taking place by the end of the seventeenth century, but the last of the piazza houses,

Plate 47 An early
eighteenth-century view
of Covent Garden. The
church of St Paul is on
the left. The ground floor
arcading to the houses
surrounding the square
can be seen, as well as the
market stalls in the
centre. Some are already
of a semi-permanent
nature

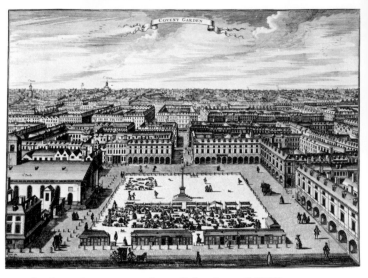

much altered, was not demolished until 1933.

Whilst the houses in Covent Garden were being built another scheme was started in the fields to the west of Lincoln's Inn. A lease was obtained in 1638 by William Newton, with permission to build 32 houses. By 1641 those on the south and west of the field were largely completed, but it was 1657 before work began on the north side, leaving a large open space in the centre. At the same time a western extension of the northern side, Great Queen Street, was being built, and was largely completed by 1640. The houses to both Lincoln's Inn Fields and to Great Queen Street were given a uniform façade in the new Renaissance-inspired designs. Inigo Jones's personal involvement is less certain there than in Covent Garden, but he was certainly one of the Commissioners on Buildings appointed by Charles I to oversee new building, especially in the London suburbs, which is what Covent Garden and Lincoln's Inn Fields were at this time; as such he must certainly have exercised considerable control over the layout of what proved to be a most influential development. Only Lindsey House, on the west side of Lincoln's Inn Fields, still survives.

On 1 September 1666, a Saturday, a baker living in Pudding Lane, in the City of London, drew his fire and went to bed. In the early hours of the next morning he awoke to find his house ablaze. It was Wednesday the 5th before the fire was finally extinguished, by which time 13,200 houses, the Royal Exchange, the Custom House, 87 parish churches and St Paul's cathedral, had been destroyed, and perhaps as many as 200,000 people had been made homeless, many camping out as best they could in tents provided by the king. The Great Fire of London presented at once an unrivalled opportunity for urban replanning on the grandest scale, and a human disaster of hitherto unheard of dimensions. That the city which eventually emerged from the ashes was a response to the human disaster and not a grandiloquent reflection of an autocratic ruler's authority tells us a great deal about the ideals, aspirations and structures of power of late seventeenth-century Britain.

A royal proclamation issued on 13 September called for rebuilding in brick and for the widening of the secondary lanes and alleys, and these requirements were eventually embodied in the Act for Rebuilding, passed in the February of 1667. The rebuilding regulations were detailed and exact, and 'knowing and intelligent persons in building' were appointed to see them carried out. The new houses were to be built of brick or stone. Wood, save for window casements and doors, was banned from the exterior of houses. Party walls were to be set out so that the boundary ran down the centre of the thickness of the wall. The first builder was to erect the entire wall, leaving toothing so that the adjoining house could be built on when its owner was ready. When he came to build on, he was to pay half the cost of the entire wall, with interest at 6 per cent over any intervening period. This meant that an owner could begin to rebuild as soon as he was ready, without having to wait for neighbours. The Act also laid down stringent regulations as to the size and structure of the houses. There were to be four kinds: houses fronting by-streets, houses fronting high and principal streets, and finally 'mansion houses . . . of the greatest bignes not fronting upon any of the streets or lanes'. For the first three kinds there were detailed provisions upon the numbers of storeys, the interior height of the rooms, the thickness of the walls, the scantlings of the timbers, and the depth of the cellars.

Charles II took an active interest in the rebuilding and at first supported the idea of a completely new plan, for which the City authorities themselves also asked on 8 September. Dr Christopher Wren submitted his new plan on the 11th, John Evelyn presented another two days later, and Robert Hooke, Peter Mills, Richard Newcourt and Captain Valentine Knight also drew up plans. Charles appointed three Commissioners, Wren, May and Pratt; the City appointed three Surveyors, Hooke, Mills and Jerman; and between them these six men set about their enormous task. By the end of November, as they began to appreciate more fully the scale of the disaster, they finally abandoned any hope of a radically new ground-plan. Instead they turned their attention to more practical and urgent problems, clearing the ruins and debris, staking out the new plots, making sure that the building regulations embodied in the Act were obeyed, and all the time the specially constituted Fire Court, with infinite patience and tact, a careful attention to the rights and the grievances of all concerned, and a refusal to become bogged down in procedural niceties, urged, cajoled and persuaded individual householders to rebuild. By the Spring of 1668 about eight hundred houses had been rebuilt, standing gaunt and solitary midst long stretches of ash and rubble, since there was no overall plan or timetable for rebuilding. It was 1673 before the great majority of houses were rebuilt, and 1696 before the last, by which time some rebuilding of the earlier ones was already taking place.

The new city certainly lacked the grandeur of the Rome of Sixtus V, or even the splendid perspective of the Champs Elysées, then being laid out in Paris by Le Nôtre; although Pepys thought the vista down Cornhill and Lombard Street 'mighty noble'. It was, however, for the great majority of its inhabitants cleaner, safer and more commodious than the old city. It was, in short, a better place in which to live, and as such an achievement quite the equal of anything else in Europe at the time.

The Great Fire was certainly a major disaster, the planning and organisation of its rebuilding an almost equally major triumph, but neither interrupted to any extent the steady outward expansion of the built-up area of London to north, east and west. East of the city for example, the site of the Augustinian priory to the east of Bishopsgate was being laid out in narrow streets by the 1640s, when there were already numerous poor silk weavers living in the district. In February 1682 the Artillery Ground was sold for £5,700 to a group of property speculators, including Nicholas Barbon, perhaps the most unscrupulous of them all, and building followed rapidly, including the market house in the Spital Fields, and by 1690 Mile End New Town was sufficiently built up to be made a separate hamlet of Stepney. In the west, immediately after the Restoration the Earl of St Albans began to lay out the area to the south of Piccadilly, and St James's Square became very fashionable over the next twenty years. At the same time, in the north, St Giles's Fields, by now called Soho Fields, was also being laid out and rapidly built up, not only by Nicholas Barbon in Gerrard Street but also by

Richard Frith in Soho Square, Frith Street, Greek Street and Compton Street, called after the bishop of London. This area, especially Soho Square, was also very fashionable when it was first built.

Altogether, very large numbers of houses were built in London in the last forty years of the seventeenth century, but in spite of the wide variety in their design and layout and the enormous social span of the people for whom they were built they had certain common characteristics. They were all built of brick, with tiled roofs and glazed windows. Some of the largest were detached but the great majority were terraced, with a modest uniformity of outward appearance and internal plan, especially the cheaper ones which were almost mass-produced. In all of this they were most influential, setting new standards of safety and amenity and new trends in design and building practice that in due course were followed all over the country.

London was by far and away the largest city in Britain in the seventeenth century, and the rebuilding of the City after the Great Fire the largest scheme of urban planning and renewal. It was however a very conservative rebuilding in that such changes as were introduced were done to remove long-standing abuses and to prevent such a catastrophe occurring again. For all its faults, which were many and manifest, Londoners were intensely proud of the city which had disappeared in smoke and flames that first week in September of 1666 – proud of the wealth of its inhabitants, the dignity of its magistrates and the antiquity of its origins, so that they believed without hesitation the story, as told by Geoffrey of Monmouth, of its foundation by Brute, the son of Aeneas, 1108 years before the birth of Christ. Stow's *Survey of London*, first published in 1598, is a sustained panegyric upon the old city.

Very similar patterns of values and beliefs are to be found amongst the inhabitants of towns the length and breadth of Britain. A number of provincial towns were devastated by fire in the sixteenth and seventeenth centuries, including Warwick and Northampton, where the administrative machinery which had served London so well was taken over following the fires in 1694 and 1674 respectively. In every case rebuilding followed in the same traditional patterns as in London. Even when the opportunity presented itself no-one wished to embark upon large-scale re-planning, and Hawksmoor's plans for the rebuilding of Oxford and Cambridge upon continental models went unheeded.

Borough magistrates had a very high opinion of their own worth and dignity, and were quick to take offence at any slight, real or imagined. As we have seen, town walls and town halls were regarded as symbols of civic pride, and there are other signs, although on a very small scale, of attempts to improve the appearance of provincial towns during this period. Most towns made some attempt to pave at least their main streets, and Cambridge, Ipswich and Windsor obtained Acts of Parliament in 1544, 1571 and 1585 respectively, to regularise what they were doing. Many regulations for the cleansing of streets were as much concerned with the abatement of nuisances as anything else, but an element of concern for appearances cannot be ruled out. At the same time, very slowly, in one town at a time, and more especially during the seventeenth century, some attention was given to the laying out of open spaces for recreation. A public walk was laid out in Exeter in 1612 at the Northernhay, and an arcaded walk, called Blagrave's Piazza, was built in Reading in 1620. There were complaints in Maidstone, in 1640, that the King's Meadow, 'beinge the auntient sportinge place for the Inhabitantes of the said Towne', had been enclosed. Sometimes these schemes were directed by the town authorities, as at Stirling, where in 1661 the masters of Cowane's Hospital were ordered to level the yard of the hospital and make a walking green thereof, and plant it about with trees, and pave the close and outwalk. More frequently they were the result of private endeavour. One of the most interesting of these attempts to improve a town was made at Ross-on-Wye at the very end of the seventeenth century, when John Kyrle, a wealthy inhabitant, took the lease of ground lying on three sides of the church and laid out a public garden, the Prospect, complete with dignified entrance gates embellished with pediments and Corinthian pilasters. Such schemes become increasingly frequent from this time onward. The Quarry, in Shrewsbury, was first laid out with avenues of lime trees in 1719, for example, in the same year that the municipal authorities in York decided to plant trees to 'beautify' the Lord Mayor's Walk, which ran just outside the city walls from Gillygate to Monk Bar. Many towns also acquired bowling greens during the seventeenth century, Bristol in 1622 for example, and Oxford in 1631, and there were seven in Cambridge in 1688. All together, many towns by the end of the seventeenth century must have been at least marginally more pleasant to live in than they were at the beginning of the sixteenth.

The moral landscape

Landscape is the autobiography of society. Successive generations write and rewrite the story of their hopes, ideals and aspirations across the landscape, without, however, being able to erase *in toto* those of previous generations. Some landscape features are profoundly satisfying and remain almost without change for centuries. The pattern of streets in a town is a good example of this. The buildings lining the streets of many English towns have been pulled down and rebuilt again and again, but only very rarely have social and economic pressures been strong enough to burst the bounds set when the pattern of plots and streets was first laid out, at any time between the tenth and the thirteenth centuries. Similarly the pattern of open fields and strips has proved to be remarkably durable: in spite of the manifest inconveniences of the system and the obvious advantages of enclosure it has persisted, although to an ever-diminishing extent, until the twentieth century.

Some features of the landscape reflect the structures created by men in order that they may earn a living from the soil, and again the open field system is a very good example of this. Other features reflect the need and the ability to manufacture goods to satisfy other demands: for clothes, tools, furniture and pottery. The ephemeral nature of so much early industrial plant tells us a great deal about the level of technology in the sixteenth and seventeenth centuries. But men are also remarkably conscious of themselves as human beings with moral, spiritual and social aspirations that transcend the satisfaction of merely physical requirements. In Chapter 5 we saw the appearance of some of these aspirations in the landscape with the slow adoption of themes in architecture which had come, often strangely metamorphosed, from Renaissance Italy and ultimately from Imperial Rome – themes in which order, balance and symmetry in buildings are seen as reflections of the divine harmony of the universe.

Men have gone to extraordinary lengths to give physical expression to their awareness of, or at least to their need to discover for themselves, a spiritual, moral, eternal world lying beyond their physical perception, as a glance for a moment at Stonehenge, Chartres cathedral or the Pyramids will reveal. In sixteenth- and seventeenth-century Britain there was a profound shift in the ordering of this scheme of values. The Reformation offered a new approach to God, and quite suddenly ancient, long revered institutions lost their meaning. Their buildings became empty shells, empty both spiritually and physically.

We are not here directly concerned with the causes and progress of the Reformation, only with its impact upon the fabric of the landscape, and this impact derives most of its force from some of the central doctrines of the Reformation leaders. The keystone to Luther's thought was the doctrine of justification by faith alone: on the one hand is the awful majesty of God, on the other a wretchedly corrupt and self-centred man. But God's mercy is infinite. If men will abandon all reliance upon personal merit and put their whole-hearted trust in the merits of Christ then surely will they be saved. Such a belief leapt like a searing flame through the heart and mind of Luther, and through the minds of thousands of those who sought to follow him. It had profound and radical consequences. It struck at the root of the luxuriant forest of intercessary practices that had grown up about the medieval Catholic church: the worship of the saints and their relics, the religious life of monks and nuns, pilgrimages, the value of good works, masses for the dead, the *raison d'être* of chantry priests, even clerical celibacy. All became unnecessary and irrelevant, and indeed, as superstitious practices, a positive hindrance to the development of the only true, reformed, religion. Increasing emphasis was placed upon the conscience of the individual Christian in direct communion with his God, with no need for any kind of intermediary, and with the Bible as his only sure guide. Tyndale's translation of the New Testament, with its studious avoidance of all reference to priests and to the organised Church, only added fuel to the flames. Many of the implications of this onslaught on long-accepted modes of thought and patterns of belief were quickly appreciated. If the prayers and the masses of the religious orders were of no value, then their considerable wealth lay defenceless. If all depended upon the individual conscience, with only the Bible for a guide, than a reading and literate laity would develop, demanding vernacular translations of the Bible; an educated ministry was essential, and religious toleration would be the long-term consequence.

The previous paragraph is of course little more than a travesty of a debate about the relationship of man with God that was conducted with monumental learning, savage intensity and brutal intolerance for nearly two centuries, and can still stir the passions and the minds of men. The impact of these doctrines upon the landscape of Britain was nearly as profound as their impact upon the beliefs of men.

The monastic ideal, which had burned so brightly in the twelfth century and had led to the foundation of the monasteries, had affected all ranks of society. Every surviving monastic cartulary contains deeds of gift of quite small parcels of land from pious peasant farmers and village craftsmen. The stern precepts of the rule of St Benedict had however long been only slackly observed by the opening decades of the sixteenth century. Only in the austere Carthusian houses was the monastic ideal still practised with something of its pristine intensity. No one was prepared to fight to save them, and it took no more than two or three of Thomas Cromwell's commissioners, together with a couple of servants and a clerk, to close proud and wealthy houses such as Shaftesbury and Oseney, St Albans and Bury St Edmunds. On 23 March 1540 Waltham Abbey surrendered to the king, the last of the religious houses in England and Wales, and a centuries-old pattern of values expressed in a unique building form, often of very great beauty, came to an abrupt end.

The dissolution of the monasteries had been envisaged for some time, but when it did come it was all over in less than four years. Lesser monasteries in England and Wales, defined as those with an annual income from lands of less than £200, were dissolved by Act of Parliament in 1536. Within weeks of the passing of this Act another was passed to create what was in effect a new government department, 'a certain court commonly to be called the Court of the Augmentations of the Revenues of the King's Crown', and it was this court that saw to the administration of the greatest programme of land nationalisation in English history. As individual houses surrendered so an inventory was made of the movable goods such as livestock, hay and grain, much of which was sold locally. Plate and jewels were listed and sent to the Master of the King's Jewel House. The lead on the roofs of the conventual buildings was valued and in due course arrangements were made for it to be removed and melted down for sale. This lead could be very valuable: that from St Osyth Priory in Essex, for example, was valued at the enormous sum of £1,044. The bells were also melted down. The buildings were defaced in order to make them unusable: the great Priory at Lewes was razed to the ground in little more than a month in March and April of 1538. For the next two centuries monastic sites became quarries for local inhabitants from miles around.

Almost from the first the Court of Augmentations began to sell the lands of the dissolved monasteries, the Act for the dissolution of the remaining ones being passed in 1539.

Plate 48 The ruins of the almost completely demolished abbey at Jervaulx, in Yorkshire

However at no time was there any real scramble to buy monastic lands; rather was there considerable pressure to sell imposed upon an almost bankrupt Crown by a grandiose foreign policy and the wars that this provoked, especially in the years between 1543 and 1547. The Crown gave very little away, perhaps little more than 2 per cent of the total, although some individuals did receive some very handsome gifts – Lord John Russell the estates of Tavistock Abbey in Devonshire, for example, and Sir Thomas Wriothesley those of Titchfield in Hampshire. The Crown never put individual properties up for sale, it was assumed almost from the first that everything could be bought and the initiative invariably came from a prospective purchaser. The normal price was fixed at twenty years' purchase, that is twenty times the assessed annual value of the property, although this assessment was often based upon out of date and uneconomic rents. Only after about 1550 did the Court of Augmentations begin to raise the number of years' purchase in order to take account of 'improved rents'. The sale, or at least the availability for sale, of so much property does not seem to have depressed prices to any extent, since twenty years' purchase seems to have been the traditional, conventional price for any land purchase.

It is impossible to generalise at all accurately as to the long-term effect upon society of the comparatively sudden release of very large quantities of land on to the market. By 1547, the death of Henry VIII, over half of the monastic lands had been sold, and over three-quarters by 1558. No families rose to great wealth simply on monastic lands. Established landed families were able to add to their possessions. Some yeoman farmers bought lands when they could raise the purchase price. Lawyers, royal officials and occasionally merchants and townsmen also bought lands. But a market for the resale of monastic lands also developed quickly, so that by the 1560s much had been re-distributed, often in quite small parcels, among a very large number of people. What is clear however is that by yielding to short-term pressures to treat capital as income the Crown divested itself of an immense source of extra-parliamentary revenue. If it had retained the monastic lands then the course of events in the seventeenth century might have been different indeed.

The fate of monastic buildings varied enormously. New dioceses were erected for Chester, Oxford, Peterborough, Bristol and Gloucester on monastic foundations, so that at least the churches of the former monasteries survived. In Oxford Cardinal Wolsey dissolved the Augustinian priory of St Frideswide in 1525 in order to endow his new foundation of Cardinal College. After his fall in 1529 Henry VIII refounded the college as Christ Church, and made the priory church into the college chapel. The diocese of Oxford was founded in 1542 with Oseney abbey, just outside the city, as the seat for the new bishop. However in 1546 Oseney abbey was leased to the clothier William Stumpe, and the bishop moved to the college chapel of Christ Church and made this his cathedral. Christ Church retained the right to take building materials from the site of Oseney, so that what had been described as the third

175

abbey in England for the splendour of its buildings had been totally demolished by 1650. At Gloucester and Chester the cloisters survive almost intact, but at Peterborough there is little more than an open square to show where once they stood. At Bristol the nave of the monastic church was demolished shortly after the dissolution, and a replacement was not built until G. E. Street undertook the task between 1868 and 1888. It was also intended that Westminster Abbey should become a cathedral, but the new diocese only lasted ten years and in 1560 Elizabeth I made it into the Collegiate Church of St Peter which it still is.

The twelve monastic cathedrals lost their monks but retained their diocesan status and their deans and chapters. In this way Norwich and Durham, Worcester and Canterbury, among others, were preserved, together with, at Norwich, their cloisters.

About a hundred monastic churches became or continued as parish churches. At Sherborne, Romsey and Tewkesbury the corporations bought the buildings, Tewkesbury paying £483 in 1542 for one of the finest examples of Norman architecture in England. At Sherborne the town bought the abbey church and demolished their old parish church, at the same time using part of the abbey premises for a school, building a new school room in 1606. The abbey church at Selby also became a parish church, the other conventual buildings disappearing. Others included Dunstable, Evesham and Pershore, and Ewenny in Glamorganshire and St Dogmael's abbey church in Cardiganshire.

In Cambridge the Franciscan house became the site for Sidney Sussex College, founded in 1589, although the buildings themselves were largely demolished to provide building materials for the Great Court of Trinity College. The buildings of the Dominican friary in Ipswich became a hospital, grammar school and town library, whilst the Carmelite house became the county gaol. In Reading the church of the Greyfriars was granted to the corporation in 1542. Part was converted into a town hall and another part became an almshouse. It was a house of correction in 1613 and was only restored to its original spiritual function in 1863. Half of the stone of the priory church at Wallingford was bought for £9 to repair the bridge over the Thames. Some monastic buildings were adapted to become private residences. In Gloucester the church of the Blackfriars was made into a town house by Sir Thomas Bell, and the Carmelite church at Nottingham was likewise converted before the end of the sixteenth century. In Exeter the house of the Blackfriars was acquired in 1539 by Lord Russell and he proceeded to convert it into a large and complex town house for himself, his family and household, a house of three storeys and garrets, a great entrance porch, fish house, wash house, slaughterhouse and stables, as much a self-contained community as any country house. At Bicester the priory church was demolished and the remaining buildings converted into a

mansion by the Duke of Suffolk. At Titchfield Sir Thomas Wriothesley converted the buildings into a country mansion, Place House. The nave of the church was rebuilt as the gatehouse, with four towers and battlemented walls, and the monastic frater, to the north, became the great hall. Much of this was demolished in the 1740s. At Bury St Edmunds the entire abbey precinct was bought for £412 19s. 4d. The abbot's lodging was turned into a dwelling house and the remaining buildings became in practice a quarry for the townsmen for something like two centuries, with two great gates still standing today to hint at splendours which have passed away. At Much Wenlock

Plate 49 Tewkesbury Abbey, Gloucestershire. Here is one of the finest Norman churches in England. The nave and tower date from the early twelfth century. The apse was remodelled early in the fourteenth century when the dependent chapels were added. It became the parish church of Tewkesbury at the Reformation

177

Plate 50 The remarkably well-preserved ruins of Fountains Abbey, Yorkshire

the magnificent late fifteenth-century infirmary and prior's lodging became a private dwelling. The site of Fountains Abbey came into the hands of Sir Richard Gresham, who stripped the buildings of anything and everything that was saleable. In 1598 Sir Stephen Proctor bought the site, and proceeded to use the abbey infirmary as a quarry for materials with which to build himself a house, Fountains Hall. Even now, however, there is more still standing at Fountains than at another great Yorkshire Cistercian House, Jervaulx. (See Plate 48.)

Thus within a very few years of the departure of the last of their inmates the conventual buildings, once so deeply embedded into the fabric of the landscape in almost every locality in England and Wales, had been dismantled, and their sites turned to profane use. Their disappearance marks the end of one pattern of ideals, practices and beliefs and the inauguration of another. In this way the changes in values and aspirations summed up in the word 'Reformation' find their visible expression in the landscape.

In England and Wales the death of the monasteries was a comparatively swift affair. In Scotland however it was much more protracted. By the beginning of the fifteenth

Plate 51 The ruins of Jedburgh Abbey, Roxburghshire. A succession of English attacks led to much rebuilding between 1480 and 1540. Part was in use as the parish church until 1875

century the practice was established in Scotland of an abbey being given to a commendator, at first another cleric of power and standing but by the end of the century often a layman. The commendator took the revenues for himself and allowed the monks such 'portion' as he thought fit. The effects upon conventual finances may be imagined. By the beginning of the sixteenth century the practice of feu-ing monastic lands had begun, partly in response to the financial difficulties commending had brought about. This resulted in the permanent alienation of endowments. In 1531 Clement VII was finally persuaded by James V to permit the taxation of the church, and feu-ing increased rapidly to meet this new demand. Between 1544 and 1549 there was a series of English invasions of lowland Scotland, penetrating as far as Dundee, where they burnt the Maison Dieu. Much destruction was caused to the monasteries, particularly those in the Tweed valley, which had scarcely recovered from similar attacks in 1523. Thus Jedburgh Abbey was pillaged in both 1523 and 1544, whilst Coldingham was attacked no less than four times, in 1532, 1542, 1544 and again in 1545. Most of what was left was destroyed in 1645. Holyrood Abbey was burned in 1547, by which time the monks had already deserted the buildings. Melrose was burnt in 1545, Haddington nunnery in 1544.

The cumulative effects of all these trends were disastrous. Buildings were neglected. Endowments were alienated to such an extent that it was not unknown for abbots to be distrained for debt. By the time the Crown annexed the monasteries in 1587 they had long ceased to function and the bulk of their property was already in lay hands. The monks themselves were not turned out: they were simply forbidden to recruit new members, and so the conventual buildings slowly fell empty. Once the monks had gone the Crown gradually disposed of what remained by creating temporal lordships. Thus Paisley Abbey was created into a barony for Lord Claud Hamilton in 1587, and Coldingham and Jedbugh were granted to the burgh in 1593, and the lands were formed into a separate barony in 1606. Arbroath became a temporal lordship in 1606, and in 1604 Dryburgh Abbey, Cambuskenneth Abbey and Inchmahome Priory were amalgamated to form the lordship of Cardross for the Earl of Mar.

There was no concerted or violent attack upon monastic buildings once they were empty, although Crossraguel Abbey was sacked in 1561 and the friaries in Perth were pillaged at about the same time. Several monastic churches became parochial: part of that at Dundrennan Abbey until 1742, for example, and the monastic frater at Sweetheart Abbey near Dumfries. A number of parish churches were built within the surviving ruins of abbey churches, as at Jedburgh in 1668, Melrose in 1618 and Kelso in 1649. The absence of any concerted attack upon monastic buildings means that no English town is dominated today in the same way that the ruins of Jedburgh abbey, gaunt and roofless, still dominate that town, and no abbey precinct in England still retains as much of its enclosing wall as does that at St Andrews, still almost complete and nearly a mile in circumference.

Change and loss also took place among parish churches during this period, although there are more impersonal economic and social forces at work in addition to the doctrinal changes brought about by the Reformation, and to all of these must be added natural disaster, especially fire.

Comparatively few entirely new parish churches were built during this period, and those which did appear were the result of population growth and change. This is particularly true of the suburbs of London, where there was much building, population increase and in due course the subdivision of parishes. Thus the parish of St Anne's Soho was carved out of St Martin in the Fields in 1686, the year in which the new church was itself dedicated, and in recognition of the extensive building which had taken place there in the previous fifteen years. Another parish carved out of St Martin in the Fields was St Paul's Covent Garden – following the development of the square by the Earl of Bedford in the 1630s, a development crowned by Inigo Jones' new church, the first in England to be built following Renaissance principles of architecture. Henry Jermyn, Earl of St Albans, began to develop the area to the south of Piccadilly, the main road to Reading from London, in the years immediately after the Restoration. The church of St James Piccadilly was consecrated in 1684 and in 1685 a new parish was created.

The East End of London was growing equally rapidly, and with the same results for the subdividing of parishes and the building of churches. Stepney parish needed at least three chapels of ease: the thirteenth-century chapel at St Mary Matfelon in Whitechapel Road became a separate parish as early as 1329. Wapping had a chapel of ease by 1617 and this became a separate parish in 1694, and Shadwell had a chapel by 1656, becoming a separate parish in 1669.

But population can ebb as well as flow. Thus Lewes lost the church of St Martin before 1545 and the church of St Nicholas had been converted into tenements before 1592. The parish church of St Lawrence Bristol had been converted into a warehouse and the parish itself amalgamated with that of St John before 1580. In Beverley the congregation of St Nicholas church began to decline in the 1540s and the church was demolished to provide building materials for the Civil War defences, the parish itself not being amalgamated with that of St Mary until 1667. In Hertford the parish of St Nicholas had fewer than ten householders in 1428 and was amalgamated with the parish of St Andrew by 1535. Another parish in Hertford, that of St John, also lost many of its inhabitants during the sixteenth century. The parish church was pulled down before 1624 and a smaller one erected in the nave. Even this had been demolished by 1679, in which year the parish was amalgamated with that of All Saints.

Disaster was sometimes natural, as when the steeple of the church at Buckingham was blown down in 1699 and never replaced, or it could be due to structural failure. The tower of St Mary's, Scarborough collapsed in 1659 and was subsequently rebuilt. The tower of St Werburgh, Derby also collapsed in 1601 and again was rebuilt, and the church of St Giles in the main street of Elgin had to be rebuilt in 1684 after a similar structural failure.

The fighting during the Civil Wars caused much destruction. The church of St Thomas in Portsmouth was severely damaged and the tower and nave were as a consequence rebuilt, although the work was not completed until 1693. At Carlisle six of the eight bays of the cathedral were destroyed by the Scots and never rebuilt. At Hereford two parish churches were damaged beyond repair during the siege of 1645, and in Nottingham the church of St Nicholas was destroyed during the Civil Wars and rebuilt in 1678.

But the largest single loss of parish churches during the sixteenth and seventeenth centuries was the consequence of fire. A disastrous fire at Northampton led to the rebuilding of the church of All Saints between 1676 and 1680, Henry Bell, the architect of Kings Lynn, adding the portico in 1701. A similar fire at Warwick in 1694 rendered so much of the church of St Mary structurally unsound that it had to be almost totally rebuilt. However the greatest destruction was caused by the Great Fire of London, when eighty-seven churches and old St Paul's were destroyed.

An Act of Parliament of 1670 provided for the rebuilding of the City parish churches. The work was to be supervised by three Commissioners, the Archbishop of Canterbury, the bishop of London and the Lord Mayor, with Dr Wren (he was not knighted until 1673), as Surveyor General, their executive officer. The Act provided for the amalgamation of a number of the parishes, so that only fifty-one churches had to be rebuilt. Money for the fabric of the church was to be provided from a fund raised by an increase in the tax on coal coming into London by sea, principally from Newcastle. This money as it was collected was paid into the Chamber of the City, that is, the city treasury. Individual parishes also raised money by whatever means they could, including the sale of rubble and old building materials from their churches. This money was also paid into the Chamber and could then be drawn upon as rebuilding progressed.

The work of reconstruction began always on the initiative of the parish. Having obtained leave from the Commissioners the parish officials, namely the incumbent and the churchwardens, approached Wren for a design and a 'model', a scale-model in wood of the proposed church. If the proposed design was accepted then building could begin. Wren himself supervised a great deal of the work and checked the accounts, but he did not do it all, and he often left matters of detail to his assistants or to the masons, carpenters and bricklayers who were doing the actual work, with the result that almost all of the churches contain some work which is crude and pedestrian along with much that is of the highest quality. By the end of 1670 fifteen churches had been started, and the work was almost complete by 1686, although Wren continued to design and add steeples for a number of years afterwards.

In designing these churches Wren was faced with a number of problems that permitted no simple or uniform solution. The first was that in many respects the traditional form of the medieval church had become obsolete. All of the Protestant churches which emerged from the Reformation laid considerable stress upon corporate worship and upon preaching, so that the nave and the pulpit became more important than the chancel, with the idea of a centrally planned church in itself going back to the Italian humanists of the fifteenth century. Up until this time there had been the opportunity to express these doctrinal changes architecturally in only a small handful of churches: Groombridge in 1623, St Katherine Cree in London, 1628–1631, St John Leeds 1632–1633. Thus Wren had no substantial body of English precedent upon which to draw, and so he had to rely upon the humanist tradition and his own sense of what was appropriate, with the consequence that the chancel all but disappeared from the designs of his churches. At St Bride's Fleet Street there is no more than a shallow recess at the east end, and at St Mary le Bow and St Mary at Hill there was not even this, with St Mary at Hill probably his most 'centralised' church.

His other problem was that of the restricted, cramped and often awkwardly shaped sites upon which he had to build a church. Here his practical, geometrical turn of mind and endless invention could be given full scope, and he produced some astonishingly ingenious solutions to what must have appeared to have been almost insoluble problems. Perhaps the oddest design of all is that for St Benet Fink, an elongated decagon, and St Antholin, an elongated octagon. Sadly, both of these have since been demolished. Fortunately, one of his smallest churches, St Benet Paul's Wharf, built between 1677 and 1683, of red and blue brick chequerwork with carved stone garlands over the windows, still stands.

At St Stephen Walbrook he first came to grips with the problem of building a central dome over a rectangular building. His solution here was to build the dome of wood and plaster on eight arches supported on eight columns, the dome itself being nowhere supported on the walls of the church. These problems he had to face again when

Plate 52 The Church of St Benet Paul's Wharf, London, designed by Sir Christopher Wren and built between 1677 and 1683

designing St Paul's.

From the middle of the 1670s there was a further development in Wren's church design, a design which came to full fruition in St James's Piccadilly, a church built outside the fire zone, and completed in 1683. Here he built a two-storeyed, galleried church with nave and aisles, a central tunnel vault for the nave and transverse tunnel vaults for the aisles, with a splendid tripartite window at the east end, with a Venetian window above, to mark where the chancel might have been. Wren was clearly very pleased with this design, he thought it both beautiful and convenient, and it served as a model for numerous churches built throughout the country over the next half-century. This church was badly damaged during the Second World War, but has since been carefully restored.

The interior woodwork, furnishings and fittings were commissioned by the parish. Wren was often consulted, but he left much of the work to individual masons, wood-carvers and sculptors. When Grinling Gibbons was employed – in fact he did far less than is generally attributed to him – then the work is of outstanding quality, as in the reredos at St James's Piccadilly.

Whilst all this work on parish churches was going on Wren was also designing, planning and supervising the building of St Paul's cathedral.

Even before the Great Fire the old cathedral was structurally in poor condition. Inigo Jones had carried out some restoration work, principally the erection of a classical western portico, but this work had been interrupted by the Civil Wars and never completed. The fire itself caused considerable damage, but at first it was hoped that reconstruction and restoration would suffice. Further falls of masonry caused irretrievable damage, and it was clear that there would have to be complete demolition followed by the building of an entirely new cathedral. The Dean of St Paul's wrote to Wren informing him of this decision and calling for 'a Design, handsome and Noble', and, with a phrase touching in its self-confidence, asking him 'to take it for granted that Money will be had to accomplish it'.

Wren produced a series of designs, plans and models. His second was completed in 1673. He used a Greek-cross plan, with a great central dome surrounded by eight smaller ones and a further dome over a vestibule at the west end. Here is the essentially congregation-focused church. It has no more than a very modest apse where a medieval cathedral would have had its choir. The wooden model of this design is still preserved in St Paul's cathedral today. It was much criticised, not least for departing too far from the traditional ideas of what a cathedral should look like. Further designs followed until in 1674 he produced what is known as the Warrant Design, because this is the one which was accepted; and in May 1675 Charles II signed the warrant for building to begin. The Warrant Design is more conventional than the Great Model design in that it has a nave of five bays, a choir of three bays, transepts, a central dome with a curious spire, and a western portico. It is essentially a medieval cathedral in classical dress.

Almost immediately Wren began to modify the Warrant Design, and the modifications gave it much greater unity. The nave was reduced to three bays, balancing those of the choir. At the west end he added a large bay with side chapels, at the east end a short bay and apse. The transepts were also of equal size, and so the great central dome

185

acted as the unifying centrepiece for a building inspired by the central principle of classical architecture: a building must be seen as an overall whole from which nothing can be taken and to which nothing can be added without destroying the whole composition.

In 1697 work had progressed so far that the first service could be held, and construction of the dome could begin. For many years Wren had been wrestling with a particularly intractable problem, and he arrived at a marvellously ingenious solution. He was well aware that a single dome cannot be effective both from the inside and the outside. There must be two, and this means that great technical problems must be overcome if the enormous thrusts of two superimposed structures are to be adequately dispersed. Wren solved this problem by building three domes. The first, interior, dome, is almost hemispherical. Above this he built a brick cone which carried the weight of the lantern, and then outside this he built a timber-framed lead-covered dome through which the lantern emerges. This splendid dome is, from the exterior, in itself a classical temple riding above the great church below.

Plate 53 Sir Christopher Wren's serene masterpiece, St Paul's cathedral, London. This photograph was taken in 1937, before Second World War bombing and subsequent rebuilding destroyed its setting

The work was finally finished in 1709, by which time Wren was seventy-seven and had spent thirty-five years superintending every detail of the construction of what is undoubtedly his masterpiece, and one of the great monuments of any age. In detail it is not above criticism, but its supreme achievement is the great dome, a re-creation of the spirit of the classical world in late seventeenth-century London, and a superb example of the spirit of the age made manifest in brick and stone, timber and lead.

The story of churches and church building in Scotland in the sixteenth and seventeenth centuries has its own unique features. The majority of Scottish parish churches were always very simple, often little more than an aisle-less rectangle. Medieval churches continued to be used after the Reformation, and indeed the *First Book of Discipline* urged the repair of churches as a matter of urgency 'in durris, wyndois, thak', unconsciously revealing a great deal about their state of repair. An Act of the Scottish Parliament of 1587 sought to resume the temporalities of the church, but without success. The chancels of churches were considered to be the responsibility of lay superiors, but there was no legal responsibility for their repair, and so they very rapidly fell into ruin. The chancel also became redundant for the same reason as in England, the new Protestant church services calling for congregational participation rather than the separation of priest and worshippers. In England, as we have seen and especially in the churches designed by Christopher Wren after the Great Fire of London, the chancel was virtually eliminated, the altar being placed at the east end of the church often without even a recess. In Scotland the solution was rather different. (See Fig. 15.) The pulpit and font were placed upon the south wall. Tables for communion were placed upon the long axis of the church, running the length of the nave, sometimes in two rows, since communicants in Scotland sat to take communion. Sometimes a central north transept was added to given an inverted T-plan, and this became a very common arrangement for many Scottish parish churches.

There was some church building in Scotland in the early seventeenth century and more in the last decades of the century, after the Restoration. It is possible to detect three plans. First of all the inverted T, discussed above, something which is a peculiarly Scottish solution to the problems of church layout posed by the Reformation. The north transept sometimes had a retiring room, approached by an external staircase, where the laird could have his lunch between morning and afternoon services. At Carrington, Midlothian, built in 1710, there is a tower on the south side of a T-plan church with a door leading to a staircase which opens on to the pulpit. The upper floors of the tower were used as a dovecot. The church at Durisdeer, built in 1699, has a south transept, since the north transept was the Queensberry burial vault. At the west end of the church, at right angles, is a two-storey block used as the village school.

15 Plan of the T-shaped church at Carrington, Midlothian.
Acknowledgement: The Royal Commission on the Ancient and Historical Monuments of Scotland

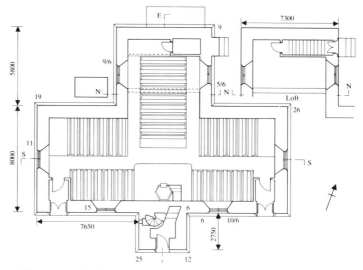

The second plan was rectangular, and a number of small churches of this kind were built in the late seventeenth century, at Auchinleck in 1683, for example, and at Duirinish in 1694, Sleat in 1687 and Southdean in 1690.

The final plan type is also the rarest. In the 1670s Sir William Bruce designed the church at Lauder in the form of a Greek cross, that is with four short arms, together with a fine steeple over the crossing. In the 1690s the Canongate church in Edinburgh was built upon similar lines. Such churches have, with hindsight at any rate, clear affinities with the 'centralised' churches of the fifteenth-century Italian humanists. How far their principles were being consciously imitated in Restoration Scotland is almost impossible now to assess.

Many of the churches described in the previous paragraphs are quite small. Where a congregation inherited a large medieval church then this posed problems of adaptation to Protestant church liturgy that were solved in a peculiarly Scottish manner. At Dunfermline the abbey nave became the town kirk, and remained so until 1821, the chancel and transepts being allowed to fall into ruin.

They were demolished early in the nineteenth century, and it was whilst this work was being carried out that the body of Robert Bruce was found, in an oak coffin. At Aberdeen, Perth and Dundee large town churches were divided up into two separate structures, at Perth into three, each with its own pulpit and communion tables.

The Reformation of the early decades of the sixteenth century brought into being numerous Protestant sects. The connection between Church and state was particularly

Plate 54 The church at Lauder, Berwickshire, built by Sir William Bruce in the 1670s

close during the sixteenth century and it was for long maintained that one could not exist without the other. Only after much fierce debate, savage intolerance and bloodshed was it finally reluctantly accepted that men should be allowed to worship according to the dictates of their own consciences and not according to the will of the sovereign or the terms of an Act of Parliament. The Toleration Act of 1689 allowed Protestants who believed in the Trinity – thus excluding Roman Catholics on the one hand and Unitarians on the other – to have their own places of worship provided they were licensed by the bishop or in quarter sessions, and provided the meetings took place behind unlocked doors. From this time Protestant dissenting places of worship begin to appear in large numbers. A few date from before this Act, many of them established after the Declaration of Indulgence of 1672. At first these nonconformist chapels and meeting houses were modest, retiring buildings of simple design and brick construction, not least because they did not wish to draw attention to themselves in a society in which the very principle of toleration had only very recently and very reluctantly been accepted. Thus there is a Baptist chapel dating from 1623 lying behind Church Street in

Plate 55 The Friends' Meeting House at Gainsborough, Lincolnshire, built in 1704

Tewkesbury. The Friends' Meeting House in Bridport dates from 1697 and that at Woodbridge was built in 1678. At Bullhouse Hall, Penistone, is a dissenting chapel of 1692 with the minister's cottage built on to the north wall. At Brigflatts, near Sedbergh, is a Friends' Meeting House of 1675, and just to the north of Farfield Hall, in the West Riding of Yorkshire, is another one of 1689. By the very end of the century toleration was being extended to other sects and religions. The Unitarian Meeting House in Friars Street, Ipswich was built in 1699, and another in Lewes in 1700, the same year in which the Jewish synagogue at Bevis Marks, in London, was built.

In 1547, shortly after the death of Henry VIII, Parliament very reluctantly passed the Chantries Act. This provided for the dissolution of colleges, free chapels and chantries, and all fraternities, brotherhoods and gilds except craft gilds. Chantries had been founded in the late medieval centuries by pious men and women who devoutly believed that by providing a small endowment a priest could be employed to say masses for their souls after death, masses which would shorten the time which the founder expected to have to spend in purgatory before he would be admitted to heaven. The Chantries Act openly denounced the superstitious nature of this belief, and the preamble to the Act spoke of converting the endowments of the chantries 'to good and godly uses, as in erecting of grammar schools to the education of youth in virtue and godliness', and the further augmentation of the universities. The statute empowered commissioners to assign lands for the support of grammar schools where such teaching was required by the foundation of the dissolved chantry, and it also specifically excluded from its operation the halls and colleges at Cambridge and Oxford, Winchester and Eton, and that called the Chapel in the Sea at Newtown in the Isle of Ely – although why this last should have been exempt remains a mystery. It makes no mention of hospitals, although some of those which incorporated a chantry were dissolved, and those schools which were not connected with a chantry in practice also escaped.

It is clear now that the Chantries Act did not destroy a national network of schools. It is equally clear that the pious hopes expressed in the Act were never fulfilled. Many leaders of the Reformation in Britain were fully aware of the importance of education for the proper training of children if they were to be instructed in the principles of true religion and to become good members of church and society, and they were equally aware of the importance of a well-educated clergy if the Reformation was to be protected from its enemies. One of the most original and constructive of these reformers writing and teaching in the 1530s was Thomas Starkey. He advocated a comprehensive plan of national, compulsory education endowed from monastic property, with provision for the proper training of clergymen in the universities. The connection between education, religious instruction, the long-term future of the reformed church and social stability, with the schoolmaster and the priest as the all-important links, was fully appreciated, and often stated, and is the reason why schoolmasters had to be licensed by the bishop from 1559 onwards. Unfortunately only half-hearted attempts were made to implement such proposals.

191

A Bill was introduced into the House of Commons in 1549 'for making schools and giving lands thereto', but it came to nothing, and in any case over half of the monastic estates which would have endowed these schools had already been sold by an impecunious and spendthrift monarch.

By this time however many individuals and institutions, especially town authorities, were beginning to attempt to salvage what they could of the old endowments of schools. In this they may have been assisted by a commission issued in February of 1550 by the Chancellor of the Court of Augmentations authorising him to 'take order' for the erecting of grammar schools. How far this represents a genuine attempt to create a network of schools is difficult to establish, but what is clear is that over the next three or four years a large number of schools were refounded on former chantry endowments – at least nine in 1551, eleven in 1552 and thirteen in 1553, so that some twenty-three English counties had schools founded by Letters Patent in these years, and six others had schools founded by other means. It would be tedious to name all of these, but they included schools at Sedbergh in 1551, Shrewsbury, Birmingham and Macclesfield in 1552, Totnes, Tavistock and Stratford upon Avon in 1553.

This initial foundation was extended and built upon by a stream of privately endowed schools during the second half of the sixteenth century and throughout the seventeenth. Thus Sir Andrew Judd founded a school at Tonbridge in 1553, John Lyon one at Harrow in 1571, Peter Blundell one at Tiverton in 1604. Charles Reed established schools at Tuxford, in Nottinghamshire and at Corby Glen in Lincolnshire, the actual buildings going up in 1668 and 1669. He endowed them in his will of 1671. At Otley, in Yorkshire, a group of freeholders asked the permission of the lord of the manor to build a school upon a piece of waste ground, and this was done in 1614. All together over 500 schools had been founded or re-founded by 1660 in ten of the English counties. If the rest of the country was equally well provided for, then by the Restoration educational opportunities must have been very widely available.

The model and inspiration for these new schools was St Paul's, founded by Dean Colet before the Reformation on new principles and with a radically new curriculum. A new school house was built in 1508, together with a house for the high master, John Lily, who was a layman and married, and another for the usher. There were to be four apartments or divisions in the school: the porch and entrance were for the youngest boys, who were to be instructed in the principles of religion. They were already expected to be able to read and write. The second apartment was for the lower boys, who were to be taught by the usher. Finally there was the upper apartment, to be taught by the high master. The boys were seated on benches, or forms, one above the other, sixteen to a form, with a head boy to each form. Colet, Lily and Erasmus cooperated to produce new textbooks for the school, and Erasmus wrote a handbook for teachers, *De Ratione Studii*. Colet believed passionately that learning, properly directed, would promote a full, Christian life from which not only would the individual benefit but also the society in which he lived. This school, after much early criticism, became the model for those reformers who believed in the value of education as the bulwark against social unrest and papal superstition, and it was increasingly widely imitated.

Perhaps the earliest of these new school buildings to survive is that at Berkhamsted, in Hertfordshire, where a school was founded in 1541 by re-establishing a chantry school. The building itself is of brick. It has a schoolroom in the middle with an open timber roof. The master's house is at one end, and the usher's at the other, both having two storeys. In other words, it is a hall-house with ceiled ends, and with very little to distinguish it from a purely domestic building of the period. Some large schools were built round a courtyard. This occurred at Guildford, where the school was begun in 1557, a west wing was added in 1569 and an east wing in 1571, the fourth side being a gatehouse with a gallery over – which was in turn, converted into a library in 1586. At Felsted, where the school was founded in 1564, the actual school room was the upper storey of a long timber-framed building with the usher's house at one end, and the ground floor occupied by another dwelling house and two shops. One of the finest groups of school buildings is that to be found at Shrewsbury. A block containing a library was added in 1594–96, and the school itself was rebuilt in 1627–30. Here the side benches still remain, since it was well into the eighteenth century before it became at all common for pupils to sit facing the master.

By the end of the seventeenth century the principles of Renaissance building had been absorbed into school architecture so that a school like that at Appleby Magna, built between 1693 and 1697, is to all intents and purposes,

Plate 56 A late nineteenth-century photograph of the school at Shrewsbury. This block, with its fluted Corinthian columns and Greek inscriptions over the doorway, was built between 1627 and 1630 as an addition to the block at right angles built in the 1590s. Together they must have made one of the largest groups of school buildings in the country at the time

at least in outward appearances, a country house.

Schools were also founded in Wales during this period, some at least upon the wreckage of monastic possessions, and again their founders were very well aware of the advantages of education as a gateway to wordly advancement, with the learning of English an added attraction. The grammar school at Brecon was founded in 1541, that at Abergavenny in 1543, and another at Bangor in 1561, so that by 1653 there were thirteen. In 1650 the Commonwealth Parliament passed an Act for the Propagating of the Gospel in Wales. This provided for the appointment of commissioners with power to establish schools, and although their functions were taken over by trustees in 1653 their work continued so that some seventy schools were established, the majority in the border counties. They came to an abrupt end in 1660. Mention must also be made of the work of Thomas Gouge, who by 1674 had become so concerned about the lack of educational facilities in Wales that he established the 'Welsh Trust', with the object of teaching poor children English and adults to read the scriptures. He claimed to have established more than 300 schools and distributed large numbers of copies of the scriptures in Welsh. He died in 1681, but his trust continued until it was remodelled in 1699 to emerge as the Society for the Promotion of Christian Knowledge.

The two English universities at Oxford and Cambridge were also affected by the Reformation, their role in educating clergymen who would defend the new religion being obvious to reformers of every shade of opinion. Henry VIII founded Trinity College Cambridge in 1546 from three medieval societies, Kings Hall, Michaelhouse and Physick Hostel, which had just surrendered. The Charter of Foundation gives a full statement of what was expected of the new college: the increase and strengthening of pure Christian religion, the extirpation of error and false teaching, the increase of godliness and the education of youth in piety and knowledge. These hopes and aspirations continue to echo through founding charters and statutes until the Civil Wars. Thus Emmanuel College Cambridge was founded by Sir Walter Mildmay with the express purpose of training clergymen for the Church of England, and the statutes of Sidney Sussex College, founded after the death of its benefactor, Lady Frances Sidney in 1589, were modelled upon those of Emmanuel.

Both Oxford and Cambridge were visited by royal commissioners in 1549, when detailed new curricula were drawn up, the teaching of Greek introduced and canon law dropped. Both were formally incorporated by Act of Parliament in 1571, and both received new statutes during the sixteenth and seventeenth centuries. The Cambridge ones of 1570 gave full authority over the administration of the university to the Vice-Chancellor and the heads of the colleges. Those for Oxford drawn up in 1636 by the Chancellor, Archbishop Laud, made such detailed provision for almost every aspect of academic life that they slowly stifled change and development. These two sets of statutes governed the universities until the reforms of the nineteenth century.

The universities were certainly seen as bulwarks of the reformed church, but they became steadily more popular in the second half of the sixteenth century as education became increasingly valued, both for its own sake and as a gateway into a career in the professions and the public service. In the 1560s there were about 300 entrants a year to Oxford, about 400 a year in the second decade of the seventeenth century, and nearly 600 a year in the decade before the outbreak of the Civil Wars. This means that there was a great deal of building at both Oxford and

Cambridge to keep pace with this increase in numbers as well as to provide the buildings for the new foundations. At Oxford some of the finest college building of this period is to be seen at Wadham, founded in 1610 and built all of a piece between that date and 1613. In concept and design the building is essentially traditional, with three-storeyed blocks erected around a central quadrangle, a hammer beam roof to the hall and fan vaulting over the gateway. The only real trace of the new Renaissance themes is in the highly rigidly symmetrical façades.

There was a great deal of rather similar, essentially traditional, collegiate building in both Oxford and Cambridge up to the middle years of the seventeenth century. Perhaps the most overtly Renaissance building before this date is to be found at Gonville and Caius College, Cambridge, where Dr Caius, who became Master of the refounded Gonville Hall in 1559, designed as part of his building programme a symbolic processional way which every student was expected to follow. It begins with a simple doorway, the Gate of Humility. This leads to the Gate of Virtue, with three classical orders of pilasters and

Plate 57 The Front Quad of Wadham College, Oxford, completed in 1613, and a striking blend of medieval and Renaissance themes

a pediment on the centre bay. This in turn leads to the Gate of Honour, which has four Ionic columns, and was completed only after the death of Dr Caius in 1573. In its concept and its symbolism this is quite new, and in its spirit there is clearly a reaching towards a fuller understanding of the underlying principles of classical architecture than is to be found almost anywhere else in England at this time, even if the reach exceeds the grasp.

Perhaps the nearest parallel to the Gates at Gonville and Caius is to be found in the Schools Quadrangle at Oxford. This block was built between 1613 and 1624. The building itself is an almost square block surrounding a central courtyard. It is three storeys high, of which the second floor was designed to house the university library, refounded in 1602 by Sir Thomas Bodley. Much is traditional in spirit, including the gatehouse with a tower. It is the decoration to the tower which constitutes an altogether astonishing, but in the end unsuccessful, essay in applied Renaissance-inspired ornament. The five classical orders are applied in succession to each of the five stages, together with a great deal of strap and foliage decoration and, on the fourth stage, a seated figure of James I attended by Fame on the one hand and the University on the other.

It was Christopher Wren who brought classical architecture to full maturity in both Oxford and Cambridge. At Oxford the Sheldonian Theatre, intended by its donor, Archbishop Sheldon, to provide a setting for university ceremonies, is almost his first work as an architect, and is deliberately classical in every way. At Cambridge the library to Trinity College, built between 1676 and 1684 and visible on Plate 1, is one of his most serene and satisfying masterpieces, a genuine recreation of the classical spirit. Wren's command over Gothic should not however be forgotten. It is apparent in his completion of Tom Tower at Christ Church, Oxford, between 1681 and 1682, although very much in his own version of 'Gothick'.

The Reformation also profoundly affected two other medieval institutions, namely hospitals and almshouses. Hospitals were in origin guest houses free to all comers, especially at town gates, as at Bury St Edmunds, or at monastery gates. St Thomas's Hospital was originally the hospice at the gate of St Mary Overy, Southwark. Medieval hospitals usually had a large hall with a chapel at the east end, with beds lying lengthwise in cubicles along the walls of the hall. St Mary's Hospital, Chichester, founded early in the thirteenth century and rebuilt at the end of that century was of this type, although the cubicles have now

disappeared. The Great Hospital founded at Norwich in 1249 consisted of a group of buildings around a cloister, and St Cross Hospital at Winchester has the same courtyard plan, a plan that will continue to be used well into the eighteenth century.

By the middle years of the fifteenth century hospitals were beginning to change their functions. Instead of being places of refuge for travellers and the sick, especially lepers, they were becoming increasingly places of retirement for the elderly infirm. One of the earliest hospitals built especially for this purpose is the almshouse at Ewelme, in Oxfordshire, founded in 1437; its buildings surround a courtyard. Many hospitals were associated with chantries and as a consequence were dissolved on the passing of the Chantries Act, but a surprising number, well over a hundred, survived. Thus the Hospital of St Bartholomew at Newbury remained unaffected, to be taken over by the corporation and its chapel turned into a school. This stock was considerably added to during the course of the sixteenth and seventeenth centuries. Some were re-foundations, as at Cobham, in Kent, where a chantry for six priests founded in 1362 was 're-edified' in 1598 as an almshouse for twenty elderly people, and the Hospital and Gild of St Helen at Abingdon was refounded as Christ's Hospital in 1553. At Warwick, the buildings of the Gild of St George were taken over by the corporation for its town hall, but the Earl of Leicester bullied the burgesses into giving him the building in which to found his hospital in 1571. Its actual contribution to the relief of poverty in the town appears however to have been strictly limited. It never had more than twelve 'brethren', all men, and fewer than half of them were ever townsmen before the end of the seventeenth century.

Many of the plans of newly founded hospitals and almshouses followed the medieval tradition of grouping buildings around a courtyard. The Coningsby Hospital at Hereford, for example, founded in 1613, is built round three sides of a quadrangle, and a similar pattern is to be found in Whitgift's Hospital in Croydon, founded in 1596, and Trinity Hospital, Greenwich, founded in 1614. Others are more simple. The almshouses at Ravenstone, in Buckinghamshire, comprise two single-storey brick-built blocks facing one another, and the Winwood Almshouses at Quainton, founded in 1687, consist of only one block of building, simple, unpretentious, and with no trace of the new classical themes in architecture, whilst the row of four single-cell cottages which form the almshouses at Cheriton Fitzpaine, in Devon, are even simpler. They are built of cob and coursed rubble, with the chimney stack projecting at the front. The fifth cottage was added in the nineteenth century.

Some hospitals and almshouses (and in practice the two names imply no difference in function) were founded to benefit the poor of a particular trade or occupation. Thus in 1696 the Bristol Merchant Venturers founded a hospital for seamen, and Sir Richard Geffrye founded the Ironmongers' Almshouses in Shoreditch in 1710, again a courtyard building. It is now a museum. The East India Company established almshouses in Poplar, and there had been an almshouse for mariners reduced to poverty by 'infortune of the seas' at Hull since 1457. Jesus Hospital at Bray was founded in 1609 for forty freemen of the Fishmongers' Company, Sir John Morden established almshouses in Greenwich in 1695 for 'decayed Turkey merchants', and in 1697 a hospital was founded in Ampthill for retired and elderly servants of Oxford colleges. The two largest hospitals founded in England in the seventeenth century were of this type.

The Royal Hospital at Chelsea was founded by Charles II for invalided and retired soldiers in direct imitation of the Hôtel des Invalides founded in 1670 by Louis XIV. Building began in 1682 to designs by Sir Christopher Wren. His building is traditional in its plan in that an ingenious complex of blocks forms the sides to no less than

199

Plate 59 The almshouses at Cheriton Fitzpaine, Devonshire. Four of the five were built of cob and coursed rubble at the end of the seventeenth century. The fifth was added in the nineteenth century. The projecting chimney stacks at the front are a common feature of vernacular building in the area

three open squares, the main one open to the south and overlooking the river Thames. The Royal Naval Hospital at Greenwich was founded in 1694 on the site of the former royal palace. The manor of Greenwich had been bought by the Duke of Gloucester in 1423 and became a favourite royal residence. Henry VIII was born here, as were his daughters Mary and Elizabeth. James I gave the palace to his wife in 1613, and it was for her that Inigo Jones designed the Queen's House, immediately to the south, in 1616, although building was interrupted at the death of Queen Anne in 1619, and not finished until 1637. The old buildings fell into disrepair during the Commonwealth and so in 1664 Charles II decided upon a complete rebuilding, even though only part of the original plan was completed. In 1694 William and Mary, finding the air at Hampton Court more to their liking, gave up the palace and Mary gave the existing buildings to form the basis of a hospital for seamen. New buildings were begun, again to designs by Sir Christopher Wren, designs which incorporated the existing buildings and provided the outline of the plan as it survives today: two groups of buildings flanking a north-south axis terminating in the Queen's

House. As at St Paul's the wooden model still survives. Work went on very slowly and it was 1750 before the main blocks were finished, their domes and colonnades forming an altogether more ostentatious group than the Royal Hospital at Chelsea, and about as far removed from the almshouses at Cheriton Fitzpaine as it is possible to be.

Schools and universities in Scotland have quite a different history. By the early years of the sixteenth century most Scottish burghs had a grammar school, encouraged by an Act of the Scottish Parliament of 1496 requiring barons and freeholders of substance to send their eldest sons to school from the age of eight or nine. In Scotland as in England leaders of the Reformation placed great emphasis upon education as the principal long-term defence of the new religion against Catholicism. The *First Book of Discipline* of 1560 called for a schoolmaster to be attached to every church, and made elaborate proposals for university education, including bursaries for poor students, enlightened and far-sighted suggestions which were never put into effect. Again as in England schoolmasters were licensed by the church authorities, and in 1693 an Act of the Scottish Parliament permitted local presbyteries to censure the schoolmaster.

In 1616 the Scottish Privy Council ordered the establishment of a school in every parish. This was confirmed by Acts of Parliament of 1633 and 1646, and in 1696 another Act of Parliament called for the building of a schoolmaster's house at the expense of the heritors. The Act also fixed the schoolmaster's salary at between one hundred and two hundred merks a year, between £5 11s. 1d. and £11 2s. 3d. sterling, again to be paid by the heritors. In spite of these measures parish schools spread only very slowly in seventeenth-century Scotland. There was certainly no national scheme of primary education in the

Plate 60 The Royal Naval Hospital at Greenwich. The King Charles Block, built by John Webb between 1662 and 1669, lies behind the left-hand pediment of the right-hand block. This was incorporated into the overall design for the Hospital made by Sir Christopher Wren, and built between 1698 and 1752, with some further building and rebuilding down to 1814. The Queen's House, designed by Inigo Jones and finished in 1635, may be seen in the distance between the two domed blocks

country, and it seems very likely that Scotland was not so well provided with schools, in proportion to its population, as was England at this time. School buildings were generally very small and often thatched, although Edinburgh Royal High School moved into substantial new stone buildings in 1578.

There were more universities in Scotland than there were in England in the sixteenth and seventeenth centuries. St Andrews was founded in 1411, Glasgow in 1451. In 1494 William Elphinstone, in due course Archbishop of St Andrews, obtained a papal bull for the founding of a university at Aberdeen. The first buildings were begun in 1505, and after 1553 it was called King's College. In 1593 a second university was chartered in Aberdeen, Marischal College, established on the site of the Greyfriars. The two were both very small – King's College had no more than twelve entrants a year in the early seventeenth century – and in 1641 the two were amalgamated, but this was revoked by the General Act Rescissory of 1661.

Glasgow University was virtually refounded by Andrew Melville in 1577, with new buildings being erected on the site of the Dominican friary. Additional buildings were put up between 1632 and 1661, and a great garden and physic garden laid out in 1704.

Edinburgh University was founded by royal charter in 1582. Teaching began in 1583 in the town house of James, the second Earl of Arran, built in 1554, together with fourteen bedchambers built on by the town. In 1617 a Great Hall with library over was built, a new library building in 1642, and houses provided for the Principal and the Professor of Divinity. More student chambers were added in the years betwen 1625 and 1685; the majority of these, however, were for study purposes, not for sleeping, since students were expected to live with their parents and there were only a few foreign students for much of the seventeenth century, principally English nonconformists, excluded from Oxford and Cambridge. The university was very much under the control of Edinburgh Town Council, which appointed the staff, decided upon the courses and awarded the degrees. This did not however stifle change and innovation. By 1700 there were eight professors, including medicine and anatomy, and about 300 students. In 1708 the regent system, under which each student was taught everything on the curriculum throughout the whole of his four year course by the same teacher, was abolished, making way for the appointment of specialist staff, and the great age of the university as a seat of learning.

The fabric of the landscape of Britain had to sustain many severe shocks during the course of the sixteenth and seventeenth centuries, whether from enclosure, the building of iron furnaces or the draining of marshes. Equally as severe were those brought about by the shifts in attitudes, values and perceptions of the world summed up in the words 'Renaissance' and 'Reformation'. The impact of these shocks upon the landscape is to be read in the prospect of Cambridge from the west which forms part of Plate 1. The chapel of King's College, a fifteenth-century foundation and one of those institutions expressly excluded from the Chantries Act, is clearly visible. When it was built, the doctrines of those who worshipped there when the prospect was drawn would have been considered heresy. Immediately to the left is the church of St Mary, the oldest visible layer in the landscape. Its tower was not completed until the end of the sixteenth century and the church was used for university ceremonies until the Senate House was built in 1730. Parishes are medieval institutions designed to minister to the spiritual needs of their inhabitants, with the parish church as the focal point of their worship. They still fulfilled this function at the end of the seventeenth century, but the perception of the needs of their inhabitants had changed dramatically. Still to the left is the library of Trinity College, the newest layer in this landscape, and the very embodiment of classical architecture and the new values of Renaissance and Reformation. In this way the themes of this chapter are given physical embodiment in the landscape.

Chapter eight

Landscapes of the mind

We have so far in this book attempted to reconstruct the landscapes of sixteenth- and seventeenth-century Britain and the processes of change that were at work in them by using two kinds of evidence: first of all such documents as directly or indirectly reveal the purpose and function of the constituent parts of the landscape, and secondly surviving relic features in the landscape today, whether buildings or boundaries, hedgerows or lanes, fields or farms. There is, however, inevitably a very real danger that when attempting to reconstruct past landscapes we shall interpret them from the viewpoint of the late twentieth century rather than from that of the men and women who, by going about the business of their everyday lives, adapted their inheritance from the past and combined it with their own unique contribution to make their immediate external world. In order to complete our reconstruction of this external world we must endeavour as far as possible to replace the gloss which our own minds place upon it with that of the inhabitants of Britain during these two centuries. In other words, we must try to reconstruct their mental landscapes in so far as this is possible. This will prevent us from placing the wrong interpretation upon what we see and, by providing a further dimension to the sixteenth- and seventeenth-century landscape, it will enhance beyond measure our understanding of the past. This is a particularly difficult task, and for two reasons. The mental world of the early sixteenth century was both rich and strange: rich in that it was emotionally and intellectually very satisfying once its basic premises were accepted, and strange in that it was quite unlike that of the late twentieth century. Secondly, the two centuries covered by this book saw a most profound and radical shift in the patterns of human thought about the world and man's position in it, a shift conveniently summarised in the phrase 'the Scientific Revolution'. At the beginning of the sixteenth century men were repeating ideas about the purpose and construction of the universe given final form and shape in the first centuries of the Christian era, over a thousand years ago. At the end of the seventeenth century the modern world picture was firmly drawn, at least in the minds of educated men.

Landscapes of the mind

The cosmology of educated men in the opening decades of the sixteenth century had its roots in Greek science and speculation. It gave an extraordinarily coherent view of man and his place in the universe, a view that was also remarkably rational, based as it was upon phenomena observed with the naked eye complemented by complex mathematical calculations. At the same time, since God

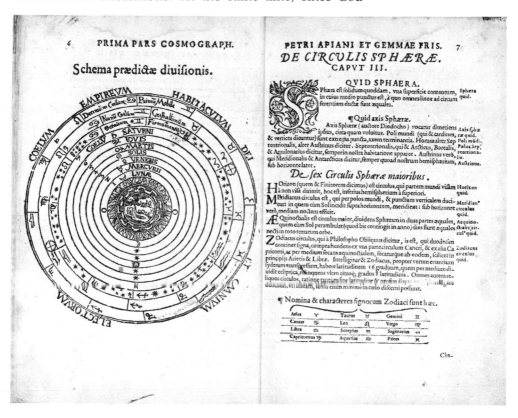

had created the universe, and the account of the creation of the world as described in Genesis was accepted without question, it existed for a purpose, namely that man might recognize God and worship Him.

The whole of the universe was composed of one *prima materia*, or basic matter. This *prima materia* had four properties: hot, cold, moist and dry. These four combined to give the four elements. Hot and dry made fire, hot and moist made air. Cold and moist made water, cold and dry made earth. Earth, being the heaviest, lay at the centre of the universe, with water on top, and then air. The earth, which was thought to be a perfect sphere, and its

Plate 61 The medieval world picture, from *Cosmographia*, by Peter Apian, published in 1584. The earth is stationary at the centre of the universe. The moon, the planets and the stars encircle the earth in perfect spheres. The last of the spheres is the primum mobile. Beyond lies Heaven, the home of God and all the elect

attendant water and air, were then completely surrounded by pure, elemental fire, which lay, transparent and invisible, in a sphere just beneath the moon. Flames were considered to be impure fire, and leaped upwards in their efforts to rejoin this pure, elemental sphere.

All that lay beneath the moon, the sublunary world, was corruptible, mutable and transitory. Everything was composed of the four elements, linked arm-in-arm 'Like countrey-maidens, in the moneth of May'. These elements, however, were in perpetual conflict because they were out of balance, and yet they were constantly seeking perfection and the stability which could come only when the right balance was achieved. It was thought that only in gold were the elements in perfect proportion. All metals were made of a combination of sulphur and mercury and were produced in the ground by the direct action of heat and cold upon an underground watery vapour. If these natural processes could be speeded up and reproduced artificially then the metals could be transmuted one into the other and gold could be made. This belief lay at the root of alchemy. The alchemist's alembic was the womb of the earth. Their theoretical belief in the transmutation of metals was reinforced by observation of the practices of miners and metal-workers. Galena (lead sulphide) when heated gives off sulphurous fumes and is transformed into lead. This often contains silver, which can be recovered after further heating and cupellation. Why cannot this process be carried further? If the four basic qualities of the *prima materia* could be removed, and then some further substance added, the result should be gold. This substance was the philosopher's stone, which would bring to perfection all imperfect bodies, human as well as mineral, that it touched. It must once have existed. Did not Methuselah live to be 969? Lamech was 182 when he begat Noah, and lived a further 595 years, begetting sons and daughters, whilst Noah himself lived to be 950. Such longevity could only derive from the philosopher's stone.

Alchemists frequently began their search with mercury, because of its superficial resemblance to silver, thought to be the metal nearest to gold, adding sulphur because of its yellowness. But their all-consuming, compulsive search had to be undertaken humbly and piously. The alchemist had to approach his experiments free from ambition or vice, since matter was itself partly spiritual and therefore sensitive to moral atmosphere. In this way their failures could be explained away: lack of success was due to spiritual turpitude, and so in time alchemical processes came to be seen symbolically, as an allegory of spiritual regeneration.

Alchemy was widely believed and practised throughout Europe during the sixteenth and seventeenth centuries, although the opportunities which it presented for fraud were equally well known, so that its practitioners and their dupes had to endure a great deal of savage and ribald mockery: one example is that portrayed in Ben Jonson's play, *The Alchemist*, where little attention is given to the distinction made by Robert Fludd between 'vulgar' alchemy and 'celestial', whose method and aim is self-knowledge. The Holy Roman Emperors Maximilian II (1564–1576) and Rudolph II (1576–1612) were both ardent believers, and their court at Prague attracted swarms of devotees, genuine and fraudulent, who gave their name to the Zlata Ulicka, the Golden Alley. There is no Alchemist's Row in the streets and lanes of London but Queen Elizabeth was deeply interested, and supported a number of alchemists, finding them accommodation in Somerset House, in London. In February of 1565 Cornelius de Lannoy promised to produce 50,000 marks of pure gold a year, but in July 1566, having 'greatly abused the Queen', he writes from the Tower begging for release; whilst in the following year Sir William Cecil noted in his diary that Cornelius had wrought in Somerset House and abused many in promising to convert any metal into gold. At about the same time Thomas Charnock described how he received instruction in alchemy from a priest in Salisbury and from a prior of Bath who, by the time Charnock met him, had become blind. Charnock lived in Stockland, near Bridgwater, and described how it cost him £3 a week to keep his furnace going. John Thornborough, successively bishop of Limerick, Bristol and of Worcester, wrote and published on alchemy, and his household in the episcopal palace at Hartlebury Castle acquired a reputation as a 'flourishing Academy' for those of like mind, including that Robert Fludd already quoted. He was a London physician and a devout believer in alchemy, astrology and the Hermetic philosophy to be described below. His interest in alchemy led him into experiments in the making of steel, for which in 1620 James I granted him Letters Patent for its commercial manufacture.

Beyond the moon lay a series of perfect, incorruptible spheres, each sphere supporting one of the celestial bodies, which were made of a fifth element, *quinta essentia*, which was pure, incorruptible and unchanging. The first seven of these spheres were the moon itself, then Mercury, Venus, the sun, Mars, Jupiter and Saturn. Both the moon and the sun were then considered to be planets circling the earth. Beyond the spheres of the planets lay the sphere of the *stellatum*, the fixed stars, and beyond this lay the *primum mobile*, and then Heaven and God. The *primum mobile*, moved by love for God, revolves from east to west once in twenty-four hours. It imparts this motion to the next sphere, and so on down to the moon, whilst the earth itself remains stationary. These lower spheres move from west to east and had to make their way against the power exerted by the *primum mobile* moving in the opposite direction. For the planets and other heavenly bodies to return again to the same position relative to each other from which they had started it was necessary to develop the idea of the Great Year, the period of time necessary for this. There was some uncertainty over its length, but Ptolemy thought it was 36,000 earth years. The idea of the Great Year would explain only some parts of the constantly shifting patterns of the planets and stars in the sky. In order to explain more fully the movements of the planets Ptolemy developed the concept of the epicycle, namely the theory that the planets themselves describe circles, the centres of which circles describe a larger circle about the earth. Given the conditions under which astronomical observations were made until the beginning of the seventeenth century this provided a satisfactory explanation of the wanderings of all the planets except Mercury, and it has justly been called 'the most mature produce of ancient astronomy'.

The spaces between the spheres were filled with light and with music, music which man before the Fall had been able to hear, but now could not because of his sins.

Within Heaven itself the angels were arranged into a hierarchy, with seraphim at the top and angels at the bottom. Of the bottom three groups, principalities were the guardians of nations, whilst both archangels and angels could appear to men as intermediaries between man and God.

This universe was a created, finite one, suffused with purpose, movement, light and music. It was created, not eternal, and would in due course come to an end, an end which God would herald with signs, portents, comets, great storms, pestilences, volcanic erruptions and similar catastrophes. It was a finite universe, but one constructed on an immense scale. There was no agreed idea as to the size of the universe, but it was generally thought that even if one could travel twenty miles a day every day it would take hundreds of years to reach the outer edge.

The influence of the sun on the earth and upon mankind was obvious, and the effect of the moon upon the tides was also known. Therefore, by analogy, the other heavenly bodies must also influence men. Upon this belief were erected the elaborate, all-pervasive doctrines of astrology. Planetary influences upon men have left a permanent mark in our vocabulary, even today, since they gave rise to adjectives describing personal traits and qualities – saturnine, jovial, mercurial, martial, even lunatic, since the moon was associated with wandering, both physical and mental. From knowledge of the exact date and time of a man's birth and the exact place, it was possible to calculate his horoscope. On the horoscope were plotted the twelve signs of the zodiac and the positions of the planets at the time of his birth. From this it was possible to make more or less detailed prognostications about his temperament and his future. This, however, if pushed too far, savoured of determinism, and left no room for free will, and so astrologers were careful to point out that the influences from the heavenly bodies can be turned to good or bad account, depending upon how we use them.

Each planet had a vast array of metals, minerals, animals, plants and colours associated with it. Each of the seven planets was associated with one of the seven metals then known: Saturn with lead, Jupiter with tin, Mars with iron, the sun with gold, Venus with copper, Mercury with mercury, and silver with the moon, whilst the precious stones took their powers from the fixed stars. All things in nature were marked with a distinctive sign indicating its use or purpose, and artificial marks could be made which would enhance these powers. Thus, by an appropriate combination it was possible to make a talisman which would concentrate, direct or divert the influences of an individual planet. In order to obtain long life an image of Saturn in the form of an old man holding a sickle, seated on a high throne and clothed in a dark robe was made, whilst Venus, associated with happiness and physical strength, would be portrayed with white and yellow robes, together with apples and flowers. At the same time the planets were each thought to influence different parts of the human body, so that talismans and appropriate metals and plants were used as a matter of course in medicine. Amethysts counteracted drunkenness, jet put snakes to flight and was used as a remedy against phantasms due to melancholy, whilst pearls were good

209

against bleeding, jaundice and diarrhoea.

It is probably almost impossible to exaggerate the importance which was attached in the sixteenth century to hieroglyphs, emblems, *imprese* and other symbolic representations of the powers of the planets and stars and their associated plants, animals and minerals on earth. Indeed it seems almost as if a statement made by way of a visual image was considered to be nearer the truth of what was being conveyed than one made in words. Such visual imagery permeates every aspect of sixteenth-century art, literature and architecture. Botticelli's painting *The Primavera* cannot be fully understood without grasping its symbolic imagery, and the paintings made for Charles I by Rubens on the ceiling of the Banqueting House in Whitehall are soaked in it. This symbolism spilled over into everyday life and everyday objects. The eagle, the hart, the spider, the ape and the dog were symbolic of the five senses. The rose, the chief of flowers, was associated with Venus, whilst the crocus was associated with Jupiter. The entire world was filled with meaning, associations, significances, with life and purpose, to be placated, directed, manipulated, feared or avoided.

It was widely accepted that the earth was a sphere. The northern hemisphere was divided into five zones. The Arctic and equatorial zones were too cold and too hot for human habitation. In between lay three more temperate zones, that in the middle being the most suitable for human habitation. Whether or not the southern hemisphere was inhabited was a matter for some debate, but in any case it was impossible to reach the Antipodes, the land of the 'opposite-footed' people, because it was impossible to cross the tropics. When in fact early sixteenth-century explorers did cross the tropics the traditional cosmography suffered one of its most severe shocks, and Godfrey Goodman in his *The Fall of Man*, published in 1616, thought that the ability of men to cross the tropics was evidence of the degeneration and imminent end of the world.

The zones were subject to planetary influences, and these in turn affected the climate and the disposition of the inhabitants. People in northern latitudes, under the influence of Mars and the moon, were dull-witted, given to fighting and to hunting, whilst those in the southern zone, influenced by Saturn and Venus, were contemplative, producing the best philosophers and mathematicians. Those in the intermediate zone, under the influence of Jupiter and Mercury, were rational and civilized. Closely associated with these planetary and climatic influences was the idea of national characteristics; all Frenchmen are rash, Spaniards proud, Dutchmen drunken, Italians effeminate, Irish barbarous, and so on. Thomas Sprat, in his *History of the Royal Society* published in 1667, wrote, in praise of Englishmen, that 'they have the middle qualities, between the reserv'd subtle Southern, and the rough unhewn Northern people'.

The landscape of the northern hemisphere was inhabited, not only by human beings, but also by animals, birds and plants. There must have been a great deal of practical knowledge of those that inhabited, not only the farmyard and garden, but also the immediate countryside. But there was in addition a vast store of travellers' tales concerning what in fact were entirely imaginary creatures, a great deal of legend and groundless speculation about real ones, and a combination of both for those animals such as the rhinoceros which in the early sixteenth century lay on the fringe of western European experience. Dragons, the basilisk, mermaids, the unicorn, the phoenix and the salamander were for many as real as the cow, the pig and the sheep, whilst it was widely believed that horses shed tears on the death of their masters, that swallows spent the winter buried in the mud at the bottom of ponds, that geese hatch from barnacles and that honey bees are generated by the decomposition of beef. The rowan tree was thought to ward off witches and it was considered unlucky to cut down holly trees.

Much medieval writing on natural history was derived more or less directly from Pliny and Aristotle and was almost totally divorced from observation and experiment. The voyages of discovery and exploration of the sixteenth century at once made things much more confused by introducing to Europeans very many more new plants and animals, sometimes more bizarre than anything to be found in medieval bestiaries, and at the same time they prompted renewed and closer study of both the familiar and the new based upon observation and not upon the repetition of ancient authorities.

Much of this interest in plants, both familiar and unfamiliar, was concerned with their medicinal properties. Botanical gardens were established in order that plants might be grown and studied at first hand. One was founded near Venice in 1533. John Gerard established his garden in Holborn and published a catalogue of the plants growing there in 1596, listing over a thousand different plants. A botanical garden was established at Oxford in

211

1621 by the Earl of Danby. The Chelsea Physic Garden was established by the Society of Apothecaries of London in 1673 and Edinburgh botanic gardens were opened in 1680.

This curiosity about the external world quickly extended beyond plants, to fossils, although their true nature was not yet understood, to coins, shells and natural curiosities of every kind. The collection amassed by John Tradescant came into the hands of Elias Ashmole. In 1675 he offered

Plate 62 The entrance archway to the Oxford Botanic Gardens, built in 1632–3 by Nicholas Stone. A bust of the Earl of Danby, who gave the site to the University in 1621, is in the niche in the pediment. It was made in 1695 by John Vanderstein

his collections to the University of Oxford provided the university would build a suitable repository. As a result the first museum was opened in 1683. Dr Robert Plot became the first keeper, and Edward Lhwyd, a Welshman with wide interests in botany and fossils as well as Welsh history and language, became the second. Sir Thomas Bodley provided a gallery for the exhibition of objects of antiquity in his new library at Oxford, and here in due course came many of the marble inscriptions collected by Thomas Howard, Earl of Arundel, in whose train Inigo Jones had made his extended visit to Italy.

From the end of the fifteenth century this traditional

world picture was enormously enriched from two directions. There is first of all that derived from the recovery of the *Corpus Hermeticum*, almost all of which was translated from Greek into Latin by Marsilio Ficino in 1463 at the direct request of Cosimo di' Medici. The writings contained in this *corpus* are by different, unknown authors, probably of varying date but certainly first to third centuries AD, writing in Greek in Egypt. The writings are intensely religious in character, within the confines of the

cosmology outlined in preceding paragraphs, and it is this religious fervour which gives them their unity. Several are pessimistic in approach, seeing the material universe as in itself evil. Others are optimistic, finding the whole universe good since it is impregnated with the divine presence. These writings were eagerly seized upon by philosophers in the last decades of the fifteenth century because it was then thought that they were all by one author, Hermes Trismegistus, an author who owes his origins to a misunderstanding of the identification made by the Greeks of their god Hermes with the Egyptian god Thoth. St Augustine referred to him on two occasions, once to

Plate 63 The original Ashmolean Museum building at Oxford. It was erected between 1678 and 1683 to house the collections given to the University by Elias Ashmole in 1677

213

condemn the magical practices he describes, and secondly to date him before the Greek philosophers and only a little after Moses. Lactantius praises him as a prophet of the coming of Christ.

Dazzled by the authority of Augustine, and misled by the blend of Platonic and Christian ideas which they found in the *Corpus* and which they thought to be prophetic insights of astonishing accuracy and prescience, Renaissance philosophers, with their reverence for everything old, accepted Hermes Trismegistus unquestioningly. For them he was the supreme philosopher, the first theologian, a man of exemplary piety and a magician of extraordinary power. By making use of the infinitely rich and complex pattern of influences emanating from the stars and the planets it was thought that he had been able to establish a channel of communication, especially by means of the making of talismans, to the heavenly bodies with the object of guiding the stellar influences and ultimately of obtaining insight into the divine. With the authority of so ancient and pious a figure the Renaissance philosopher turned with increasing self-confidence to magic, in spite of the terrifying prospect of calling up demons instead of benign spirits and the much more real danger of being accused of witchcraft and sorcery. Although profoundly misguided this new direction was also profoundly important, since it meant that men were ceasing to be passive spectators of the natural world and were coming instead to accept the idea that they might be active manipulators. The power upon which this idea was based was at first grounded in a delusion, but it also, as we shall see, had practical consequences which would make this power increasingly real.

In 1614 there appeared *De Rebus Sacris* by Isaac Casaubon, perhaps at that time the most learned man in Europe, in which he proves convincingly that the *Corpus* cannot be pre-Christian. This discovery was in due course seized upon by the French monk Marin Mersenne. His *Quaestiones in Genesim*, published in 1623, mounted a massive attack upon the whole Renaissance Hermetic/ Cabbalistic philosophy, and more especially upon its leading contemporary exponent, Robert Fludd. Mersenne was a friend and admirer of Descartes, and his work cleared the way for the acceptance of the mechanistic Cartesian world picture.

The second of the two late fifteenth-century streams of thought to enrich the traditional world picture derives from the Cabbalistic studies of Pico della Mirandola, a younger contemporary of Ficino. Cabbala was a Jewish mystical tradition believed to have been handed down by word of mouth from Moses himself. Thus for Pico and those who followed him Cabbala had as much authority as Hermes Trismegistus, but had more to commend it because it aimed higher, beyond the natural world to the angelic hierarchy and to God himself. This was done through the magical and mathematical manipulation of the Hebrew alphabet. God 'spoke' when He created the world, and He spoke in Hebrew. Thus the Hebrew alphabet had magical properties. Its twenty-two letters could be rearranged to reveal hidden secrets about God and His created world, and a further dimension was added by the practice of Gematria. This assigned numerical values to the Hebrew letters so that, when words were converted into numbers and numbers into words, following mathematical calculations of staggering complexity, the entire organization of the universe could be laid bare, with the further possibility of being able to harness its powers in the service of man. Pico saw the connections between Hermetic and Cabbalistic teachings, both in religious experience and the prospect of the magical control over the forces of the universe. This led him to an almost ecstatic vision of man as the centre of the universe and with full control over his destiny. 'O highest and most marvellous felicity of man! To him it is granted to have whatever he chooses, to be whatever he wills'.

Cabbala became almost as widespread and as influential as Hermetic philosophy, and the two streams of thought came together in the strange and yet brilliant mind of John Dee, at once a naive and gullible believer in magic and astrology, and a mathematician of the first rank, whose interests in the problems of navigation and map-making kept him at the centre of English efforts at overseas exploration for a generation. Mathematical skills developed for Cabbalistic purposes were applied to the solution of practical problems.

This then was the mental framework within which the changes described in previous chapters were taking place. Amongst the educated minority it was accepted, although with much controversy over details and increasingly heated debate over the problems of accommodating the new knowledge flooding in from astronomical discoveries or from voyages of exploration. The extent of the comprehension and understanding of this mental landscape even among the educated literate minority is impossible to measure. Further, the distance between Milton and

Newton on the one hand and an illiterate ploughboy on
the other admits of no clear break or division, so that the
extent of its penetration amongst the half-educated, semi-
literate and wholly illiterate is again impossible to
measure. Nor can one speak of two separate worlds, one
of educated opinion and the other of popular belief.
Instead they are probably better seen as lying at the
opposite ends of a continuum linked, or separated by, an
infinitely complex tangle of ideas, practices and opinions,
frequently only half-understood, often contradictory and
inconsistent, and certainly beyond any glib generalisation.

There is a mass of evidence testifying to the existence
of a wide range of popular beliefs in magical and supernatural powers, beliefs which sometimes show a garbled,
distorted connection with the cosmology outlined above,
although it is clear that the vast bulk have their roots in
medieval and even Anglo-Saxon practices.

These popular beliefs were nourished from at least two
sources. First of all it is very clear that among the poorest
sections of society church-going was rare, and that in any
case many of those who did go found what was taught
incomprehensible. Very many of those learned and
lengthy sermons published by seventeenth-century clergymen in search of preferment must have been way over
the heads of the vast majority of the congregation before
whom they were delivered. Ignorance of the basic tenets
of Christianity, even of the Lord's Prayer itself, was widespread among many sections of the community, and to
ignorance must be added scepticism and disbelief.

Secondly, awareness of the very real limitations of man's
power over his environment, not only over the weather
and its effects such as storms, floods and droughts, but
also over disease, human and animal, insect pests, vermin
and weeds, was combined with an almost unquestioned
belief that the natural world was populated with spirits,
hobgoblins, fairies, ghosts and other supernatural spirits,
good and evil, and that many natural events were in fact
portents or omens of future events.

Scepticism, disbelief and ignorance of Christian teachings added to a mental landscape that gave full scope for
supernatural powers of every kind meant that very many
men and women, from all ranks in society and of every
level of education, looked to astrology, magic and the
comforts and cures offered by cunning men, wise women,
fortune tellers and their charms, incantations, spells, love
potions and weather predictions to cover every possible
event and circumstance of everyday life, every domestic

crisis, every ache, pain or illness, in men or in animals. It
was widely believed that scrofula, or the King's Evil, the
tubercular inflammation of the lymph glands of the neck,
could be cured by the king touching the sufferer. Thousands of victims of the disease flocked to the court of
Charles II, 8,577 in one year alone, 1682–83. Queen Anne
was the last British monarch to touch in this way, and her
most distinguished patient was the young Samuel
Johnson, in 1712, when he was two and a half years old.
In addition to royalty having healing powers for this one
disease, it was also widely believed that seventh sons had
powers of healing by touch, and those who were seventh
sons of seventh sons were thought to be especially well-
endowed with magical powers.

There could have been few towns and villages without
their cunning men or wise women, although we know all
too little about them since they preferred not to publicise
their activities for fear of prosecution for witchcraft. Such
men and women claimed to be able to heal the sick, to
find lost or stolen property, to provide amulets that would
give protection against disease, shipwreck and other
misfortune, even to discover lost or buried treasure. Belief
in astrology was reinforced by the teachings of Hermetic
and Cabbalistic philosophers, and the association between
the signs of the zodiac and various parts of the human
body meant that physicians almost as a matter of course
looked to astrology for help when diagnosing or
prescribing for illnesses. Governments were particularly
sensitive to astrological predictions with a political bias,
and almanacks continued to be censored until the end of
the seventeenth century.

Many of these supernatural practices were believed to
be beneficent by those who performed them and by those
who sought them, but everyone was well aware that they
could also be directed towards malevolent ends. It was
maleficium, the power and the intention to harm, that
turned these practices into witchcraft. Accusations of
witchcraft seem very frequently to be the result of popular
fear and mistrust of some elderly woman of eccentric
appearance living on her own, more especially if the
accusor had experienced some unaccountable personal
misfortune after being guilty of some hostile or unchari-
table act towards the accused. As long as men believed
that material misfortune could be caused by some breach
in the moral order then a guilty conscience would find
some relief in making an accusation of witchcraft.

In England the persecution of witches never reached the

hysterical proportions it did on the continent, and there
was only one really notorious witch-finder, Matthew
Hopkins, who was at work in East Anglia in 1645. Not all
accusations of witchcraft ended with a conviction by any
means, and, as far as the evidence allows us to judge,
acquittals always exceed convictions, even during the
height of Matthew Hopkins's activities. The witchcraft
cases tried in the sessions court of Ipswich, in Suffolk,
may well be typical, both of the nature of the accusations
and of the kinds of punishments inflicted and the numbers
acquitted. All the cases were heard in September of 1645,
whether or not under the influence of Matthew Hopkins
it is impossible now to say. There were seven cases, in
three of which the accused persons were found guilty.
Alice Denham was found guilty of feeding imps and was
sentenced to be hanged. Jacob Emerson and Maria his wife
were found guilty of sending lice to Mary and Robert
Wade, for which they were sentenced to a year's imprison-
ment and to stand four times in the pillory. Maria Lakeland
was indicted for witchcraft, casting away a ship,
nourishing evil spirits, wasting the bodies of John Beale
and Thomas Holgrave, and for the murder of her husband.
It was for the last offence that she was found guilty and
sentenced to be burned, the normal punishment for the
murder of her husband by a woman. All the other accused
were acquitted.

This ancient, traditional world picture crumbled only
very slowly, as a very wide range of solvents, often
working insidiously on some one thread of the whole
gorgeous fabric, in due course deprived it of its astonishing
intellectual coherence. By the end of the seventeenth
century its credibility, at least in educated circles, had been
largely destroyed. Nevertheless much still remains, even
today, in a broken, fragmentary form, whether in our
vocabulary, our superstitions, the continuing popularity
of horoscopes, or an imponderable psychological malaise,
the consequence of the dissolution of a purposeful
universe in which man occupied the centre of the stage.

The solvents came from many sources: new discoveries,
whether in astronomy or from the voyages of discovery
of the late fifteenth and sixteenth centuries, the search for
practical solutions to practical problems in mining, engineering, map-making and surveying, solutions which gave
men increasing mastery over the physical world, or the
ferment of ideas loosely encompassed in the words
'Renaissance' and 'Reformation', including the reactions
which these ideas provoked. There was, finally, an even

more subtle 'mole in the cellarage' at work. Men had slowly to change their ways of thought. The traditional world picture had been built up on the basis of thinking by analogy, to which was added a reverence for ancient authority. The entire fabric of Hermetic/Cabbalistic philosophy was erected in this way, and thus represents the last flowering of traditional modes of thought. Channels of thought had slowly and painfully to be realigned. Analogy and authority had to be replaced by experiment and observation, weighing and measuring. The changes were made very slowly. Copernicus looked back to Greek astronomers to support many of his ideas. Tycho Brahe computed horoscopes and Sir Isaac Newton was a close student of alchemy for many years. The break between the old and the new in the minds of men has never been either clean or sharp.

Copernicus had by about 1512 arrived at the idea that the earth revolved round the sun, but the idea was based upon the reinterpretation of observations already made, a reinterpretation that gave a better fit to these observations. He spent the next thirty years observing and measuring carefully the movements of the planets and stars, and when finally he published his work in 1543 in *De Revolutionibus* it was this part which was quickly and readily accepted. It formed the basis upon which Erasmus Reinhold drew up the Prutenic tables, replacing the thirteenth century Alfonsine tables of eclipses, solar altitudes, planetary conjunctions and so on with more accurate data. His heliocentric theory on the other hand was considered interesting, eccentric, but wholly unacceptable.

In 1572 Tycho Brahe saw, along with almost everyone else in western Europe, a bright new star in Cassiopeia. What did it mean? What calamities did it foretell? By a series of careful and accurate observations he was able to show that it was a star, an immense distance beyond the moon, and therefore in the translunary world where, according to Aristotle, there could be neither change nor corruption. By 1574 the new star had disappeared, and in the same year Brahe could write that to deny the forces and influence of the stars is first of all to undervalue the divine wisdom and providence and secondly to contradict experience. It was inconceivable that God could have made such marvellous and brilliant stars for no end or purpose. The ancient world picture was so deeply entrenched in his mind that his own careful observations of natural phenomena, which to the modern mind seem so clearly to destroy its entire fabric, failed to dislodge it. Two years

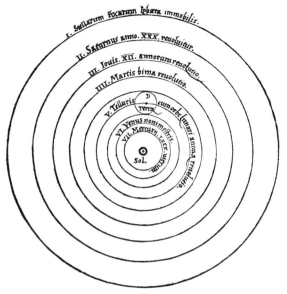

NICOLAI COPERNICI

net, in quo terram cum orbe lunari tanquam epicyclo contineri diximus. Quinto loco Venus nono mense reducitur. Sextum deniq; locum Mercurius tenet, octuaginta dierum spacio circũ currens. In medio uero omnium residet Sol. Quis enim in hoc

pulcherimo templo lampadem hanc in alio uel meliori loco po neret, quàm unde totum simul possit illuminare? Siquidem non inepte quidam lucernam mundi, alij mentem, alij rectorem uo= cant. Trimegistus uisibilem Deum, Sophoclis Electra intuentẽ omnia. Ita profecto tanquam in solio regali Sol residens circum agentem gubernat Astrorum familiam. Tellus quoq; minime fraudatur lunari ministerio, sed ut Aristoteles de animalibus ait, maximã Luna cũ terra cognationẽ habet. Concipit interea à Sole terra, & impregnatur annuo partu. Inuenimus igitur sub hac

later he built his observatory upon the island of Hven, near Copenhagen, the first purpose-built astronomical observatory in the western world. One of his visitors was James VI of Scotland, in Denmark in 1589–90 to bring home his bride, Anne. A hundred years later John Flam-steed was at work in the Royal Observatory built at Green-wich in 1675 by Sir Christopher Wren.

In the last years of the sixteenth century, from a combi-nation of clear argument and careful experiment, Galileo worked through to a better understanding of the laws of motion, and an appreciation of the futility of the objections to the motion of the earth. In 1609 he made his own

telescope and turned it towards the moon and the stars. To his astonishment he saw that the moon was not a pure, incorruptible crystalline sphere, but that its surface was pitted with mountains and valleys. On 7 January, 1610 he saw three small stars near Jupiter. Successive nights revealed four. By the end of the month he was convinced that they were satellites revolving round Jupiter in the same way that the moon revolved around the earth. In March he published his discoveries in a little book called *Sidereus Nuncius*. It caused a sensation. His colleagues at the University of Padua refused to believe him. Aristotle had not mentioned any planets to Jupiter and therefore they could not exist. When invited to look through his telescope they refused to do so. In the following year he observed spots upon the surface of the sun. The entire fabric of the traditional world picture was now under threat, and the guardian of the tradition, the Church, moved to its defence. In 1616 the theory that the sun is at the centre of the universe was declared heretical, and the writings of Copernicus were placed upon the Index. They were not removed until 1835.

But the discoveries had already spread far beyond Italy. In September of 1610 Kepler in Prague succeeded in seeing the satellites of Jupiter, and Thomas Harriott in England had seen them by the end of the same year.

In 1601 Johannes Kepler, at the instigation of Tycho Brahe, was appointed Imperial Mathematician to the

Plate 65 Flamsteed House, the Royal Observatory at Greenwich, from a print of 1824. It was built in 1675 to designs by Sir Christopher Wren

Emperor Rudolph II in Prague. Here he set to work upon Tycho's observations, adding more of his own, especially upon the movements of the planet Mars. Eventually, after an astonishing intellectual effort, he wrote: 'it was as if I awoke from sleep and saw a new light'. The motions of the planets were not spherical, but elliptical about the sun. He published his results relating to Mars in 1609 as *Astronomia Nova*, and for the other planets in 1618 as *Epitome Astronomiae Copernicanae*. As Kepler himself wrote, nature could no longer be regarded as divinely animated (*instar divini animalis*), but as a piece of clockwork (*instar horologii*). The traditional world picture lay in ruins. A new one had yet to be constructed to take its place.

The contribution of the voyages of discovery was almost as significant. How could the new races of men discovered in the Americas have got there, since all men were descended from the eight persons who had survived the Flood? Many thought that they were descended from the lost tribes of Israel, and attempts were made to find references to the New World in the Bible. It was widely believed that, although they were truly men, following the papal Bull *Sublimis Deus* of Paul III in 1537, they were in thrall to the Devil. The discovery of America had not been a chance event but an example of God's providence since it had been designed by Him for the purpose of bringing enlightenment to them. By the end of the sixteenth century some more sensitive Europeans were more than a little ashamed of the appalling consequences of this 'enlightenment' upon the aboriginal inhabitants of America.

At the same time the voyages dealt a further blow to the traditional world picture. It was now clear from observation that men could live in the torrid zone. It was not too hot for human habitation. This, however, was used to support the idea, widely held, that the world was in decay. That the tropics were now inhabitable was evidence that the world was losing its pristine strength. Its end could not be far off. The theory that the world was fast approaching its dissolution was most cogently put forward by Godfrey Goodman, in his book *The Fall of Man*, published in 1616. Much of what we have considered, not only in this chapter but also through much of this book, he used as evidence of the imminent end of the world: the social upheavals brought about by enclosures, sun spots and the scarred face of the moon, the loss of ten days when the Julian calendar was reformed, the diversity and extravagance of fashion, the use of tobacco, the popularity of theatres, the 'new star' of 1572. His world was wholly geocentric, and Copernicus was merely absurd. His melancholy and sense of foreboding were widely felt and were not dispelled before the end of the seventeenth century.

The voyages of discovery made use of and at the same time stimulated the more accurate astronomical observations described in previous paragraphs. Without their aid the long transoceanic voyages would have been very much more dangerous than they already were. The voyages also promoted improvements in navigation and in map-making, where success depended upon empirical observation rather than upon conceptual speculation, compelling a slow change in man's vision of the external world. Magnetic variation of the compass from true north was already known by the middle years of the fifteenth century, for example, and the Casa de Contratación was established at Seville in 1503 to give purely practical training to the navigators and pilots of ocean-going ships. Attempts to found a similar school in England were entirely without success and English navigators had to learn their art from individual mathematicians, of whom John Dee was one of the most influential for much of the second half of the sixteenth century. Richard Chancellor, Stephen Borough, Leonard and Thomas Digges and Thomas Harriott were all his friends, and he was visited at his home in Manchester in 1596 by Christopher Saxton.

Late medieval maps do little more than set out information in picture or diagram form, and often as a bird's eye view, a form of map-making that persists right through the two centuries covered in this book. (See Plate 34.) Much practical work had to go into establishing surveying techniques and into making accurate instruments before such diagrams could become true maps, the work of surveyors being much eased by a number of improvements in mathematical techniques. The decimal system was devised and published by Simon Stevin in his book *De Thiende*, first published in 1585 and translated into English in 1608 by Robert Norton, who also wrote on surveying. Logarithms were invented by John Napier of Merchiston in 1614, and from the second decade of the seventeenth century pocket editions of trigonometrical and logarithmic tables were being published; Henry Briggs's *Arithmetica Logarithmica*, published in 1624, contained logarithms calculated to 14 decimal places. It was Kepler who thought that logarithms tripled the life of an astronomer.

Gemma Frisius published in 1533 an account of triangu-

lation as a technique for the making of maps, and one of
his pupils at the University of Louvain was John Dee.
Another was Gerard Mercator. Triangulation established
itself only very slowly because of the difficulty of measuring angles accurately, but a theodolite had been
described by Leonard Digges, another friend of John Dee,
and the earliest dated English example to survive was
made by Humfrey Cole in 1574.

The making of maps was much stimulated in England
in the 1530s and 1540s by the need to make accurate plans
of the fortifications along the south-east coast, but it is the
1570s before map-making becomes at all common. Lord
Burghley was one of the first statesmen to appreciate the
value of maps, and he accumulated a large collection
during the course of his long years in office. The mapping
of the English counties was well under way by the 1570s
and it was under royal patronage that Christopher Saxton
completed and published his *Atlas* in 1579. Here, for the

Plate 66 Christopher
Saxton's map of
Wiltshire, published in
his *Atlas* in 1579.
Although it is a very
simple map and the
pictorial element is
strong, especially in the
representation of hills and
churches, it is more
realistic than that in Plate
67

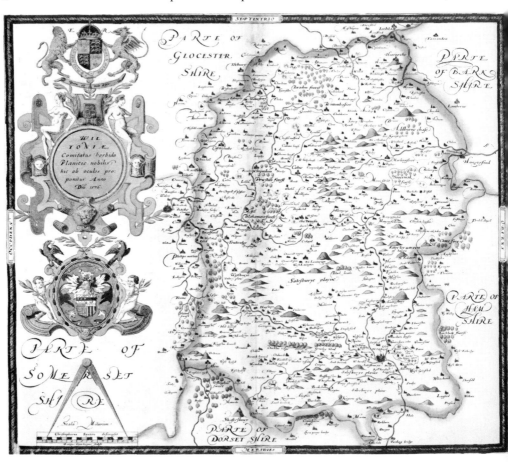

first time, the landscape of England lay before his contemporaries reduced into an easily comprehensible, symbolic form upon sheets of paper. The effects upon men's mental landscapes is almost impossible for us today fully to grasp.

Saxton's map needs to be compared with the map of the same part of England that appears in Michael Drayton's immensely long topographical poem, *Poly-Olbion*, published between 1613 and 1622. Here is a world of water nymphs, woodland goddesses and mythological figures as far removed from the Wiltshire of Saxton as it is possible to be, but nevertheless of considerable significance as a representation of a world that was slowly passing away.

By the end of the sixteenth century map-making and surveying had reached a very high standard of accuracy. The long detailed written descriptions of estates and manors characteristic of the late fifteenth and early sixteenth centuries were at first supplemented by maps and then to all intents and purposes replaced by them. John Walker prepared both map and written survey of the manor of Boxted, in Essex, in 1586, a little after Ralph Agas had made an astonishingly detailed map of the village

Plate 67 The map of Wiltshire and Somerset used to illustrate Michael Drayton's long topographical poem *Poly-Olbion*, published between 1613 and 1622. This is the ancient, living landscape, with each river and hill having its own spirit or deity, that was fading rapidly at this time

and fields of Toddington, in Bedfordshire, on which are marked several thousands of plots and strips of land. His achievement is matched by that of Thomas Langdon, who in the 1590s made a number of very detailed maps of the estates of All Souls College, Oxford. Such maps were frequently prompted by the need to establish property boundaries accurately, to resolve disputes or to signal changes in estate management practices.

Nevertheless the pictorial element in maps is slow to

Plate 68 Part of William Morgan's map of London, published in 1681–1682, a town plan from which the pictorial element has all but disappeared

disappear. The town plans in John Speed's *Theatre of the Empire of Great Britain*, published in 1611 (see Plate 34), are essentially bird's eye views, and even the remarkably accurate map of London published by William Morgan in 1681–1682 still contains some pictorial elements, the barges on the Thames for example, and elevations of the Bridewell, the King's Printing House, the Temple Church and the Duke's Theatre. By this time however the pictorial element is little more than decoration, pretty and attractive but not germane to the purpose of the map, which presents a matter-of-fact, prosaic view of London. Similarly, the road maps published by John Ogilby in *Britannia* in 1675 (see Plate 71) show windmills and churches in elevation but as such they are almost irrelevant to the underlying purpose of the maps, which was to make it easier for travellers to find their way about the roads of late seventeenth-century England. The ancient, haunted landscape of *Poly-Olbion* has passed away.

The needs of navigators, surveyors and map-makers both compelled and produced a more accurate, systematic and more realistic approach to the external world. The discovery of the rules of perspective and their application to painting in Italy early in the fifteenth century is a further facet of this growing realism, although one which was of little significance in England before the seventeenth century. The painting of Lord Darnley and his brother, made in 1563 by Hans Eworth, a painter trained in Antwerp but at work in England between 1549 and 1574, is one of the earliest examples of the use of perspective in a painting executed in England. It is however a very stiff application of the rules and its impact must have been slight, since painting, except portraiture, especially in miniatures, was unimportant in England before the 1620s, and painters remained craftsmen rather than artists. Nevertheless in due course the rules of perspective compelled a new, more realistic look at the external world.

There was at the same time a growing awareness of man's increasing mastery over nature. This awareness is to be found first of all in the solution of practical problems in engineering, whether in the construction of drainage works in the fens, or in the careful and accurate laying out of aqueducts to bring water into towns, such as the New River works for London, or for more frivolous purposes such as the application of the power of water or compressed air in garden fountains and automata such as hissing animals or birds that flapped their wings. Greater precision in the making of scientific instruments meant the more careful cutting of screws and gears. The pendulum clock was invented in 1659, and improvements to escape mechanisms meant that clocks and watches became more reliable. Time itself could now be measured more accurately.

The world picture described so far in this chapter was the product of a long period of intense speculation and intellectual effort based upon argument by analogy, observation made by the unaided human eye and a profound respect for ancient authority, especially the Bible and the writings of Aristotle. Much of this speculation was of the most abstract kind, but much was also dedicated to purely practical purposes. Natural philosophy and technology were never completely separated from one another. After all, the ultimate object of medicine, in which the humours and astrology played such a large part, was to cure the patient, and much writing on astronomy was directed towards practical ends: the calculating of Easter, determining the true north, even if only to be able to orientate churches approximately correctly, telling the time by means of the astrolabe. The medieval centuries saw important technological innovations – wind and water power were harnessed to an increasingly wide range of functions, the mechanical clock was invented, spectacles and balance scales came into general use. More important however, was the slow recovery of the geometry of Euclid and the logic of Aristotle, and with them an appreciation of the possibility of discovering the rational structure of the universe through experiment and measurement, to which mathematics held the key. That in due course scientific investigation might lead to an increase in man's power over nature for the ultimate benefit of mankind was an idea first put forward in the thirteenth century.

The sixteenth century was marked by a long series of purely practical books written, not in Latin, the international language of learning, but increasingly in English, French, German, Italian (the vehicle for much of Galileo's discoveries), and Dutch (in which Stevin wrote his book on decimals). They were designed to solve purely practical problems, whether in mining or military engineering, surveying or land mensuration, navigation and agriculture. Although many of these manuals drew upon theoretical work in mathematics and astronomy there was as yet no coherent statement of the benefits that might accrue to mankind from the marriage of scientific experiment and speculation to technological innovation. It was here that Francis Bacon made his most significant contribution. He often failed to appreciate the work of others, had no conception of the importance of mathematics as the language of nature, and made no important scientific discovery. His significance lies in his advocacy of scientific research and its application to improving the condition of mankind, and the immense power and persuasiveness with which he put forward his ideas. They are most fully stated in his *Advancement of Learning*, published in 1606:

But if my judgement be of any weight, the use of history mechanical is of all others the most radical and fundamental towards natural philosophy; such natural philosophy as shall not vanish in the fume of subtile, sublime, or delectable speculation, but such as shall be operative to the endowment and benefit of man's life. For it will not only minister and suggest for the present many ingenious practices in all trades, by a connexion and transferring of the observations of one art to the use of another, when the experiences of several mysteries shall fall under the consideration of one man's mind; but further, it will give a more true and real illumination concerning causes and axioms than is hitherto attained.

Even here, however, in his emphasis upon practical and mechanical arts, he is often doing little more than summarizing, albeit in a majestic prose far beyond the capabilities of most other men, a debate among his contemporaries as to the value and the antiquity of such arts. Adam in the Garden of Eden was widely considered to have practised all 'lawful and profitable Arts', and the power and splendour of the court of Solomon as described in *The First Book of the Kings* was commonly thought to be the consequence of his mastery over nature. This finds a direct echo in Bacon's *New Atlantis*, published in 1627, the year after his death, where the House of Solomon has every appearance of a research institute for the applied sciences. Its object, according to its Father, was 'the knowledge of causes, and secret motions of things; and the enlarging of the bounds of human empire, to the effecting of all things possible'.

It is the 1640s before Bacon's influence becomes at all noticeable, and then it is to be found among several groups of scientists and reformers whose interests cut across the Royalist/Parliamentarian divide of those years. From their numbers was formed in 1662 the Royal Society, of which Joseph Glanvill wrote in 1665 that Francis Bacon's 'Salmon's House in the *New Atlantis* was a Prophetick Scheame'. In its early years the Society was fired with enthusiasm for utilitarian and commercial projects of every kind, some genuinely useful, many rather trivial. Its Georgical Committee, for example, established in 1664, circulated a questionnaire calling for information upon agricultural practices throughout the country. Reports survive for parts of Yorkshire, Kent and Gloucestershire. However the early expectations that it would itself act as a research institute soon faded, in spite of the skill and zeal of its Curator of Experiments, Robert Hooke, although it did assume a vague responsibility for the management of the Royal Observatory at Greenwich, founded in 1675. It became instead a centre for the criticism and the diffusion of the work of scientists at large, both in England and on the continent, something in which it was assisted by the enormous range of the correspondence of its first Secretary, Henry Oldenburg, and the publication, from 1665, of its *Philosophical Transactions*, among the earliest of scientific periodicals, starting only two months after its French rival, the *Journal des Scavans*. It became as much a social club as anything else, wealth and birth being as important for aspiring Fellows as intellectual distinction. Amateurish, dilettante dabbling in scientific matters became fashionable in court circles, and both Charles II and the Duke of Buckingham had some pretensions to interest in chemistry, but the patient accumulation of facts and testing of hypotheses lay far beyond their capabilities or powers of concentration. Thomas Sprat, chaplain to the same Duke of Buckingham, was the first historian and apologist of the Royal Society, his *History* being published in 1667. When writing his book he was very conscious of following the precepts of Francis Bacon, more especially in his emphasis upon the practical value of the work of the Fellows of the Society, who sought 'to make all their Labours unite for the service of mankind'. At the same time 'they meddle no otherwise with Divine things than onely as the Power, and Wisdom, and Goodness of the Creator, is display'd in the admirable order, and workmanship of the Creatures'.

The old, traditional world picture was now fading fast, and as it did so God was pushed further and further into the immensities of space, making the prospect of divine intervention in everyday events on earth more and more remote. Calvin took strong exception to the medieval concept of the ordered hierarchy of the universe. Instead, in his view, God was the lawgiver of the universe and ruled directly, with no need of the medieval hierarchy of angels. God had predetermined all events from the beginning. His laws were the laws of nature, and 'theological doctrines of predestination thus prepared the way for the philosophy of mechanical determinism'. The concept of the laws of nature is first fully developed by Descartes, for whom the universe was governed by the laws established in nature by God. The Cartesian world picture was rigidly deterministic. Everything, including mental events, was governed by the laws of mechanics, orderly, natural processes, independent of God, leaving no room for teleological explanations. The Renaissance concept of the *anima mundi*, the idea that the world is infused with spirit, living, breathing, even thinking, is replaced by a universe constructed on geometrical lines, a cosmic machine worked by divine immutability, one totally devoid of magic, sensibility or purpose.

Galileo wrote in 1623 that 'Nature is written in mathematical language'. Descartes and Kepler held the same view, and it is given its fullest expression in the title of the book that finally brought the new world picture into full focus. Newton's *Mathematical Principles of Natural Philosophy* was published in 1687. His theory of gravitation gave a full explanation of all astronomical phenomena. By 1666 he had deduced that the forces keeping the planets swinging for ever around the sun were reciprocally as the squares of their distances from the sun. But he himself did not dismiss God from his universe, because, as he wrote, 'the motions which the planets now have could not spring from any natural cause alone, but were impressed by an intelligent Agent'. Not even Sir Isaac Newton could abandon entirely the concept of a purposeful universe.

By the end of the seventeenth century the medieval world picture had lost almost all of its credibility in educated circles, and with its passing a thousand years of learning lost its immediacy, to become of interest only to historians of ideas. One tightly organized explanation of the external world and of man's role in it had been replaced by another that gave a more convincing explanation of the facts which thrust themselves upon men when they began to look in a new way and with heightened curiosity at the world that lay about them. The medieval world picture provided for comparatively few contacts between ideas and the reality of the physical world, although during the course of the fourteenth and fifteenth centuries the range of these contacts was slowly extended; this happened more especially when Italian painters at the beginning of the fifteenth century discovered the rules of perspective and so came to look at their external world with a fresh eye. The artist's perception was sharpened when, like Leonardo da Vinci, he turned to anatomy and botany in order to improve this contact with reality. Mapmakers, striving for ever greater accuracy, contributed immeasurably to this heightening awareness of the external world. At the same time man's mental landscape was enormously extended in its range. By the end of the seventeenth century the concept of an infinite universe was widely accepted and men were just beginning to grasp something of what the words 'infinite universe' meant.

The sun was thought to be between 80 and 90 million miles away from the earth, and Newton accepted that first magnitude stars must be about 80 million million miles away, or 14 light years, a term not used until the end of the nineteenth century. From the vastness of telescopic space men had to turn their minds to the vastness of microscopic space. The Dutchman Antoni van Leeuwenhoek published regularly in the *Philosophical Transactions* of the Royal Society accounts of the astonishing discoveries he was making through his high-powered single lens, and it is clear that he was seeing things that were less than 1/10,000 of an inch across.

In some ways this chapter has done little more than flit from one book to another, from *De Revolutionibus* to *The Advancement of Learning*, from *Sidereus Nuncius* to *Principia Mathematica*. Books of this kind are of enormous significance when plotting the direction of men's thoughts about their world, and the invention of the printing press meant that such books, and the ideas which they contained, could spread easily and rapidly throughout Europe. But such 'book-hopping' can also be very misleading. The reading public was then very small indeed, a very much smaller proportion of the total population than it is today. This means that the extent to which the intellectual developments of the seventeenth century penetrated the ranks of the shoemakers and husbandmen, cottagers and tailors who made up the bulk of the population of Stuart Britain is impossible now to measure, although individual life stories of men such as John Flamsteed seem to indicate that it should not be minimized. What is clear is that popular rituals and superstitions, the dependence upon charms, spells and horoscopes, and the belief in fairies, spirits and ghosts was scarcely touched. Only witchcraft declined, and then largely because the judiciary before whom accusations of witchcraft came for trial refused to countenance it. The last execution for witchcraft took place in 1685 and the last recorded trial was held in Leicester in 1717, when the jury rejected the charge. The Witchcraft Act was repealed in 1736, without bringing a belief in witchcraft and magic to an end. The formal, polished, elegant Ptolemaic world picture has long disappeared into history. Such broken remnants as lie scattered through the minds of men today must be among the oldest elements of their mental landscapes.

Communication Chapter nine

Previous chapters have been concerned to analyse certain facets – by no means all – of the landscape of Britain in the sixteenth and seventeenth centuries, whether fields and farms, churches, houses, cottages, towns, windmills, forges and furnaces, or woods and fens. The analysis has been concerned with reasons, motives and the processes of change, the slow materialisations in physical form of changes in man's perception of his world, of his role in it, of his command over it. Much has of necessity to be described at a level of abstraction that disguises the men and women whose lives provide the raw materials for this analysis. At the same time the nature of the historical sources for the period means that it is impossible to arrive at any accurate statistical basis. Instead it can only be illustrated by example, with the attendant dangers that the example may not be truly representative, that it conceals regional and local variations, and the even more subtle snare of the very act of choosing an example giving it an importance and significance it almost certainly did not in itself really possess.

Analysis also destroys many of the thousand subtle and complex links over time and space between men and their environment. The fields and farms, churches and mansion houses, towns and windmills of the previous chapters were not discrete entities. Instead they formed a dense matrix within which the landscape was shaped, moulded and changed. They were linked in the minds of men by assumptions, experiences and codes of practice, whether formally established by law or informally recognised by custom and long usage. But these linkages can only be formed and sustained by physical and intellectual contact between individual human beings and it is with the channels through which these contacts were made that this chapter is concerned.

The Tudor and Stuart centuries see Britain move from being a comparatively backward island on the periphery of a western European civilisation which was essentially Mediterranean in its focus, to being a world power. It is particularly difficult to arrive at a balanced picture of human mobility in this period. By the end of the seventeenth century many Englishmen had sailed round the world, and the registers of wills proved in the Prerogative Court of Canterbury show men from this country dying in the West and East Indies as well as over much of Europe, while both men and women were settled along the eastern seaboard of North America. At the same time the registers of many rural parishes show families born, marrying and dying in the same parish for generations. Thus the descendants of William Paling can be traced in the parish registers of Hoby, in Leicestershire, from the seventeenth century to the end of the nineteenth and the descendants of Anthony Draycott, husbandman, lived in Seagrave, also in Leicestershire, over the same period. In contrast, apprenticeship registers of the London livery companies show boys and young men drawn from the length and breadth of England to the capital in order to learn a trade; London was not the only magnet – it was merely by far and away the most powerful. Four-fifths of the boys apprenticed to mariners in Ipswich in the first half of the seventeenth century came from Suffolk, but the other fifth came from as far away as Devonshire and Westmorland, with the record unfortunately giving no hint as to the reasons which could compel young men to travel so far in order to learn to be seamen in a second rank provincial town. Studies of lists of inhabitants can show, by comparing surnames, that even though the total population of a village may not increase very dramatically, a period of about ten years can be marked by an astonishing rate of turnover in individuals. In 1676 the rector of Clayworth, in Nottinghamshire, made a list of the inhabitants of his village. There were 401 persons. In 1688 he repeated the exercise. This time there were 412 persons, a very modest increase in total numbers. The feature of the two lists which is of the greatest interest however is that of the 401 people listed in 1676 no less than 244 had disappeared by 1688, with fewer than 100 being buried in the parish churchyard, their places being taken by 254 newcomers to the village. Again, as with almost all of the examples given throughout this book, there is no reason to think that the experience of Clayworth was unique in any way. We must accept that there was very considerable geographical mobility throughout this period among all ranks of society as well as very considerable geographical stability.

Men and women, their possessions, their ideas, skills, attitudes and assumptions could, in the sixteenth and seventeenth centuries, move either by land or by water. On land they had to rely either upon their own efforts, in other words they could walk, or else they had to make use of horses, either to ride on, to draw their carriages and wagons (see Plate 1), or else to carry goods and merchandise in packs upon their backs. Stories are legion as to the bad conditions to be found on the roads of Britain, and the dangers which travellers had to face, but there is equal but less dramatic evidence of travellers, goods and letters reaching their destinations safely and without undue delay. What is clear from this conflicting evidence is that roads were quite unlike those of today. We expect a road to have a hard, firm surface, a camber to throw rainwater into ditches and drains at the sides, footpaths and kerb-stones to separate wheeled vehicles from foot passengers, a welter of signposts to tell us exactly what to do and where we are, and above all we expect the road itself to be clearly separated off from the surrounding countryside by its hard, metalled surface and its boundary walls and fences. Tudor and Stuart roads were quite unlike this. They were often earthen tracks which could become impassable in bad weather. They were almost entirely without signposts of any kind, and there was often no clear boundary between road and countryside.

An Act of Parliament of 1555 imposed responsibility for the repair of roads upon the parish. Each parish was to choose two Surveyors of Highways each year. The Surveyors could compel their fellow parishioners to work upon the repair of the roads, at first for four days in each year, and from 1563 for six days. The Act was made perpetual in 1586, and in 1662 the Surveyors were empowered to levy a rate in order to meet expenses over and above the six days' statutory labour of the inhabitants. In 1697 another Act of Parliament stipulated that roads should be no more than eight yards wide, and gave the county Justices of the Peace the power to order Surveyors of Highways to set up signposts, although the first milestones to be erected in Britain since Roman times were not set up until 1729, along the London road out of Cambridge. It was 1835 before the system was changed. The Surveyors themselves lacked any kind of engineering knowledge. Suitable roadmaking material was often not available locally. Parishioners were very reluctant to perform their statutory labour, and what was done was often done badly. The result was that the quality of the roads could vary enormously from parish to parish, and was as much dictated by the season of the year and the underlying subsoil and geological structures as by any attention to their duties on the part of Surveyors of Highways.

Supervision of the work of the Surveyors was entrusted to the county Justices of the Peace and to the Justices of Assise, and this supervision could take up a great deal of the time of the courts. The Western Circuit Assise Judges were told in 1634 that the statutory labour of the parishioners of Calne, in Wiltshire, was insufficient to keep in repair a three-mile stretch of the London to Bristol road, and in 1638 that the highways in Brislington, in Somerset, were in a constant state of disrepair owing to a 'great resort of colliers' to coal pits. At the assises held in Rochester in March 1605, the Grand Jury presented that the road near Lamberhurst, on the road between Rye and London, was decayed and dangerous. At the Kent assises in July 1617 and again in July 1619 the inhabitants of Northfleet were indicted for not repairing the Dartford to Gravesend road. At quarter sessions held for Northamptonshire at Michaelmas 1630, the inhabitants of Collingtree were presented for not repairing the common highway in Collingtree, being the road between Welling-borough and Towcester. In 1647 the Western Circuit Assise Judges were told that the parish of Widcombe, in Somerset, was crossed by three main roads and that their repair was beyond the capacities of the parishioners.

This system may have worked reasonably well within the expectations of the times in a remote, rural parish, far from any busy thoroughfare. But, as the examples quoted in the previous paragraph show, parishes on main high-ways could find the burden intolerable. The parish of Stanton, in Hertfordshire, on the Great North Road, was indicted at quarter sessions for failing to repair its roads more times than any other. In 1660 the parishioners threw up their hands in despair and appealed to Parliament for help. They repeated their petition in 1663, when they were joined by parishes in Cambridgeshire and Huntingdon-shire. The result was the first turnpike act, passed in the June of that year. Toll gates were to be erected at Stilton, Caxton and Wadesmill. Receipts from the tolls were to be used by specially appointed county surveyors to repair and maintain the road, with power to use, if necessary, the ancient statute labour of the parishioners, and also to levy a parish rate. All of this was to be done under the supervision of the county Justices. The Act was to be in force for eleven years. In 1665 it was extended for twenty-one years for the Hertfordshire section and the Caxton gate was moved to Arrington in Cambridgeshire.

No further turnpike acts were passed until the 1690s, when there were a number, including ones for the Colchester to London road, the Wymondham to Attleborough road in Norfolk, the Reigate to Crawley road, and that between Birdlip and Gloucester, and others. All gave the county Justices powers to appoint surveyors who were, in the case of the Wymondham road, 'to view and survey the said ruinous places and consider the defects thereof'. They could make use of the old statutory labour, but turnpike gates were to be erected, and tolls charged, the proceeds to go towards the repair of the roads. On the Wymondham road the tolls were fixed at a penny for a horse, 6d. for a stage or hackney coach, a shilling for a wagon, and 6d. for every score of oxen. Carts carrying hay at haymaking time and corn in the straw at harvest time, soldiers on the march and their attendant wagons, and persons riding post, were to go free.

A new development took place in 1706. In that year a private Act of Parliament was passed creating a body of trustees with power to manage a stretch of road quite independently of the county Justices of the Peace. This Act was for the Fonthill to Stony Stratford road, and served as the model for the turnpike trusts of the eighteenth century, which, by 1830, numbered over 1,100 with responsibility for 22,000 miles of road, and this in spite of considerable opposition which was often violent, so that in 1735 destruction of turnpike gates, locks or floodgates erected under authority of an Act of Parliament was made a felony punishable by death.

The 1555 Act thrust the responsibility for the repair of roads firmly on to the parish. Only at the very end of the seventeenth century was this burden eased very slightly with the beginning of the turnpike system, but even here the trustees could call upon the statutory labour if necessary.

In contrast, the repair of bridges, except those in corporate towns, was, by a statute of 1531, made the responsibility of the county. There were however a number of local exceptions to this general rule. One of the most ancient bridges in England was that at Rochester, with nine piers and over 400 feet long. From before the Norman Conquest each pier was repaired at the cost of the tenants of a separate estate in Kent. The bridge was rebuilt in stone at the end of the fourteenth century and the Wardens responsible for its repair were incorporated by an Act of Parliament in 1421. The bridge over the river

Leen at Nottingham, again a very long one with twenty stone arches, was repaired at the charge of different authorities: the town of Nottingham was responsible for the north end of the bridge and the first two arches, a length of 46½ feet, the remainder being divided up among the wapentakes of Nottinghamshire, so that Broxtall Hundred for example was responsible for the next 81½ feet, and so on. Similarly, if a bridge spanned a river separating two counties, then both would be responsible for its upkeep. Chepstow bridge, for example, was repaired by Gloucestershire and Monmouthshire. At Gateshead however the bridge over the Tyne was lined with shops, eighteen on the western side and thirteen on the eastern side, a number with dwelling rooms over, and the rents went towards the costs of repairing the bridge. There were also houses along East – now Magdalen – Bridge, in Oxford, which was in the sixteenth century over 500 feet long with twenty arches.

The Justices of the Peace in quarter sessions were kept as busy attending to the repair of bridges as they were to the repair of roads. In Warwickshire, for example, in 1625 the justices found that Edmonscote bridge over the Avon was now so ruinous that to repair it would cost three times what it would have done to repair it 'within these five years past', and so it was decided to levy a rate upon the whole county to pay for its repair. The Hundred Jury for Norton Hundred, Northamptonshire, presented at the quarter sessions held in Michaelmas 1630 that the inhabitants of Towcester had failed to maintain a sufficient footbridge at Swineford, and at the same sessions the Grand Jury presented that the bridge on the common way leading from Brackley to Banbury was out of repair in the parish of St James, Brackley by reason of the failure of the parishioners to repair it. It was reported in 1648 that the New Bridge between Dunster and Porlock, in Somerset, was so out of repair that several people had died attempting to cross it, and the Grand Jury for the Kent assises presented in February 1609 and again in June 1611 that the bridge at Newenden, between Kent and Sussex, was in decay and the road on either side seriously flooded.

The story of roads and bridges in Scotland is quite different. Successive Acts of the Scottish Parliament, beginning in 1587 and repeated in 1609, 1617, 1630, 1633 and 1661 attempted to establish Justices of the Peace in the Scottish counties on the same lines, and with the same responsibilities for roads and bridges, as those in England. The office was accepted only very slowly and reluctantly, and it was only after the Act of Union of 1707 that Justices of the Peace began to make any significant contribution to Scottish affairs. In theory they had authority to order the repair of roads and bridges, and an Act of Parliament of 1669 provided for six days' statutory labour on the English model. In practice they were unable to do anything. Only when James VI proposed to visit Scotland in 1617 was some meagre attempt made to improve the roads in eastern lowland Scotland, in particular that from Berwick to Edinburgh, and from Falkland to Dundee. Similar half-hearted attempts were made to repair these roads when Charles I proposed to visit Scotland in 1628 and for his actual visit of 1633.

This almost total absence of any effective authority for the repair and maintenance of roads in Scotland meant that they were almost non-existent. Wheeled traffic was almost unknown outside the major towns, and merchandise had to travel by packhorse or by sledge. Even at the end of the seventeenth century the Selkirk to Edinburgh carrier is said to have used the bed of the river Gala Water in dry weather as being 'more traversable than the main road'. In 1692 it was said at Kirkcudbright that its inland trade was very inconsiderable, and goods that they wanted came on horseback from Leith or Dumfries; and of Haddington it was said at the same time that it too had only an inconsiderable inland trade, 'not worth the

Plate 69 A view of Aberbrothick, from Slezer's *Theatrum Scotiae* of 1693. It illustrates the close relationship of town and country in the seventeenth century, the nature of the Scottish run-rig system and the poor state of the roads

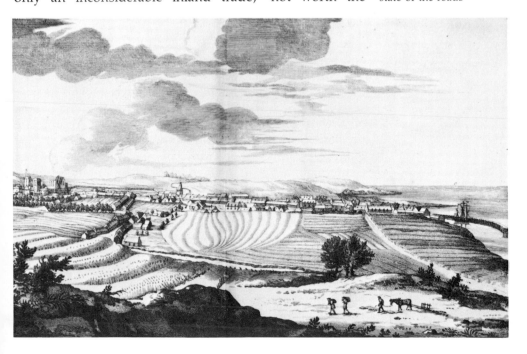

noticing being only managed by poor mean packmen'.

There were some bridges in lowland Scotland, but they were usually the responsibility of individual burghs, and so were often neglected for long years together owing to a lack of resources with which to pay for their repair. Peebles for example complained in 1692 of the burden of keeping in repair the bridge over the Tweed. The history of the bridge at Perth is a long story of disaster. Three arches were swept away by flood in 1573. It was 1617 before repairs were complete, and the whole bridge was destroyed in 1621. It was 1722 before a new bridge was built. Glasgow Bridge was kept in reasonable repair from the tolls charged for its use, but further up the Clyde, at Lanark, there was no bridge until the early eighteenth century, and passengers and horses had to use the ferry.

As we have already seen, there was considerable geographical mobility in Tudor and Stuart Britain, and the Act for the repair of the road between Wymondham and Attleborough mentioned previously gives, in its list of tolls to be paid, an outline sketch of the travellers to be found on the roads. There were however very many travellers who would pass toll-free, especially those on foot, to their destinations, although many who were to be found on the roads were vagrants and so it is probably misleading to talk of 'destinations' since they were often wandering in search of work, food or shelter, or to avoid the consequences of their own misdeeds. At the Warwickshire quarter sessions held at Easter 1625 an order was made for the relief of Joyce Harrice, who had come wandering and begging from London. She had been born in Kingsbury, in the county, and so the inhabitants were ordered to provide for her maintenance. Occasionally quarter sessions records reveal something of the variety of people who were on the roads of Stuart England. Among the petitions filed in the Northamptonshire Michaelmas 1630 quarter sessions is one from Thomas James, yeoman, of Cambridge. He had arrived at Stanion, in the county, some three months ago, with his bears. He had been called before Dr Dalby, a Justice of the Peace, and committed to gaol and then bailed, but 'hauing not his comission from his Maiestie under broade seale ready to shewe for his travelinge', he was committed to the house of correction, from which he petitioned to be released.

Those who could afford to do so travelled on horseback. Many shopkeepers and craftsmen in the lower to middle ranks of society kept horses as a matter of course. Mark Ebelwhite, a tanner of Denham in Buckinghamshire, died in 1690, leaving personal possessions worth £603, including three horses and their harness worth £10; and Richard Cox, a bricklayer of Eton, also in Buckinghamshire, died in 1676 leaving personal possessions worth only £23, his horse in the stable being worth £1 16s. Horses were not, of course, kept merely for riding. They were also working horses. Thus John Knight, the incumbent of Calverton, in Buckinghamshire, who died in 1661, left personal possessions worth £676, including eight geldings and mares valued, with the harness, at £5 13s. 4d., but these would have been used to pull his two ploughs, three barrows, three long carts and two dung carts in the cultivation of his glebe land, some 28½ acres in the common fields of Calverton.

Those who were in a hurry and did not wish to wear out their own horses could, and again if they could afford it, hire horses, either from those who made a living hiring out horses – and there were 'horsehirers' operating under the control of the municipal authorities of Southampton and Newcastle upon Tyne – or else from postmasters. The Comptroller General of the Posts, certainly from 1583, required all his deputy postmasters to keep four horses for those who wished to ride post. Everyone who did so was to be accompanied by a guide, who was to blow his horn at least three times every mile, as well as on entering a town or on meeting travellers. Those travelling post on royal business were to pay 1½d. a mile, those on their own business paid 2d. a mile, with 6d. for the guide, who returned with the horses on completion of the stage. They could expect to cover 7 miles in an hour in the summer and 5 in the winter. The rates were raised to 2½d. a mile in 1603 and 3d. a mile in 1609 when travelling on royal business. It was also possible to hire horses by the day, week or month. In exceptional circumstances travelling post could be very fast indeed. In 1603 Sir Robert Cary carried the news of the death of Queen Elizabeth to her successor, James VI of Scotland, in three days, a rate of 130 miles a day, travelling in this way.

Horses were also used to carry goods and merchandise, and it is clear that a great deal of the commerce of Britain in the sixteenth and seventeenth centuries was moved by packhorse, and not only in the Highland Zone. William Rand, of Stewkley, in Buckinghamshire, had five horses and mares and pack saddles at the time of his death in 1683, and goods could only be brought to Dorking market across the heavy clays of the Weald in wintertime by packhorse. Packhorse trains must have been encountered the

241

length and breadth of Britain. It was, for example, reported to the Royal Society in 1675 that when sea-sand was transported inland to spread on the fields of Cornwall to improve their fertility, it was first of all carried by lighter as far inland as the tides would permit, and then despatched by packhorse 'by reason of the hilliness, narrowness and badness of the ways', each horse carrying 13 or 14 gallons of sand, and seven or eight horses tailed together to make a train. Almost all of the raw materials for the Staffordshire pottery industry were brought in by packhorse, and the finished products taken out, principally to Willington, on the Trent, for transport by water to London. Packhorse trains frequently covered long distances. Shrewsbury cloth was taken regularly to London by this means, and Kendal packhorsemen travelled to Southampton almost as a matter of course, taking a month over the round trip.

The oldest form of public wheeled vehicle on the road was the carrier's wagon. A regular service was running between Oxford and London as early as 1398, and by the opening years of the seventeenth century there was a dense network of services linking most parts of the country, with the longest regular run said to be that from Kendal to London. The services were so regular that it was possible for John Taylor to publish in 1637 *The Carrier's Cosmography*, in which he listed the days of arrival in London of carriers from various parts of the country and the inns where they were to be found. Thus the Ipswich carrier arrived at the George in Lombard Street on a Thursday, the same day that the Maldon carrier reached the Cross Keys and the Bury St Edmunds carrier the Dolphin in Bishopsgate, where the Norwich carrier arrived on Mondays and Tuesdays. Those from Oxford to London were licensed by the university, and, in 1626, one carrier was required to have twelve horses, make two return journeys each week and keep a shop in the town.

Various attempts were made during the seventeenth century to regulate the size of the carriers' wagons and the numbers of horses which might be employed. Thus a royal proclamation of 1621 forbade the use of four-wheeled wagons altogether, but it seems to have been largely ignored, as was a similar proclamation of 1629. A statute of 1662 laid down that no wagon was to be pulled by more than seven horses, or carry more than than a ton weight in merchandise between October and May, or more than a ton and a half between May and October. As a further attempt to prevent heavy wagons from damaging the roads it was also required that their wheels be at least four inches in breadth, in the pious hope that they would roll the roads rather than churn them up into ruts as narrower wheels would do. Another statute of 1670 required that no more than five horses were to be harnessed nose-to-tail to wagons. Any more were to be harnessed in pairs, and a statute of 1696 stipulated that no more than eight horses, harnessed in pairs, were to be used to draw wagons. These statutes, all part of a vain attempt to mould traffic to the roads, rather than the other way round, reveal indirectly the limits to the technology of the time.

Another Act of 1691 empowered Justices of the Peace to fix the rates to be charged by carriers. The Justices of the Peace for Ipswich met in June of 1694 to set the rates for carriers working from the town. From Ipswich to London the rate was to be 5s. the hundredweight for solid and compact goods, but for pictures, chairs, couches, squabs (that is, sofas), looking glasses, tables, stands and 'other cumbersome goods of the like nature' it was to be 8s. For the carriage of all small wares, boxes and parcels of goods under 28 lbs the rate was 6s. the hundredweight if brought into the town by wagon but 8s. the hundredweight if brought in by a common stage coach or any horse or horses only. The rate for the carriage of all goods under 14 lbs. in weight was to be a penny a pound, and for goods under seven pounds weight it was fixed at 2d. the pound, except letters 6d. each parcel and 2d. for every letter. Rates were much cheaper from Bury St Edmunds and Botesdale, a shilling every hundredweight, and from Stowmarket and Woodbridge 6d. the hundredweight, and from Eye and Colchester 1s. 6d. the hundredweight. The rates were to be written out and hung up in the market place for all to see.

As the previous paragraph illustrates, merchandise of every kind was transported in the carriers' wagons. Further evidence from Ipswich reveals just how extensive and varied this merchandise could be. By the 1680s, the Port Books for Ipswich, in which are recorded the goods landed at the quayside, also note those goods which were to be sent on to London by the carrier's wagon. They included in one year alone 22 goshawks, twelve gross of glass beads, 7000 crystal beads, numerous pieces of wrought silk, 2 falcons, 18 peregrine falcons, 34 reams of maps and prints, on one occasion 1188 ells of silk, and on 3 May 1681 582 lbs. of silk. Wagons were leaving every three or four days.

In addition to the horses of the carriers' wagons plodding their way across the countryside, other kinds of animals were also to be found on the roads of Britain. By the end of the sixteenth century the cattle trade between Wales and England was well-developed, and thousands of cattle and their drovers moved slowly across midland and southern England from the hills of Wales to be fattened on pastures in the Home Counties before making their final journey to Smithfield market. A statute of 1597 required the drovers to be licensed in quarter sessions, to be married men and householders and over thirty years of age, and another Act of 1628 forbade drovers, carriers and wagoners to travel on a Sunday. Numerous drovers' routes crossed the Welsh border, from Chester to the Severn, where the passage across the river was made from Beachley to Aust. One of the main routes, from northern Wales, came through Sutton Coldfield, Southam, Sulgrave and Biddlesden to Buckingham, and much of this road to the north of Buckingham is still called the Welsh Road. From Buckingham, where there was a big cattle fair, the animals went on to Barnet. Another route came from Builth Wells through Leominster and Worcester to Banbury. The drovers also used Watling Street until it was turnpiked and the cost of the tolls forced them to use alternative routes. The Act of 1597 which called for the reconversion of pasture to tillage exempted land converted from tillage to grass within two miles of Watling Street and being within five miles of Dunstable in order that the drovers might be able to find grazing for their herds and flocks. A map of Shenley, in Buckinghamshire, made in 1693, shows numerous small fields and closes flanking both sides of Watling Street, closes which must have served this purpose, and many have survived to the present although they are now threatened by the building of the new city of Milton Keynes.

Droving from Scotland into England was well established by the middle years of the fourteenth century, and cattle were being drawn from the Isle of Skye by the beginning of the sixteenth. Export of livestock to England was forbidden in the middle years of the century because of food shortages in Scotland, but an Act of the Scottish Parliament permitted the trade again in 1607, although cattle and sheep still had to pay customs duties. By the 1660s thousands of cattle were passing through Carlisle each year and in 1669 duties on the export of cattle to England were abolished. The Act of Union with England gave a great impetus to the trade. In 1672 another Act of the Scottish Parliament granted a fair and market at Crieff to James, Earl of Perth. This became the most important assembly point for cattle destined for England, its rival and eventual successor, Falkirk Tryst, not starting until after the Act of Union. From Crieff the herds crossed the Pentland Hills by Cauldstane Slap, and made their way to Peebles via Romanno before turning south for Dryhope, Tushielaw and Deanburnhaugh. Once into England numerous routes led south, and there were many big cattle fairs, at Northallerton, for example, and at Stagshaw Bank, outside Corbridge, at Appletreewick, Boroughbridge, Middleton Moor, Wibsey, Skipton and Malton. Many herds came down the Great North Road to the big fair at Barnet, whilst others went into East Anglia to the fair at St Faith's, just outside Norwich, and the rich pastures of Norfolk and Suffolk. There must have been thousands of cattle and sheep on the move at any one time, especially during the summer months, and not only cattle and sheep. Defoe records in the early years of the eighteenth century the flocks of geese and turkeys which were driven from East Anglia to the London market. It was not unknown for drove ways to be deliberately laid out in the lowlands of Scotland, 'raiks', up to a hundred feet in width with turf dykes on either side. Such a drove road was made from Annan to Gretna in 1619, for cattle making their way from Galloway into England, and drystone walling marks both sides of the drove road going south from Deanburnhaugh over Muselee enclosed ground, and also the road crossing Whitehaugh Moor towards Hawick.

Carriers' wagons were not the only wheeled vehicles to be found on the roads. Two-wheeled farm carts were common in country districts of lowland England by the end of the sixteenth century, by which time the four-wheeled farm wagon had also appeared (see Plate 1). In hilly districts however, wheeled transport was much less common, not least because it was difficult to handle over steep and uneven ground, and instead sledges were used, called 'slide butts' in the Gower peninsula. John Evelyn, in his proposals for the rebuilding of London after the Great Fire, suggested that sledges should be used instead of carts. Sledges were still in use in Cumberland and in Bristol in the nineteenth century. In Great Yarmouth the narrow Rows of the town were sometimes no more than three feet wide, and never more than six. This compelled the use of a special narrow cart in which the wheels were under the seat rather than projecting at the sides.

It seems very likely that four-wheeled coaches were first

seen in England in the 1560s, and their use, amongst those who could afford them, spread very rapidly – so much so that a Bill was introduced into the House of Commons in 1601 to restrain the excessive use of coaches, but it was rejected. By the 1620s hackney coaches were available for public hire in the streets of London, much to the indignation of the London watermen, who saw their livelihood, gained by transporting people up and down the Thames by boat, threatened by this intrusion into the already over-crowded, narrow streets of the city. Various attempts were made to control the numbers of hackney coaches in London by requiring that they should be licensed, but the staggering increase in the number of licences to be issued, it rose from fifty in 1637 to 800 in 1715, and the cost of the licence, fixed in 1694 at £50 for twenty-one years, with a further payment of £4 a year, to be collected by five commissioners especially appointed for the purpose under an Act of Parliament of that year, illustrates vividly how popular and how profitable this mode of transport had become, and loud and bitter complaints from licensed hackney coachmen show how frequently unlicensed ones were prepared to face the possibility of a £5 fine for each offence. By this time hackney coaches were to be found in provincial towns. Two were licensed in Windsor in 1687. Yet further confusion was introduced into the streets of London with the coming of sedan chairs in the 1580s, Sir Saunders Duncombe being granted a patent to let them for hire in 1634.

By the 1630s public coaches were working from London to provincial towns, the earliest recorded service being to St Albans in 1637. A network of coach services grew up during the Commonwealth years, so that by 1658 a coach travelled to Salisbury in two days and to Exeter in four, the same time it took to reach York, and there was a coach every fortnight to Edinburgh, for which the passenger fare was £4. In the years after the Restoration, coach travel became an accepted mode of transport, and those who used it could expect to do between thirty and forty miles a day, depending upon the weather and the state of the roads (see Plate 71). By 1715 there were some 900 coach services a week out of London serving over two hundred towns. In other words an entirely new industry has appeared and reached maturity within the space of about seventy years. By the end of the seventeenth century there were specialised coach-harness makers, coach builders and coach masters in many towns throughout England.

Coaches started and finished their journeys at inns, and

as roads improved and travel became easier so the numbers of inns grew, as did their prosperity. A census made in 1577 over 27 counties in England records 14,000 alehouses, 2,000 inns and 300 taverns. Like all lists and surveys of the period it is almost certainly incomplete, but the numbers do give some impression of the extent of the provision made for travellers, and numbers increased rather than diminished during the seventeenth century, a phenomenon not always wholeheartedly welcomed. It

Plate 70 The George Hotel, Northampton, from a print of the early nineteenth century. It was this inn that Defoe likened to a palace

was suggested in 1641 that the four alehouses and one inn at Puddletown, in Dorset, were too many, and the reason why the town had become a very disorderly place. Another survey made in 1686 is not strictly comparable because it is concerned with the numbers of guest beds and the stabling for horses in towns, but the figures are in themselves interesting and show the extent to which travel had come of age. Cambridge, Exeter, Winchester, Leicester, Bristol and Warwick all had stabling for more than a thousand horses, whilst Norwich had room for 930, Lincoln for 894 and Salisbury for 865. Bristol had 1019 guest beds, Exeter had 866, Great Yarmouth had 687, Derby had 841 and Northampton had 289. Towns on the main roads of the country, those to Norwich, to York,

Chester, Bristol, Portsmouth and Dover, flourished on the trade that travellers brought, and their inns were often large, well-furnished establishments, their owners suitably prosperous and suitably respected. The Rose and Crown in Northampton was three storeys high and thirteen bays wide, the Angel, on the south side of Oxford High Street, had 100 feet frontage, whilst the George, also in Northampton, was said by Daniel Defoe to 'look more like a palace than an inn'. Towns like Towcester and Stony Stratford had numerous inns on the Chester road, whilst Foster's Booth, a few miles to the north of Towcester, owes its origins entirely to the growth of travel in the sixteenth and seventeenth centuries. Newport Pagnell was also a 'thoroughfare' town, being on the main road from Oxford to Cambridge, and at least one inn here, the Saracens Head, is fifteenth century in origins. In Cambridge the George Inn, owned by the most famous carrier of them all, Thomas Hobson, stood where St Catherine's College now is.

There were many large inns in London, and some streets had several so that traffic congestion must have been very real. In Gracious Street in the 1630s were four inns, the Spreadeagle, the Tabbard, the Cross Keys, and the Saracens Head, all being frequented by carriers from towns in East Anglia, from Sudbury, Maldon, Long Melford, Braintree, Bocking, Colchester, Coggeshall and Ipswich. In Holborn there were three such inns, the Chequers, the Bell and the Cross Keys, and in Bishopsgate there were two, the Four Swans and the Green Dragon.

In Scotland, however, inns, even at the end of the seventeenth century, were almost entirely unknown, and this in spite of successive Acts of the Scottish Parliament from 1366 to 1567 to encourage their establishment.

Coaches, carriers and their wagons carried both passengers and goods. The sixteenth century also sees the beginnings of a postal service for the delivery of letters. There was a system of posthorses along the roads to Berwick and to Dover by 1516, and by the end of the sixteenth century the system had been extended to the Exeter, Bristol and Holyhead roads, with another for the road from Carlisle to Newcastle upon Tyne, by which time private as well as royal and government letters were being carried. In 1635 a proclamation empowered Thomas Witherings to set up a new Letter Office, with authority to carry letters for up to 80 miles for 2d. Witherings was already in charge of foreign letters. It was hoped that he would be able to provide a letter carrier to every shire

town and a footpost to every market town. The *Carriers'*
Cosmographie of John Taylor, published in 1637, and
already quoted, reveals that he had some success, since it
notes that the footpost from Bury St Edmunds arrives
every Wednesday at the Green Dragon in Bishopsgate, 'by
whom letters may be conveyed too and fro', while the
footpost from Nottingham came every second Thursday,
as did that from Walsingham and from York. In 1660 an
Act of Parliament established a General Post Office. A
letter of a single sheet would be carried 80 miles for 2d.,
and then the charge rose to 3d. During the 1660s byposts
were established for the carriage of letters to destinations
off the six post roads, which by this time were those to
Chester, to Berwick, to Exeter, Bristol, Yarmouth and
Dover; a service from London to Sheffield was added in
1663, three years after a service from Towcester to Derby
was started. By the 1670s a letter took five days to reach
Edinburgh, and only two to go to Chester. By this time
also there were several letter receiving offices in London.
In 1680 William Dockwra began a penny postal service in
London, in defiance of the monopoly of the General Post
Office. Legal action brought his service to an end in 1682,
but it was in fact taken over by the General Post Office,
and by the end of the century nearly a million letters a
year were being carried for a penny over London. In 1709
another attempt was made to break the monopoly of the
delivery of letters in London, but again a court case
brought the offender, Charles Povey, to heel, although
again the General Post Office took over his idea, namely
the collection of letters street by street by a collector ringing
a bell. The Letter Bell became a part of London life and
survived well into the nineteenth century, providing
Hazlitt with the title for an essay.

In Scotland, an Act of Parliament of 1695 established a
General Letter Office, but the only posthorse road was
that from Edinburgh to Berwick. All the others, including
that from Edinburgh to Glasgow and to Perth and Aberdeen, were by foot.

In Restoration Britain letters and parcels, goods and
merchandise of every kind moved from one end of the
country to the next without any very disconcerting delay.
Indeed correspondence of the time gives every impression
that it is expected to arrive at its destination safely and
without loss. What this meant for the dissemination of
ideas, opinions, news and gossip is impossible for us now
to appreciate. Henry Oldenburg, first Secretary of the
Royal Society, carried on an enormous correspondence

with scholars and scientists throughout western Europe. Edward Lhwyd, second Keeper of the Ashmolean Museum in Oxford, kept up an extensive correspondence with clergymen, antiquaries and naturalists over much of Wales. He sent collecting boxes for botanical specimens by the carrier, and could expect to receive them back in due course, the carrier having been asked to 'besprinkle a handful or two of water every night' over the contents of the boxes in order to keep them fresh. He could even ask to be sent birds' eggs, two of each kind, and gave instructions as to how they were to be blown and how they should be packed, asking for the name of the bird in Welsh in the covering letters.

So busy were the roads of England and Wales in the years after the Restoration that in 1675 John Ogilby found it worth his while to survey and then to publish a series of road maps. The maps are in strip form, with important landmarks, including bridges, ferries, mills of every kind, country houses, even gallows, set down so that the traveller could find his way. There are often notes as to whether the country is open or enclosed, wooded, pasture or heath, and the roads themselves are marked out in furlongs, Ogilby being one of the first map-makers to use the mile of 1760 yards laid down in a statute of 1593 in a consistent manner. For the student of the landscape of late seventeenth-century England and Wales these maps are an almost inexhaustible quarry. For the contemporary traveller they must have been a godsend.

Overland communication was clearly very important in the sixteenth and seventeenth centuries, but for the movement of bulky goods over any distance at all – and this meant no more than five or six miles – it quickly became very expensive, and so merchants and dealers in grain or coal, bricks, sand, timber or iron wares, gravitated to the nearest navigable waterway. Britain has a long coastline in proportion to its area, and a number of river systems, parts of which are navigable. By the end of the sixteenth century only Dartmoor, Salisbury Plain, the Northamptonshire uplands and the Pennine chain were more than about twenty miles from navigable water, together with the central mountain massif of Wales.

The main rivers and many tributaries in England were navigable after a fashion during the medieval centuries, but rivers were, and continued to be throughout the sixteenth and seventeenth centuries, important not only as 'moving highways', but also as sources of food and power, and these functions often conflicted. Millowners built dams and sluices to ensure a steady supply of water, and hence of power, for their mills. Fishermen built traps and snares, whether for eels or for salmon. Landowners whose properties bordered on rivers were reluctant to see their fields and meadows used as towpaths, and at the same time saw sluices, traps and dams as obstacles that would cause the river to flood. To all these man-made hazards in the way of barges and boats must be added the natural ones: shoals and rapids, drought in summer and flood and frost in winter. In 1677 barges were aground for a month in the Thames at Oxford following a long dry spell, and the Severn at Tewkesbury froze in the winter of 1607–8. Millers, bargemen and landowners were often in conflict; lawsuits, deliberate obstruction and as deliberate destruction, together with physical violence, were commonplace.

Most rivers of any size were from time to time in the charge of Commissioners of Sewers, groups of local landowners appointed by the Crown with the duty to prevent flooding by clearing and maintaining drainage channels. They could order the removal of obstacles of every kind, including dams and weirs, and the dredging of ditches, drains and the river bed. Such orders were often bitterly opposed, after all one man's obstruction might be another's livelihood, and in practice little or nothing was done for years together. Occasionally some groups of Commissioners attempted to improve a river for navigational purposes. This occurred for the Medway from Maidstone to Tonbridge in 1600, for example, but their opponents questioned the basis of their authority to do so and they were compelled to admit that their duties ran only to cleansing the river. Commissioners of sewers were also authorised in 1608 to provide a water supply for Cambridge, which they did by means of a channel of running water down the middle of Trumpington Street.

By the end of the sixteenth century there was widespread interest in the problems and the opportunities for river improvement. Perhaps the most significant publicist was Francis Mathew, who advocated a scheme for joining the major rivers by artificial waterways, including the Thames and the Severn by means of a cutting from the Bristol Avon to the Thames at Lechlade or Cricklade. He even suggested that the state should undertake the work, but in this he was far in advance of his time.

As the inadequacy of Commissioners of Sewers to undertake river improvement for navigation was progressively revealed, so people began to turn elsewhere for authority to carry out the necessary works, obtaining either Letters Patent from the Crown or else an Act of Parliament. One of the earliest Acts for the purpose was that of 1539 for 'mending of the Ryver of Exetor'. This empowered the city authorities to make the river Exe navigable from the sea at Topsham to the city, removing the weirs and mills that obstructed it. The work however proved beyond their capabilities, and nothing was accomplished until in 1563 John Trew of Glamorgan, having undertaken to bring

Plate 71 The Custom House, Exeter, built between 1679 and 1681

boats carrying 10 tons of cargo as far as the city, began work on an entirely artificial waterway. Within three years he had dug a canal, 16 feet wide, 3 feet deep and just under 3 miles long, running parallel to the river and yet bypassing the principal obstructions. Water was diverted into the canal by means of a weir built across the river, and along the canal itself were six sluices arranged in pairs so that in practice they formed three pound locks. Although the canal proved difficult and expensive to maintain, having to be closed for long periods, in the long term it turned out to be reasonably successful. Extensive improvements were carried out in 1698 and again in 1829, altering the original canal out of all recognition. The canal terminated in Exeter at a basin where warehouses and quays were built, and in 1679–81 a Custom House. This basin is now the home of Exeter's Maritime Museum.

Letters Patent were obtained in 1619 to make the Bristol Avon navigable as far as Bath, but nothing was achieved. Other Letters Patent were obtained in 1634 to make the River Soar navigable from the Trent to Leicester. About six miles were improved but then the money ran out and the work had to be abandoned. In 1636 William Sandys obtained Letters Patent to make the Warwickshire Avon navigable. Here, after enormous expense, he was eventually successful and barges could make their way up from Tewkesbury as far as Stratford. Another fairly successful scheme was for the improvement of the river Wey from Guildford to Weybridge, where it joined the Thames. Guildford at this time was an important trading centre, drawing manufactures and merchandise from a wide region: guns from the Weald ironmasters, gunpowder from mills at Chilworth, paper from mills at Byfleet, timber from the Weald for the naval dockyards at Deptford and Woolwich, together with grain and malt, all found their way down the river, and there is still on the quayside at Guildford a wooden eighteenth-century treadmill crane employed in loading and unloading the barges.

Navigation on the Thames revived in the second half of the sixteenth century after a long period of decline. The head of navigation was Burcott, and goods had to be landed here for onward carriage to Oxford. However, two Acts of Parliament, in 1605 and 1623, provided for the improvement of the river as far as Oxford, and this work was eventually completed. Pound locks were built at Culham, Sandford and Iffley, and the wharf at South – now Folly – Bridge, Oxford, had a wet dock and a crane. The river was very busy in the seventeenth century, with barges carrying grain and timber to London and bringing a very wide range of goods, including coal, back on the return journey. Places like Marlow, Wooburn and Henley became important river ports, and bargebuilders were to be found at Burnham and Pangbourne.

Traffic along the Thames was particularly plagued with weirs and high tolls at locks and along towpaths. In about 1578 there were said to be twenty-three locks, sixteen floodgates, seven weirs and more than twenty mills on the stretch of the river between Maidenhead and Oxford. An Act of Parliament passed in 1695 made the Justices of the Peace of the neighbouring counties commissioners for regulating these charges, but the Act seems largely to have been ignored.

Probably even more important as a navigable river was

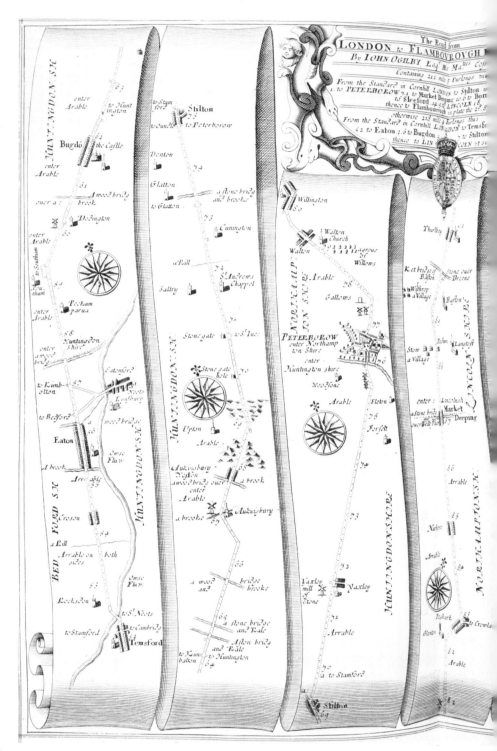

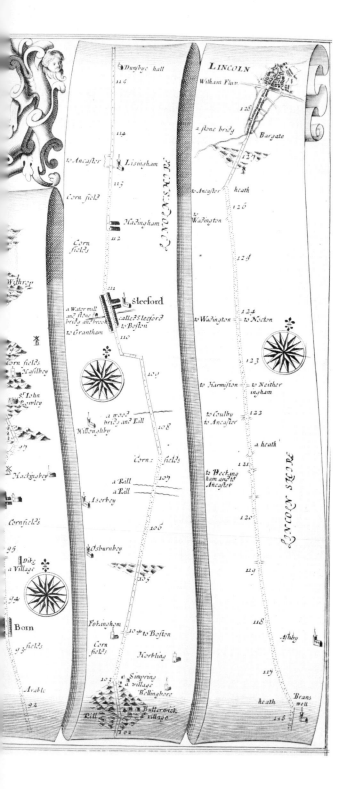

Plate 72 A page from Ogilby's *Britannia*, the first book of road maps published in England. The main emphasis is upon guiding the traveller on his way and so there is a great deal of evidence as to what he can expect to see on his journey

the Severn, which was navigable as far as Shrewsbury, from which rafts of logs were being floated downstream in the late sixteenth century. The river was also much used by Shropshire and Worcestershire ironmasters to move raw materials and finished products. The Severn had one great advantage over other English rivers in that an Act of Parliament of 1532 had made it toll-free. It could also be a dangerous river to navigate, especially towards its estuary, where there were sandbanks, shoals and rapids, hazards compounded by the tidal bore. The Severn barges, or 'trows', had a square rigged sail. They had to be hauled up river against the current by teams of men using a towrope fastened to the mast. When going downstream they were, in the absence of wind in the right direction, hauled by men rowing in a small towboat.

There was also considerable traffic on the Trent. Sea-going ships could reach Gainsborough, as well as the single-masted square rigged Humber keels. From Gainsborough to Nottingham flat-bottomed ketches were used, drawing no more than three feet of water and yet capable of carrying anything up to 50 tons of cargo. Navigation above Nottingham was much more difficult, and for long the corporation fought every attempt to improve it. By the middle of the seventeenth century smaller boats could reach Wilden Ferry, where packhorse trains from the North Staffordshire potteries brought pots and dishes for shipment down the Trent to London. When in 1699 renewed attempts were made to obtain legislation to enable the Derwent, a tributary of the Trent, to be made navigable as far as Derby, the corporation of Nottingham planned to put chains across the arches of the Trent bridge, but the Bill was rejected in the House of Commons. In the same year Lord Paget obtained an Act of Parliament to improve the river from Wilden Ferry as far as Burton-upon-Trent. In 1711 he leased out his rights to two men, George Hayne and Leonard Fosbrooke, who had what amounted to a monopoly along this stretch of the river. It was now that Nottingham bargemen found the boot on the other foot. Hayne and Fosbrooke refused to allow them to come further upriver, and blocked it off with boats and ropes.

Further downstream it was Gainsborough that prospered on the river traffic. Wharves and warehouses were built along the river, ship-building was flourishing by the middle of the seventeenth century, and in 1683 it was reported that 30 ships, of between 30 and 80 tons burden, belonged to the town.

The Trent comes out into the Humber, which is also joined by the Aire and Calder – made navigable as far as Leeds and Wakefield in 1699 – and by the Yorkshire Ouse, navigable to York since medieval times and now rapidly silting up. This river network had its parallel to a large extent in that which flowed into the Wash. By the time Daniel Defoe was writing, early in the eighteenth century, Stamford, Peterborough, Bedford, Cambridge, Bury St Edmunds and Thetford could all be reached by barge from the Wash. King's Lynn, at the head of much of this network, prospered, and the Custom House, built in 1683 as an Exchange, is still witness to this prosperity.

As merchants and dealers sought navigable waterways as the cheapest way of moving their bulkier goods, so ultimately the waterways came out to the sea, and the final link in the communication network that enmeshed seventeenth-century Britain, namely the coastal shipping that worked in and out not only the big ports like London and Newcastle, Hull and Bristol, but also scores of small creeks and harbours lining the coasts: Wells Next-the-Sea and Blakeney in Norfolk, Southwold and Walberswick in Suffolk, Minehead and Watchet in Somerset, Maldon and Brightlingsea in Essex, Milnthorpe in Westmorland. Beaumaris, in Anglesey, was importing French wines early in the seventeenth century. Stirling town council was, at about the same time, spending money building a pier for the haven on the Forth, buying a lighter and regulating the charges of carters and sledmen bringing goods up from the shore, and ships from Ayr were sailing to Carolina and the West Indies at the end of the century.

The larger ports had stone quays to which ships could, if there were sufficient water, be moored. In London certain quays were recognized as places for loading and unloading specific classes of merchandise. Bear Quay, for example, was for 'Portingall commodities by reason the merchants of that country do lye and had there ware howses'. Gibsons Quay was for lead, tin and coastal wares, Smarts Quay 'altogether with fish', Somers Quay, 'wholly for Flemings', and so on. Quays were often provided with cranes, and there is one, a treadmill of 1667, still preserved at Harwich, where it was once used in the former naval dockyard. Smaller ports might have only one or two quays: Southampton at the time of Charles II had two, Watergate, some 223 feet long and ranging from 190 to 63 feet wide, and West Quay, 225 feet long by 58 feet wide at one end and 37 at the other. Southwold at about the same time had only one quay, Blackshore, 100 feet long and between

30 and 21 feet wide. There was a tackle house on the south-east, and a dwelling house and warehouse on the north-west. Other ports had only a pier and at low tide ships lay stranded in the mud. Occasionally the building of a stone pier would create an entirely new harbour, as occurred at Clovelly, in North Devon, where the local squire, George Cary, built a massive granite pier, together with warehouses and cottages, and the new community flourished on trade with South Wales, as did Barnstaple, Ilfracombe, Minehead and Harland, where a new quay was built in 1566. Yet other ports had to use lighters. It was said of Dumfries in 1692 that there was no harbour with any quay, there being only shallow water with many sandbanks, and so lighters had to be used. At Glasgow at the same date the Clyde was rapidly silting up and no vessel of any burden could come within fourteen miles and so cargoes had to be unloaded and brought to the town on rafts or in small cobbles.

Another coastal town to develop during the seventeenth century was Falmouth. Fortifications were built at the entrance to Falmouth Haven in 1539–46. The haven was increasingly used by ships during the course of the sixteenth century and the enterprising Sir John Killigrew built four inns to serve the seamen in 1613. Houses followed, and by 1660 there was a population of about 700 inhabitants. A charter of incorporation was obtained the following year, when the name Falmouth was used for the first time, the settlements having previously been called Smithwick. In 1674–6 a new quay was built, and a packet station for the service to Corunna was established in 1689. The service was extended to Jamaica in 1703.

The pier at Clovelly still survives today, but it is the exception. The technology of the period could scarcely keep pace with the rate at which the sea destroyed harbour works, and *The Statutes of the Realm* for the sixteenth and seventeenth centuries contain numerous Acts of Parliament in which a coastal town attempts to raise sufficient money to repair the devastation brought by storm to its harbour works. Thus an Act of 1697 provided for a duty of a farthing to be levied on every chaldron of coal loaded at Newcastle upon Tyne for the repair of the pier at Bridlington, thrown down by a great storm in November of 1696. There are similar Acts for Great Yarmouth, Minehead, Whitby, Watchet and Dover.

For many harbours the problems brought by wind and tide were insufficiently understood and attempts to remedy a difficult situation served only to make matters worse. Those harbours on the coasts of Sussex and Kent were particularly badly off in this respect. The English Channel acts as a great funnel. As tides come in from the Atlantic so they are increasingly confined as they approach the Straits of Dover. Shingle and sand are brought ever eastwards, and attempts to build piers out into the sea serve only to create eddies in which the sea deposits its load, choking up the newly built harbour. The problem is compounded if at the same time there is a river bringing down silt. Rye and Winchelsea were badly affected in this way. Attempts to scour the River Ouse at Newhaven and build a pier and lighthouse, following a licence of 1664, were only partially successful. Storms destroyed that part of Brighton which lay below the cliffs, and Hastings lost its harbour pier in a storm in 1578. The problems and difficulties were just as severe at Dover, and it was only the importance of the harbour as the nearest point to the Continent that made the effort to keep its harbour open worthwhile. Again and again piers and breakwaters were constructed, only to pull shingle and sand into the harbour and choke it. In the 1590s Thomas Digges planned and built an immense sea-wall, some 1980 feet long, from the foot of Castle Hill westwards across some two-thirds of the shallow bay which served as a haven. This led to a considerable extension of the town to the west of the Town Wall, whilst the seaward side of the sea-wall was used as a rope walk. The new land beyond Snargate, some sixteen acres, was vested in 1605 in the Harbour Commissioners, and the rents provided at least part of their income. The whole of the town from Townhall Street and Snargate to the sea has been reclaimed from the sea, unintentionally, since the sixteenth century.

The first dry dock in Britain was built at Portsmouth in 1495. The growth of Deptford, Woolwich and Chatham during the sixteenth century led to the decline of Portsmouth as a naval town and the dry dock was eventually filled in in 1623, just as its fortunes began to revive. A new one had to be built in 1656–7, and a second in 1698. The first purely civil dry dock was built at Liverpool in 1710, following an Act of Parliament.

The dangers and hazards of navigating the coasts of Britain were slowly diminishing during the course of the Tudor and Stuart centuries as lighthouses were built and beacons set up. There was a lighthouse at Winchelsea in 1261, and one at St Catherine's Head, in the Isle of Wight, in 1328, and the medieval chapel lighthouse of St Nicholas, Lantern Hill, Ilfracombe, is still working. Another chapel lighthouse was that of St Ninian, Castle Hill, Aberdeen, provided with a lantern by the burgh in 1566. In 1514 the medieval gild of seamen at Deptford was refounded as Trinity House. Its chief concern at first was to establish a monopoly of the right to provide pilots for the Thames estuary, and it was only after an Act of Parliament of 1566 that it was authorised to set up beacons and marks. The first lighthouse built by Trinity House was that at Lowestoft, built in 1609, although it had taken over two

Plate 73 The medieval chapel lighthouse of St Nicholas, Lantern Hill, Ilfracombe, Devon. The lantern on the top is eighteenth century

towers at Caister in 1607, which had been built six or seven years earlier by Thomas Bushell. Trinity House Newcastle upon Tyne received a charter in 1536 and with it licence to build two towers, of stone, at North Shields, charging English ships which passed 2d. and foreign ones 4d. This was the usual method by which lighthouses were financed in this period, and a number of private lighthouses were built in this way, their owners drawing what could at times be a considerable income from them. These private lighthouses were not bought out until 1836, by which time that at Dungeness was worth about £7,000 a year to its owner, Thomas Coke of Holkham. In this way Sir John Killigrew built a lighthouse on the Lizard, and in 1618 Sir William Erskine and John Meldum received a patent to build two lighthouses at Winterton with the right to collect dues from ships which passed it. Trinity House had just built a lighthouse nearby, but such was the influence of the patentees at court that their grant included a clause forbidding Trinity House to maintain it. Perhaps the most famous seventeenth-century lighthouse was that built on the Eddystone Rock by Henry Winstanley. He began work in 1696, but was captured by French privateers, who demolished what he had built. On his release he began again, and the lighthouse was finished in 1698. He perished in the storm which swept the lighthouse away in 1703. It was rebuilt by Trinity House, and an Act of Parliament passed in 1707 gave them authority to collect a penny per ton from passing ships, with coasters paying no more than 2s., all to be collected at the ports of arrival or departure.

This then was the traffic to be found on the roads of Britain in the sixteenth and seventeenth century: men and women, walking and riding, thousands of horses pulling carts, wagons and coaches or struggling along a narrow stone causeway under heavy packs and panniers, cattle and sheep, ducks and geese, and in some parts of Britain, around London for example, or in the Black Country and the dales of the West Riding, the Cotswolds and East Anglia, the traffic was very intense indeed. It is a matter for some astonishment, not that the inhabitants of the parish of Stanton finally threw up their hands in despair in 1660 at being unable to cope with the burden of their roads, but that they had managed for so long, and that their example was not followed by scores of other parishes similarly burdened.

This traffic carried not only men and women, but also their letters, their possessions and their manufactures, whether woollen cloth, nails, saucepans, kettles or candlesticks, imported goods from Europe, from the New World and from the East, so that by the end of the seventeenth century shopkeepers all over the country were stocking raisins, prunes, sugar and tobacco, brandy and tea. When Alexander Ethersey of Buckingham, draper, died in 1706 he had in his shop and warehouses Kidderminster stuffs, Yorkshire cloth, West Country narrow cloth, silk, fustian, calico, linen and Hamburg cloth. When Silvester Widmore, of Great Marlow, mercer, died in 1668 he had in his warehouses grey, brown, red, nutmeg, and lead-coloured kerseys; green, red, blue, lemon and ash-coloured perpetuanas; Dutch serges, cambric, Scottish cloth, dimitties, linen, canvas, white mercury, treacle, verdigris, Valencia almonds, raisins, prunes, currants, sugar, wine glasses, pepper, tobacco, coriander seeds, cloves, nutmegs, carraway seeds, cinnamon, dates, tennis balls, nails, knit-

261

ting needles, paper, hops, rice, cochineal, fishing hooks – the list is almost endless. Merchandise was brought to Great Marlow by road and by water, much of it by barge up the Thames, Buckingham was accessible only by road. Neither Alexander Ethersey nor Silvester Widmore was unique in his time. It is their probate inventories which reveal just how efficient the communication network of late seventeenth-century Britain must have been.

Britain in 1700 Chapter ten

Britain in 1700 was quite unlike Britain in 1550. Change is a continuous process, even in the most traditional and conservative societies, where it can be so gradual as to be scarcely noticeable from one generation to the next. Many sections of British society were both traditional and conservative in the opening decades of the sixteenth century, but change came rapidly and often dramatically to almost every community in sixteenth- and seventeenth-century Britain, and there can have been few parts of the island, even in the remotest and most isolated localities of the Highland Zone, which had not experienced at least one aspect of the total spectrum of change that occurred across the period.

One of the most potent factors making for change in the rural landscape was enclosure. We saw in Chapter 3 that this had been taking place almost continuously in many districts of England and Wales throughout the entire period covered in this book. In some villages it could be a gradual, piecemeal process spread over a century or more. In others it could all be over in two or three years. This enclosure could affect not only arable but also meadow and pasture, wood and wasteland. In Wales in particular, large areas of upland common grazing were enclosed at this time. In Scotland however enclosure has not the same long history that it has in England and Wales, but it had certainly begun to take place by the end of the seventeenth century, and it was advocated by James Donaldson in his book *Husbandry Anatomised*, published in 1697 – the first book on agriculture published in Scotland.

It is very important to appreciate that enclosure was very unevenly distributed during this period. As late as 1795 nearly half of the area of Cardiganshire, some 206,000 acres, was said still to be common waste, and nearly 80 per cent of the total area of Westmorland was also said to be common waste at the same period. In Oxfordshire 54 per cent of the total area remained to be enclosed by private Act of Parliament in the eighteenth and nineteenth centuries, and about 35 per cent of Buckinghamshire. But figures at this level are far too coarse, concealing the subtle local variations which have always been so characteristic of the British landscape. In Buckinghamshire, for example, parliamentary enclosure was particularly widespread in the north of the county, and yet very few parishes were entirely without pre-parliamentary enclosure. Padbury, for example, was totally enclosed by Act in 1795 and yet all the neighbouring parishes had some ancient enclosures. By the middle years of the eighteenth century, if not before, Padbury must have seemed rather old-fashioned to many of its neighbours.

Large tracts of Royal Forest were disafforested in the seventeenth century, the trees felled, the land divided up into fields and farms and brought under cultivation. We have seen this taking place in Wiltshire, for example, where the last Royal Forest, Clarendon, was granted to the Duke of Albemarle in 1664. Again this is a process which must not be exaggerated. Timber was still valuable, especially for ship-building, and between 1660 and 1700 Acts of Parliament were passed for the enclosing and planting of about 11,000 acres in the Forest of Dean, and some 1400 acres in the New Forest, where pollarding was forbidden in 1698. Steps were also taken to preserve the timber in Alice Holt and Bere Forests, in Hampshire. It was hoped that these woodlands would make Britain self-sufficient in naval timber, although in fact this did not happen.

Extensive areas of woodland and of Royal Forest still survived in the landscape at the beginning of the eighteenth century. Enfield Chase, for example, was not enclosed until 1777, and Hainault Forest, in Essex, had to wait until 1851. The Great Forest of Brecknock still extended over 40,000 acres in 1815. Epping Forest was vested in the Corporation of London by an Act of Parliament in 1878, and Hatfield Forest, also in Essex, remained largely uncleared at the end of the seventeenth century; twelve of its seventeen coppices survive today, in the care of the National Trust.

A very similar story is to be told of the draining of marsh and fen. We spent some time in Chapter 3 looking at the drainage of the Bedford Level in the middle years of the seventeenth century, but the work created as many problems as it solved, and there was a long, slow deterioration during much of the eighteenth century. Drainage work elsewhere in the fens was bitterly opposed and certainly not completed before the middle years of the nineteenth century, and the last native Large Copper butterfly in Britain was taken in Bottisham Fen in 1851.

The draining and enclosing of Holland Fen, following an Act of Parliament in 1765, led to serious rioting, and there was no real progress until the introduction of steam pumping-engines in the early years of the nineteenth century. Similarly, in the Somerset Levels King's Sedgemoor remained largely untouched at the end of the seventeenth century, in spite of nine special commissions for the work from Charles I and an Act of Parliament of 1669. Chat Moss, in Lancashire, also remained undrained until the nineteenth century, and presented enormous problems for George Stephenson when he was building the Liverpool to Manchester railway in 1830.

Enclosing, felling and draining considerably modified the landscape of many districts of Britain in the sixteenth and seventeenth centuries, but much of this work was carried out on a very local scale. The largest scheme by far must have been the draining of the Bedford Level. The nearest approach to a concerted attack at national level aimed at draining marsh and clearing woodland is probably to be found during the 1630s, when Charles I made a very real attempt to achieve solvency in order to avoid having to go to Parliament for money. Much woodland was cleared as a result, but marshland drainage was generally of little effect before the 1650s. In this way the short-term political aims of men can have a long-term impact upon the landscape.

The absence of any concerted, large-scale attack upon common arable, waste, woodland and marshland means that there were still very large areas of Britain where traditional peasant economies – based upon a close and subtle relationship between men and their environment and yet well beyond subsistence levels of production – still flourished at the end of the seventeenth century. The two centuries covered in this book had brought great changes into many of these communities, as we have seen, and yet attempts to force the pace of change, for whatever reason, could still provoke violent opposition. Almost every community, township, parish, hamlet and farmstead has its own unique history in this respect, so that generalisations based upon a handful of examples often fail to convey the richness and diversity of experience and the subtle variations in the pace of change to be found from one district to the next and from one decade to the next.

With these reservations in mind some broad generalisations can nevertheless be made. Marshland survived beyond the end of the seventeenth century because the technical problems involved, especially the pumping away of flood water, lay beyond the technology of the time. Woodland survived because timber was still a valuable resource for a wide range of purposes, including fuel, house and ship-building. Why some villages clung tenaciously to their open fields whilst their close neighbours enclosed is more difficult to explain, but is perhaps to be found in the understandable reluctance of some communities to abandon well-tried ways and leap into an uncertain future where survival was by no means assured. Again as with so many other facets of landscape history, any ultimate explanation is to be sought in mental attitudes, fears and preoccupation rather than in the workings of impersonal economic forces.

The more obviously man-made parts of the sixteenth- and seventeenth-century landscape, namely its houses, churches and other buildings, also experienced considerable change. Purely domestic building was transformed almost out of recognition during the course of this period, although again as with every other component of the landscape the old was never entirely replaced by the new. By the end of the seventeenth century brick had become the most widely used building material, although stone continued to be used where it was locally available, as in the English limestone belt, the Lake District, the Pennines and much of Wales. New houses were frequently tiled. Chimneys, ceilings and staircases were built in as a matter of course. Glass became cheap and so windows could be glazed, and the sash window came from the Netherlands at the very end of the seventeenth century. There was much rebuilding and alteration as well as a great deal of new building. Glebe terriers, which are descriptions of the possessions of the parish church, including the glebe land and the parsonage, highlight the reality of these changes. In 1607 the vicarage at Chalfont St Peter, in Buckinghamshire, was described as containing five bays of timber-framed and tiled building with eight rooms, including hall, kitchen, parlour, and two chambers, the last two being the only rooms lofted over and with three chambers above. In 1694 the vicarage was a six-bay brick-built house of three storeys, with kitchen, hall and parlour on the ground floor, three lodging chambers on the first and three garrets above. Here the vicarage has clearly been rebuilt, the new bearing little resemblance to the old, and both it and the church were to be rebuilt again in the 1720s. In contrast, at Hughenden, also in Buckinghamshire, the parsonage was only altered. In 1607 it was described as a house of six bays of timber framing, with walls of plastered earth and mortar. There was a tiled roof, and four of the six bays were lofted over. In 1690 it was reported that the parlour and hall had been new floored, and the kitchen and butteries new paved in brick in that year. The four chambers and study on the first floor had also all been newly floored and the walls plastered. This building has also entirely disappeared.

These improvements in methods and materials of construction and in layout were to be found in the houses of almost all ranks in society and in many parts of Britain. But again there were many regional and local variations. Squatters' cottages on Welsh hillsides and the cabins of grassmen and cottars in the Highlands and Islands of Scotland remained untouched, and there were still very many one and two-roomed cottages in lowland England with mud and stud walls, thatched roofs and earthen floors. Nevertheless, even with these reservations in mind, it is probably not too much of an exaggeration to say that more people now lived in houses with some modest pretension to comfort, privacy and cleanliness than ever before.

Many of these improvements came about as a consequence of industrial expansion. More bricks, tiles and glass were being made, more nails, locks, hinges and hasps, than at any time in the past. Many of these improvements were absorbed into the vernacular tradition without difficulty, and we saw in Chapter 5 how this tradition adapted itself to new requirements by incorporating ceilings, chimney stacks and staircases without having recourse to foreign models. The rich variety of the vernacular tradition was however under attack, more especially from the middle years of the sixteenth century as an entirely new range of attitudes towards and expectations from building was slowly adopted. These new values were based upon a growing awareness of the principles of classical architecture as expounded and elaborated by fifteenth-century Italian humanists. These values first entered Britain at the highest levels in society and gradually percolated down the social scale, helped by the publication of pattern books – which made the decoration, if not the spirit, of classical architecture accessible to country masons, bricklayers and carpenters – by the considerable geographical mobility of building craftsmen, and finally by a growing awareness in almost all levels of society of new tides in taste and fashion, so that by the end of the seventeenth century almost all new building and much rebuilding was almost entirely in the new styles, even if quite often crudely and inaccurately done.

Domestic building at almost all levels of society flourished during the sixteenth and seventeenth centuries. There was a pause during the Civil Wars, but shortly after the Restoration building began again and continued almost without pause until the end of the seventeenth century and beyond, a period which also saw the greatest single rebuilding in Britain before the Second World War with the rebuilding of London after the Great Fire. The years after the Restoration also saw the emergence of the English country house as epitomised in Coleshill (see Plate 32) and by the end of the century houses as big as any prodigy house of the late sixteenth century were being built, although the architectural principles which underlay the design of a house like Blenheim Palace were far removed from those underlying Theobalds or Hatfield.

The housing stock of late seventeenth-century Britain was probably its largest gross fixed investment. The social infrastructure into which so much capital has been poured today – roads, railways, electricity supply stations, gas works, airports, public buildings of every kind – either did not yet exist or had reached only a very rudimentary level of development. Perhaps the next largest investment was to be found in church buildings, ranging in size from Canterbury cathedral to the mud-walled church at Aberlady, in East Lothian.

The stock of church building saw considerable and often very dramatic change in these two centuries, reflecting in a peculiarly intimate way the changes in doctrine and liturgy associated with the Reformation. The ruins of the monastery at Jervaulx (see Plate 48) and the simple brick meeting house at Gainsborough (see Plate 55) reveal with astonishing clarity just how effectively the most abstract patterns of thought and belief can find echo in the landscape. By the end of the seventeenth century the new principles of architecture have been absorbed into the building patterns considered most appropriate as the setting for the practice of these beliefs, and St Paul's cathedral (see Plate 53) is at once a monument to and a summation of a shift across a very wide range of values and ideals. To compare it with the view of the ruins of Fountains Abbey in Plate 50 is to be immediately made aware of just how radical this shift in values had been across the period covered by this book.

Other kinds of buildings lose their functional significance during this period, more especially after the Restoration, and these include castles and town walls. Developments in siege artillery made such buildings obsolete during this period and long years of internal peace, broken only by the violence of the Civil Wars in the 1640s, made them increasingly anachronistic. Like monasteries, however, they were often too substantial to be completely demolished save at great cost, and so they were simply neglected until a later age rediscovered them, not for practical purposes but as symbols of a distant, sentimentalised, past. It is probably entirely appropriate that it is only the mound of the long dismantled castle at Cambridge that can be seen on Plate 1. It was being used as a quarry for building materials for King's College in the fifteenth century, whilst the castle gate-house was used as the county gaol until the end of the eighteenth century.

It is always easy, when describing and analysing change of any kind, whether enclosure or forest clearance or the introduction of new designs in buildings or new practices in farming and manufacture, to forget that these changes are invariably due to men and women, their ideas, attitudes and values, the way in which they organise themselves into groupings, apportion power and authority and provide for the transmission of these ideas, attitudes and values. Patterns of family life, the boundaries within which political power is exercised and the machinery through which political decisions are implemented, changes and developments in the most abstract speculations about man's place in the universe and his relationships with God, all find visible reflection in the landscape, which is why some appreciation of demographic trends, however hazy in detail, is essential for a full understanding of its history.

We saw in Chapter 1 that the population of England in 1550 may have been about 3 million, and that of Wales perhaps 275,000. The sixteenth century seems to have been marked by strong population growth, so that totals may have reached four million by 1601, with perhaps 370,000 in Wales. There was probably some slackening in the rate of growth in the 1620s and 1630s but it is estimated that the population of England may have reached 5.3 million in 1656. After this there is a period of stagnation, perhaps even decline, with some recovery in the 1680s, so that numbers may have reached only 5 million in 1701, with something over 400,000 in Wales. The 1660s were years of plague and the 1690s of poor harvests, factors which may have adversely affected population in the last half of the seventeenth century, but there were also other factors at work. London at this time was growing faster than the national rate of increase, and was obviously exercising a severe drain upon population numbers elsewhere in the country since urban conditions at this time meant that no town could maintain its population by natural increase alone and any growth was dependent upon immigration. London was growing so rapidly that it was consuming almost the entire natural national increase in the last decades of the seventeenth century. There was at the same time considerable emigration from Britain, especially to North America. It has been estimated that perhaps 300,000 people left Britain in the second half of the seventeenth century.

We have already seen that there are no statistics, not even unreliable ones, from which to estimate the population of Scotland before the middle of the eighteenth century. To say that it may have reached a million by the opening years of the eighteenth century is no more than a guess. Plague was absent from Scotland after 1649, unlike England where there was a severe outbreak in 1665–6, but the 1690s saw a particularly severe crisis of mortality with very bad harvests and famine conditions in many parts of the country. It has been suggested that Scotland may have lost 15 per cent of its population at this time.

By far the largest town in Britain in 1700 was London, with a population of perhaps 600,000. Next was Edinburgh, with perhaps 40,000. Third was Norwich, with about 30,000 inhabitants at this time, followed by Bristol with about 20,000. Some industrial towns were growing rapidly by the end of the seventeenth century. Manchester, Leeds and Birmingham had all reached eight to ten thousand inhabitants, and their growth is to be matched by that of a number of ports, including Glasgow, Liverpool, Hull, Exeter and Newcastle upon Tyne. The naval dockyard towns of Deptford, Chatham, Portsmouth and Plymouth were experiencing almost boom conditions in the 1690s, as a consequence of the wars of William III. Other ports did not share in this growth. Southampton for example had no more than 3000 inhabitants at the end of the century, and Grimsby, where the harbour was rapidly silting up, had only five hundred. At the same time both Bath and Tunbridge Wells were becoming popular spa towns. Brighton however was still only a stagnant fishing town with about 1500 inhabitants, the same number as were to be found in the large parish of Cheltenham. Many county towns, such as Shrewsbury, Bury St Edmunds, Northampton and Warwick, flourished as social centres for the local gentry, and it became common practice for many of them to buy a town house and avail themselves of the facilities for business and pleasure that many towns could now offer – attorneys and physicians, newspapers and coffee houses, shops, horse-racing, assemblies, balls and card parties. Nevertheless, in spite of all of this activity, towns still remained very small by modern standards. Fields and farms, horses and middens were never very far away from even the most elegant town houses, as Plate 1 shows; and Bath was still almost entirely confined to the limits of its medieval walls as illustrated in Plate 34.

It is clear that the whole of the seventeenth century, and especially the second half, was marked by distinct growth in some, but by no means all, towns. Very many towns saw a great deal of rebuilding on sites which had long been occupied – in York for example – but there is little expansion in the built-up area before the 1670s, as almost all population growth was accommodated by infilling on vacant spaces or by subdividing large houses. Only in London is there large-scale outward growth in newly built suburbs. The King Street and Queen Square area of Bristol saw only very modest building before the 1690s, and no real development until the first decades of the eighteenth century. Some modest developments were laid out in Birmingham, the Old Square in 1713 and Temple Row in 1719, but no new street was laid out in Leeds between 1634 and 1767. Overall, it seems very unlikely that more than a quarter of the population of England lived in towns at the end of the seventeenth century, and the proportion in Scotland was almost certainly very much less.

At the beginning of the eighteenth century the population of Britain may have been about 6.5 million. There was considerable diversity in the traditions, customs, ways of life, speech and dialect of these people. The development of printing and the book trade in the sixteenth and seventeenth centuries had brought a measure of standardisation to the spelling and punctuation of printed English by the end of the seventeenth century, but levels of accuracy and consistency in private, handwritten documents such as letters and diaries vary enormously, even among educated people. Thus the great Duke of Marlborough remained an erratic speller through his life.

Very large numbers of books, pamphlets, broadsheets, proclamations and newspapers were published during this period. This is the age of the first and the finest flowering of English literature, the age of Spenser and Shakespeare,

Milton and Dryden, Sir Thomas Browne and Andrew Marvell. The Authorized Version of the Bible was published in 1611, and Newton's *Principia Mathematica* in 1687. Hakluyt's *Principal Voyages of the English Nation* was first published in 1589 and Sir William Dugdale's *Antiquities of Warwickshire* in 1656. This is also the great age of English music, from Tallis and Byrd to Gibbons and Purcell, whose gifts may not unreasonably be compared with those of Mozart.

Books of this quality are but a small minority of the total mass of publication in the sixteenth and seventeenth centuries, as they would be in any period. The great majority of books and pamphlets were works of religious or political controversy, and it is often impossible to separate out the two, or else they were broadsheets of a more or less sensational nature, dealing with murders and hangings, monsters, disasters, storms and fires. It is impossible now to assess levels of literacy for this period at all accurately, but it seems very likely that more people could read than could write, since the two were taught quite separately in schools, and that perhaps as many as a third to a half of men could sign their names, the only indicator of literacy that can be measured for this period and that a very basic one, since it carries no implication of any ability to read texts of any complexity. Thus it is very likely that the audience for literature as opposed to sensational ephemera was very much narrower than it is even today and also very much more related to position in the social hierarchy. Labourers had no need for literacy and no encouragement to acquire it.

English was not, however, the only language in use in Britain, even at the end of the seventeenth century. The official languages of law and government continued to be Law French and Latin until their use was abolished by Act of Parliament in 1730. Thus many manorial courts and quarter sessions continued to use Latin for the formal record of their proceedings, although it bears little resemblance to the language of Caesar and Cicero. Lawyers in particular were most indignant at the passing of the 1730 Act since it deprived them of a technical jargon, and a further Act passed two years later permitted the continued use of legal terms for which there was no satisfactory English equivalent, including, for example, the writs of *nisi prius*, *fieri facias* and *habeas corpus*.

In Scotland Gaelic was widely spoken, by perhaps a third of the population, and English was unknown among the great majority of the inhabitants of the Highlands and

Islands. A further language was spoken in Orkney and Shetland. These islands had come to the Scottish Crown only in 1469, and their links with Norway remained strong until the early years of the seventeenth century. Thus appeals against rulings in the Shetland *lawthing* continued to be heard in the king's court in Bergen until well into the sixteenth century. In 1611 the Scottish Privy Council ruled that the Norse laws of Orkney and Shetland should be replaced by Scottish laws, but this was very slow to take effect. The last Shetland document to be drawn up in Norn, the island variant of Norse, is dated 1607, but Norn continued to be spoken on Foula until the nineteenth century.

Richard Carew, writing in his *Survey of Cornwall* at the very end of the sixteenth century, noted that English had driven Cornish 'into the uttermost skirts of the shire', and it seems to have disappeared as a spoken language from the westernmost parts of Cornwall by about 1800.

Welsh was widely spoken throughout Wales, even though its use in administration and the law was formally abolished in 1542. In 1563 an Act of Parliament provided for the translation of the Bible into Welsh, and the revised edition published in 1620 gave Welsh a standard literary language. The ancient poetic metres continued to be cultivated, and it is only from the early seventeenth century that it is possible to detect a decline in both the quantity and the quality of Welsh poetry. The *cywydd*, an elaborately structured poem celebrating an idealised view of the heroic deeds, open-handed hospitality and complex genealogies of noble and gentry households, was still composed whenever occasion arose, and many Welsh gentry and antiquaries such as Robert Vaughan of Hengwrt and Sir John Wynn of Gwydir made large collections of Welsh poetry at this time.

We spent a long chapter at the beginning of this book looking at the political, legal, social and ecclesiastical institutions of Britain in the middle years of the sixteenth century. Their role in moulding and shaping the landscape must by now be obvious.

The most powerful of these institutions must undoubtedly have been Parliament. It was only by means of Acts of Parliament that the monasteries were dissolved in England and Wales between 1536 and 1540, and the chantries in 1547. It was Acts of Parliament of 1536 and 1542 that provided for the union of England and Wales, regrouping very ancient administrative units into counties, recasting the laws of inheritance in Wales and replacing one language by another for administrative and legal purposes. Similarly, another Act of 1545 provided for the amalgamation of parishes where two parish churches were less than a mile apart and one was worth less than £6 a year. Again it was Parliament which provided the machinery and the funds for the rebuilding of London, its parish churches and St Paul's cathedral after the Great Fire. In this way Parliament could bring about major shifts in the landscape, reflecting new attitudes to old institutions at national level. Further the attempts on the part of the Scottish Parliament described in Chapter 3 to remove some of the more obvious barriers to agricultural improvement must represent a growing awareness of the backward state of Scottish agriculture. Parliament could also legislate in quite personal and local matters, and these again could have a consequential impact upon the landscape. Thus an Act of 1543 provided for the division of Wapping marshes, which had been enclosed and drained at great expense by Cornelius Wanderdelf of Brabant, and another of 1540 provided that Royston, a market town in five parishes, should be a parish of itself, and the priory church, which the inhabitants had just bought, should be the parish church. Other Acts of Parliament dealt with individual roads, waterways, harbours, hospitals, schools, woods, fens and bridges, even to the extent of providing, in 1545, that the burning of frames of timber made or prepared for the building of houses was a felony punishable without benefit of clergy.

In this way Parliament had a considerable influence over the evolution of the landscape. It is for this reason that the study of its composition is of such importance for landscape historians. Its members are, after all, human beings and Parliamentary legislation very frequently reflects their assumptions, values and aspirations. In the seventeenth century members of Parliament were drawn from a much narrower section of society than they are today, namely the landed gentry, and so their actions and decisions almost always represented the aims and ideals of that social grouping rather than any other, and it was a long time before it was recognised, let alone accepted, that other social groupings might have a point of view worth attending to.

Both the monarchy and the House of Lords were abolished in February of 1649, leaving the House of Commons undisputed master of the field. The next ten years were marked by successive attempts on the part of Oliver Cromwell to stabilise, broaden and legitimise this seizure of power on the part of one organ of the constitution, but to no avail. The Restoration brought back both monarch and House of Lords. Although everything possible was done to turn the clock back, in fact the experiences and the lessons of the previous twenty years could not be forgotten. John Pym in 1641 had called for the king to have as his ministers such men as Parliament could confide in, and this was a principle which slowly came to be accepted. The same year saw the first Triennial Act, requiring Parliament to meet every three years. In due course Charles II was able to side-step this and rule without a Parliament from March 1681 until his death in February 1685, the last English monarch to dispense with Parliament for so long a period of time. After the accession of William III, Parliament met every year, and the Triennial Act of 1694 provided that no Parliament should last longer than three years, an unlooked-for interpretation of the 1641 Act, so that until 1714 there were general elections every three years.

The most important change in the structure of Parliament came with the Act of Union with Scotland in 1707. We saw in Chapter 1 that an Act of Parliament of 1536 declared 'the king's dominion of Wales to be incorporated united and annexed to and with his Realm of England' and provided for the representation of Wales in the Parliament of Westminster. The Act was imposed by the English Parliament by right of conquest. No one thought of consulting the inhabitants of Wales on the matter.

Things were quite different when it came to the union of England and Scotland. Scotland was an independent sovereign state with its own monarch, Parliament, law courts and other institutions. The union of 1603 was a union of the Crowns in one person, no more and no less, and there was no union of institutions of any kind. The immediate benefit to the two countries was the fairly rapid cessation of border raiding. James I certainly wanted a more intimate political union, something which is represented symbolically in the paintings executed by Sir Peter Paul Rubens on the ceiling of the Banqueting House built by Inigo Jones in Whitehall. The union of 1707 was negotiated by commissioners from both kingdoms and was embodied in a treaty and an Act of Parliament. It provided for the abolition of the Scottish Parliament and the addition of 45 new members to the English House of Commons, composed of thirty county members and fifteen from the royal burghs. One seat was given to each of the twenty-seven largest Scottish counties, the remaining six were grouped into pairs, Nairn and Cromarty, Clackmannan-shire and Kinross, Bute and Caithness. Each pair had one seat, the two counties of each pair taking it in turns to elect the member. The burghs were arranged into fourteen groups, each group electing one member, and Edinburgh taking the fifteenth seat. The Act also provided that the 150 or so Scottish peers should elect sixteen representative peers to sit in the English House of Lords. These changes brought the largest accession of numbers to the Westminster Parliament before the Great Reform Bill of 1832, but they brought very little change to its social composition. Parliament remained very much in the control of the propertied classes in society, and more especially the landed interests, and would remain so until well into the nineteenth century.

We also looked in Chapter 1 briefly at the Privy Councils of England and Scotland, the supreme administrative bodies in both countries for the years up to 1640. The Privy Council was also restored in 1660 but very quickly grew so large that it ceased as such to have any significant role to play, and instead an inner, cabinet council, composed of only a handful of the king's most trusted advisers, came to take the lead, although the king still remained very much in control. Only with the accession of Queen Anne in 1702 does the day-to-day intervention of the monarch in the business of government start to diminish in any way.

We also saw in Chapter 1 that one of the dominant threads in English political life from the 1530s to 1603 was the question of the succession to the English throne. This problem appeared to be solved in 1603 when James I came to the throne, since he had two sons and a daughter living. But the elder son Henry died in 1612, and so it was the younger son who succeeded as Charles I in 1625. Charles in his turn had two sons and a daughter. Charles II succeeded *de facto* in 1660, *de jure* in 1649, but he had no legitimate offspring. The conversion of his brother James to Catholicism was suspected by the end of the 1660s and appeared to be confirmed by his marriage to a Catholic bride, Mary of Modena, in 1673, raising the spectre of a Catholic monarch and memories of the persecution under Mary. Once again the succession to the throne became a matter of increasing political importance, and a series of Exclusion Bills was brought forward to keep James from the throne, but in vain. He succeeded in 1685, and had forfeited every claim to loyalty from the great majority of his subjects by the end of 1688, when William of Orange, the son of Charles I's daughter Mary, was offered the throne. He was married to another Mary, the daughter of James II by his first wife, Anne Hyde. William died childless in 1702, and the throne passed to the younger daughter of James II by his first wife, Anne. Anne was married to Prince George of Denmark, and lost seventeen children before any of them could reach their teens. When it became apparent that she would not leave a direct heir, the Act of Settlement of 1701 provided that the grandson of Elizabeth, daughter of James I, should succeed, and, as George I, he did so in 1714.

Thus the succession question occupied in the late seventeenth century the same dominant position in English political life that it had done in the sixteenth. That it was provoked by the conversion to Catholicism of James II illustrates the depth of the divisions in men's views of their spiritual goals created by the Reformation, and the Act of Settlement in 1701 may be seen as a confirmation of the changes these divisions had brought into the fabric of Britain over the previous two centuries.

In spite of its claim to political omnipotence Parliament in practice saw its role in the national life as being very much more limited and restricted than it is today. Defence and foreign affairs, the maintenance of law and order and the administration of justice were about the limits of its vision. Efforts to legislate people into religious conformity had been largely abandoned by the end of the seventeenth century. Almost all of its legislation affecting the social and economic life of Britain was particularistic rather than universal in its application. It made no attempt to provide a national transport system, for example. If an individual stretch of road became almost impassable then it would establish a turnpike trust to take care of it. If an individual harbour was damaged in a storm then it would make provision for its repair. But there was no overall central direction in such matters, and nothing approaching the national programme of canal building inaugurated by Colbert in the France of Louis XIV.

There were of course many other facets of the landscape over which Parliament could have no control: the development of the vernacular tradition in building for example, its regional variations, and the slow infiltration of the ornament and the principles of classical architecture. Parliament laid down the sizes of the houses to be built after the Great Fire but made no attempt to legislate upon the style or the spirit in which they were to be built. These were dictated as the response to one of those profound movements in human thought which no society, however hermetically sealed from its neighbours, can entirely exclude.

Courts of law have their own role to play in shaping the landscape, more especially by adjudicating upon claims to exploit parts of it, and by maintaining and enforcing codes of practice drawn up to regulate its division and its use. Thus in the years up to 1640 the Court of Star Chamber was punishing those who took the law into their own hands by tearing down enclosing hedges and fences, something Parliament was also trying to do but by coercing those who had carried out the enclosures in the first place to dismantle the enclosures themselves. At the same time other courts of law were beginning to extend their protection to enclosures made by agreement. Such agreements, as we saw in Chapter 3, were becoming increasingly common by the end of the sixteenth century, and the parties to them were applying to the Court of Chancery for a decree that would make them legally binding. By the end of the seventeenth century, however, Parliament had abandoned its hostility to enclosure on social grounds; its members were now well aware of its advantages and so they were prepared to consider favourably legislation for the enclosure of particular parishes. But it was the nineteenth century before a General Act was passed to simplify the passage of enclosure acts and no Act has ever been passed calling for the abolition of the open field system as a whole.

Much of this book has been concerned with boundaries of every kind, whether of parishes, manors, boroughs, counties, dioceses, cantrefs or baronies. This may seem rather strange since boundaries as such are very rarely clearly marked for any length upon the landscape itself, their very existence can often pass unnoticed on the ground, and they appear in full only on maps. But boundaries, like placenames, are among the most important intangible elements of the landscape, and they can also be among the most ancient. The rural landscape is today in many respects much more uniform than it was even a hundred and fifty years ago, when the enclosure of the open fields was by no means everywhere complete. However in Plate 3 we can see where field boundaries mark the level of cultivation up the steep slopes of the chalk scarp even today, and in Plate 74 we can see sharp boundaries between unenclosed open fields, the closes where enclosure has already taken place and the coppices and rides of the woodland of Whaddon Chase. Boundaries

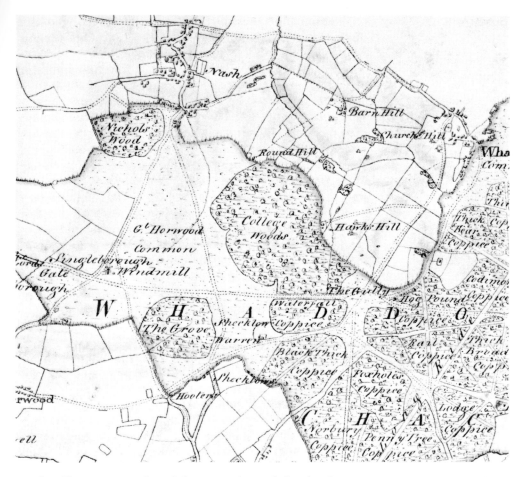

Labels on map: Nash, Nichols Wood, Barn Hill, Church Hill, Wha Com, Round Hill, College Woods, Hawk Hill, Thi, Thick Cop, Bear Coppice, G.ᵗ Horwood Common, Singleborough Windmill, Gate borough, The Gully, Hog Pound Coppice, Codimo, W H A D D O N C H A S E, The Grove, Sheckleu Coppice, Waterfall, Tail Coppice, Thick Broad Cop., Warren, Black Thick Coppice, Foxholes Coppice, Lodge Coppice, rwood, Sheckloe, Hootens, Norbury Coppice, Penny Tree, Cop pice, Coppice, ell, rwood

mark off one area of social perception of the landscape from another, and in this respect their study is of the first importance for a fuller appreciation of the way in which landscape evolves.

The decline in the effective powers of the Privy Council in the years after the Restoration meant that the bodies which exercised administrative and judicial authority within these boundaries became increasingly autonomous, their rights increasingly entrenched, their views of their responsibilities increasingly narrow and legalistic. The officers responsible for the administration of parishes, manors, boroughs, burghs and counties carried out their duties largely as they thought fit. Such control over them as remained was exercised only through legal process and it took writs of *certiorari* or *mandamus* issued from the court of Kings Bench at the suit of an aggrieved, and wealthy, private person following a flagrant breach of the law, to bring their actions under scrutiny.

Plate 74 The two inches to the mile drawings made for the first edition of the one inch to the mile Ordnance Survey map early in the nineteenth century of an area in north Buckinghamshire. At this time the open fields of Great Horwood had not yet been enclosed and Whaddon Chase was still thickly wooded over much of its area. This map illustrates vividly the last fragments of the medieval rural landscape before they disappear for ever

The structures and functions of the family changed little during the course of the sixteenth and seventeenth centuries and the informal links of the kinship network continued to be of great importance in the functioning of almost every facet of the social organisation. Outwardly at any rate the structure of society continued unchanged. The upheavals of the Civil War years had brought many men of the middle and lower ranks of society to the fore and the Restoration was in part a reaction against this breach of what was considered the natural order of things. Thus Restoration society continued to lay heavy stress upon the hierarchical nature of social organisation, although in fact there had been some movement, of which many contemporaries were aware. The great noble and landed families continued to exercise great influence and to command considerable deference, but they never constituted a rigid caste and so they could neither protect their peers against the consequences of their own folly, nor prevent the rise of outstandingly successful men into their ranks. Thus the second Duke of Buckingham squandered an immense fortune in the course of a notoriously reckless and dissolute life, whilst more successful and level-headed politicians such as the Earl of Halifax and the Duke of Leeds were rising from the lesser gentry.

The expansion of English trade overseas in the years after the Restoration brought great wealth to a fortunate few and comfortable affluence to very many more. Financiers and merchants became a group to be reckoned with in government circles since they provided the loans without which government itself could not have operated. The establishment of the Bank of England in 1694 brought much greater certainty and stability into what had been a very treacherous and speculative field of enterprise. The wealth and influence of the new moneyed interests were very much resented by the country gentry who had to shoulder the burden of the Land Tax, the only form of direct taxation then imposed, and at the same time watch men making fortunes by what appeared to be very dubious means.

The gentry/non-gentry distinction continued to be the great divide in English society, but very many more men now claimed to be gentlemen than would have dreamed of doing so before 1640. This is especially true in towns, where it became quite usual for successful craftsmen shop-keepers to call themselves gentlemen on the basis of their success in trade, and with neither the education, the descent nor the landed estate upon which the country gentry based their claims. An example may illustrate this point. Luke Jours, gent., of Ipswich, died in 1678 leaving personal possessions worth £1,265 5s. 4d. He began life as a brewer and a turner, and it was as a turner that he sent his son John as pensioner to St Johns College Cambridge. By 1661 he was sufficiently well-to-do to claim to be a gentleman, and he was recognized as such in the lists of those paying to the Royal Aid of that year, to which he contributed £20. By the time of his death he owned three inns in Ipswich, shares in five ships, and property at Alderton, Cattawade, Clapton and Grundisburgh. In spite of its hierarchical nature, and the frequency with which the word continuity occurs in the preceding paragraphs, the society of Restoration Britain was sufficiently open to allow men like Luke Jours to push their way up the social ladder.

Land nevertheless continued to be the basis of social organisation. By the end of the seventeenth century however money made in commerce, especially overseas trade and finance, was beginning to become both respectable and influential, and the creation of the Bank of England and the continued prosperity of the East India Company provided for the first time facilities for investment other than in a landed estate. In contrast, industry as such was still comparatively unimportant as a gateway to wealth and social mobility. Only the Foleys and the Crowleys rose to real wealth solely from an industrial base, and it is for this reason that they are worth a line or two. Richard Foley was working a slitting mill in the Stour valley by the 1620s and in due course moved into iron making, so successfully that by 1633 he claimed to be employing 800 persons a week. He died in 1657 and the family business was taken over by his son Thomas, who partially retired in 1669, by which time it is likely that he controlled the largest iron producing business in England, an integrated system of furnaces, forges and slitting mills, with assured supplies of ore, charcoal and water power. In 1669 he handed over control of four furnaces, seventeen forges and three slitting mills, together with a warehouse at Bewdley, all in the Stour valley, to his third son Philip, then aged seventeen – assets worth a total of £68,830 8s. 8¾d. Philip, in spite of his years, proved to be a remarkably successful businessman and extended the family business into the Forest of Dean. He died in 1716, by which time he had been overtaken in terms of personal wealth by another ironmaster whose origins also lay in the Stour valley, Sir Ambrose Crowley. After an apprenticeship to a London ironmonger he established a warehouse in 1686 at No. 151 Thames Street, London, by which time he had also established a nail works at Sunderland, moving to Winlaton in 1691, four miles west of Newcastle upon Tyne, and had broken into the lucrative business of supplying nails to the Navy. By the end of the 1690s he had built a forge and slitting mill at Winlaton Mill on the Derwent, about two miles above its confluence with the Tyne. In 1701 he built a warehouse at Blaydon and in 1704 another at Greenwich, where he also built for himself a splendid house, being by this time one of the wealthiest men in England. He died in 1713, aged 55, leaving his son John in control of a business with capital assets alone worth in excess of £100,000.

The years of the Civil Wars and the Commonwealth had brought very great disruption to the established Church. An ordinance of October 1646 abolished bishops, and deans and chapters were abolished in 1649 and their estates sold with the promise, unfulfilled, that, like the lands of the chantries a hundred years before, they would be applied to the improvement of education. The Church recovered its possessions at the Restoration but any claim that it might have made to exercise a monopoly over people's religious beliefs was abandoned by the Act of Toleration of 1689. The establishment of the Church of England showed extremes of wealth and poverty. Some, but not all, bishoprics were very well endowed, whilst the majority of country clergymen had to endure varying levels of poverty. We saw in Chapter 7 that the main thrust of church building in the seventeenth century was directed to the rebuilding of the churches destroyed in the Great Fire of London. Building and rebuilding in the rest of the country was on a comparatively modest scale, although it is probably more extensive than is generally thought. Thus churches were rebuilt at Newent, in Gloucestershire, Minsterley and Whitchurch, both in Shropshire, Ingestre, in Staffordshire, Honington in Warwickshire and Farley in Wiltshire in the years after the Restoration. There was also a great deal of piecemeal repair and patching, and it is clear that very many churches were in a sorry state physically owing to lack of money to carry out even essential repairs in time to prevent yet further deterioration.

The difficulties were exacerbated by the fact that responsibility for the repair of the church was shared. The rector – and by the seventeenth century this often meant an absentee lay impropriator – was responsible for the chancel, the parishioners, through the churchwardens, were responsible for the rest of the church and the church-yard. It is clear that sometimes conditions were very bad indeed. It was reported of the church at Upmarden, in Sussex, in 1625, that the chancel was so badly out of repair and

> so undecently and beastly kept both in healing and otherwise that through the pigeons dung and other filth in the same the people are not able to endure the ill and noysome smell thereof but are inforced to stop their noses or carry flowers in their hands to prevent the ill smell thereof.

At Lancing, also in Sussex, in 1624 it was reported that the vicar had caused all the trees of the churchyard to be felled so that the churchyard walls were beaten down and the churchyard filled with saw pits, logs and trees so that it looked more like a wood yard than a churchyard. The church itself was in grave disrepair notwithstanding the efforts of the churchwardens, who were rebuilding 'as fast as we can rayse meanes to goe on with the same'. At Llan Egwod, in the archdeaconry of Carmarthen, it was reported in 1710 that the floor of the church was of earth and uneven, the graves being left so that ordinary people could see where their friends were buried, and skulls and bones were piled eight feet high. At Warborough, in Oxfordshire, the church in 1673 was said to lie like a barn, in a 'desolatly neglected and ruinous condition', whilst the church bells had been lying in the churchyard for five years unhung.

All together, it seems to have been an almost continuous battle to keep the church watertight, decently glazed and reasonably well paved, a battle which the churchwardens were often in danger of losing.

The parish church, in spite of the changes in religious beliefs and practices of the period and its often doubtful physical condition, remained in most districts the centre of communal activities of every kind. The ceremony of beating the parish bounds at Rogationtide served to emphasise a sense of parochial exclusiveness, and was often an occasion for much eating and drinking. In a number of Sussex parishes the custom was well-estab-lished that those going round the bounds should be given cakes and drink at certain farmhouses which traditionally had to provide this hospitality, and loud and bitter were the complaints when a farmer refused to meet this tax on his generosity. At Rustington, also in Sussex, the parson was expected to provide meat and drink when the harvest was in, and at Storrington in the same county, the parishioners claimed that the parson by ancient custom had to provide bread, cheese and a barrel of beer in church on Easter Day immediately after evening prayer. At Merthyr, in the archdeaconry of Carmarthen, it was the custom for a year after the funeral of persons of better fashion for the grave to be strewn with herbs every Saturday night, and an arched bier set over it every Sunday morning, covered with black, unless it was a maiden's grave when it would be covered in white. At Wing, in Buckinghamshire, the Lord and Lady of May were still being chosen, May ale celebrated and a maypole erected until well into the seventeenth century, and in 1661 the men of Horwood, Whaddon and Swanbourne were in trouble for stealing maypoles out of Horwood Wood. A rich and varied pattern of traditional custom and practice still clung about each parish church even at the end of the seventeenth century.

It has been one of the principal themes of this book that it is men and women living in society who mould and shape the landscape according to their abilities and their perceptions of their needs within parameters set by the constraints and the opportunities presented by their environment. Three further corollaries depend upon this statement.

First of all the study of social, political and legal structures is a necessary part of landscape history, since it is through these structures that men, in the way in which they apportion power among themselves, regulate access to the resources and to the authority necessary for the manipulation of their environment. Speed's plan of Bath (Plate 34) is a diagrammatical representation of marvellous subtlety and complexity of the interaction of the whole range of Jacobean institutions across one small fragment of the landscape frozen at one point in time.

Secondly, levels of technology are important determinants of man's ability to change his environment. Skills in mining and metal-working, engineering and ship-building, agriculture and surveying, are often closely inter-related, and castles, windmills, lighthouses and bridges are the visual evidence of the contribution of technology to the landscape.

Thirdly, some of the most abstruse speculations by men about their purpose in life, their role in the universe, their relationships one with another and with a divine eternity can make an equally powerful contribution to the shaping of the landscape, as we have seen when assessing the visual impact of the changes in values and ideals summed up in the words Reformation and Renaissance.

All three of these corollaries interact in the most complex fashion, as a glance at any of the illustrations to this book will reveal, and more especially at Plate 1. In many ways this book has been an extended commentary upon this Plate, and it is still by no means exhausted, but perhaps the landscape which it represents is now a little less unfamiliar than it was at the beginning of this book.

Further reading

The sixteenth and seventeenth centuries, the age of Shakespeare and the Civil Wars, the colonisation of America and the Reformation must be among the most intensely studied of any periods of British history. Some of the greatest of English historians have spent their lives on these two centuries: Macaulay and S. R. Gardiner, Sir Charles Firth and G. M. Trevelyan. Generations of scholars have published whole libraries of books and other materials devoted to the period, whilst national and local record repositories contain miles of shelving housing archives and documents, many still unlisted, let alone fully explored. Fortunately there a number of very good guides through this overwhelming wealth of material. Conyers Read, *Bibliography of British History, Tudor Period, 1485–1603*, published in 1933 with a second edition in 1959, is still very useful, in spite of its age. G. Davies, *Bibliography of British History, Stuart Period, 1603–1714*, second edition by M. F. Keeler, 1970, is even more useful.

The following general surveys will be found of value:

G. R. Elton, *England under the Tudors*, 1955, second edition 1974.
G. Davies, *The Early Stuarts*, 1937.
J. R. Jones, *Country and Court, England 1658–1714*, 1978.
W. Ferguson, *Scotland, 1689 to the Present*, 1968.
G. Donaldson, *Scotland, James V – James VII*, 1965.
T. C. Smout, *A History of the Scottish People, 1560–1830*, 1969.

The pioneering work in landscape history, W. G. Hoskins, *The Making of the English Landscape*, first published in 1955, can still be read with pleasure and profit. A series with this title comprising a volume on each of the English counties is now in progress. There is further M. Williams, *The Making of the South Wales Landscape* (1975), R. Millman, *The Making of the Scottish Landcape* (1975), and M. L. Parry and T. R. Slater, eds, *The Making of the Scottish Countryside* (1980).

The Victoria Histories of the Counties of England is an invaluable series for reference purposes, and more recent volumes such as *Warwickshire*, Vols VII and VIII, *Oxford-shire* Vol. X and *Wiltshire* Vol. X contain well-documented studies of agriculture, trade and industry as well as histories of individual towns and villages.

The publications of the Royal Commissions on the Ancient and Historic Monuments of England, Scotland and Wales are indispensable, as are the volumes by Sir Nikolaus Pevsner on *The Buildings of England*, and the splendid *Survey of London*.

The remainder of this reading list is divided up according to the chapters of the book, and the list for each chapter has been deliberately restricted to about a dozen items which have proved particularly useful for the themes of that chapter.

Chapter 1

G. R. Elton, *The Tudor Constitution* 1960.

G. R. Elton, *Reform and Reformation, England 1509–1558* 1977.

M. W. Flinn, ed., *Scottish Population History*, 1977.

W. Harrison, *A Description of England*, 1577, ed. G. Edelin, 1968.

P. Laslett, *The World We Have Lost*, 1965.

P. Laslett, *Household and Family in Past Time*, 1972.

G. D. Owen, *Elizabethan Wales*, 1962.

W. Rees, *An Historical Atlas of Wales*, 1959.

L. Stone, *The Family, Sex and Marriage in England, 1500–1800*, 1978.

A. E. Trueman, *Geology and Scenery in England and Wales*, revised edition by J. B. Whittow and J. R. Hardy, 1971.

J. B. Whittow, *Geology and Scenery in Scotland*, 1977.

J. Wormald, *Court, Kirk and Community: Scotland 1470–1625*, 1981.

E. A. Wrigley and R. A. Schofield, *The Population History of England, 1541–1871*, 1981.

Chapter 2

M. L. Anderson, *A History of Scottish Forestry*, 1967.

D. G. Barron, ed., 'Court Book of the Barony of Urie, 1604–1747', *Scottish History Society*, Series 1, Vol. 12, 1892.

C. Brears, 'The Fen Laws of Common', *Lincolnshire Notes and Queries*, 20, 1929, pp. 58–64, 74–7.

T. Cave and R. A. Wilson, 'Parliamentary Survey of the lands and possessions of the Dean and Chapter of Worcester, 1649', *Worcestershire Historical Society*, 1924.

Further reading   F. V. Emery, 'West Glamorgan Farming, 1580–1620', *National Library of Wales Journal*, 9, 1956, pp. 392–400; 10, 1957, pp. 17–32.

B. M. Evans, 'The Commote of Cyfeiliog in the late sixteenth century', *Montgomeryshire Collections*, 60, 1967–8, pp. 28–46.

T. H. B. Graham, ed., 'The Barony of Gilsland, Lord William Howard's Survey taken in 1603', *Cumberland and Westmorland Antiquarian and Archaeological Society*, Extra Series Vol. 16, 1934.

D. A. Kirby, ed., 'Parliamentary Surveys of the Bishopric of Durham', *Surtees Society*, Vol. 183, 1971 and Vol. 185, 1972.

T. I. J. Jones, 'Exchequer Proceedings Concerning Wales *in tempore* James I', *Board of Celtic Studies, History and Law Series*, Vol. 15, 1955.

W. Linnard, *Welsh Woods and Forests*, 1982.

N. J. Pounds, ed., 'Parliamentary Survey of the Duchy of Cornwall', *Devon and Cornwall Record Society*, 1982.

W. Rees, ed., *Survey of the Duchy of Lancaster Lordships in Wales, 1609–1613*, 1953.

F. Shaw, *The Northern and Western Islands of Scotland: their economy and society in the seventeenth century*, 1980.

W. J. Slack, *The Lordship of Oswestry, 1393–1607*, 1951.

J. Thirsk, *English Peasant Farming*, 1957.

I. D. Whyte, *Agriculture and Society in Seventeenth Century Scotland*, 1979.

Chapter 3

A. R. H. Baker and R. H. Butlin, eds, *Studies in Field Systems in the British Isles*, 1971.

D. G. Allen, 'The Rising in the West, 1628–1631', *Economic History Review*, Series 2, Vol. 5, 1952–3, pp. 76–85.

H. C. Darby, *The Draining of the Fens*, 1940, second ed. 1956.

G. Hammersley, 'The Crown Woods and their Exploitation in the Sixteenth and Seventeenth Centuries', *Bulletin of the Institute of Historical Research*, 30, 1957, pp. 136–61.

E. Kerridge, 'The Revolts in Wiltshire against Charles I', *Wiltshire Archaeological Magazine* 57, 1960, pp. 64–75.

F. H. Manley, 'The Disafforesting of Braden', *Wiltshire Archaeological Magazine* 45, 1932, pp. 549–67.

J. Porter, 'A Forest in Transition: Bowland 1500–1650', *Transactions of the Historic Society of Lancashire and Cheshire*, 125, 1975, pp. 40–60.

G. Stovin, 'A Brief Account of the Drainage of the Levels of Hatfield Chase', *Yorkshire Archaeological Journal*, 37, 1951, pp. 385–91.

J. Thirsk, 'The Isle of Axholme before Vermuyden', *Agricultural History Review*, 1, 1953, pp. 16–28.

C. Thomas, 'Enclosure and the Rural Landscape of Merioneth in the Sixteenth Century', *Transactions of the Institute of British Geographers*, No. 42, 1967, pp. 153–62.

C. Thomas, 'Colonisation, Enclosure and the Rural Landscape', *National Library of Wales Journal*, 19, 1975, pp. 132–46.

M. Williams, *The Draining of the Somerset Levels*, 1970.

Chapter 4

A. I. Bowman, 'Culross Colliery: A Sixteenth Century Mine', *Industrial Archaeology*, 7, 1970, pp. 353–72.

D. W. Crossley, 'Glassmaking in Bagot's Park, Staffordshire in the Sixteenth Century', *Post-Medieval Archaeology*, 1, 1968, pp. 44–83.

D. W. Crossley, ed., 'The Sidney Iron Works Accounts, 1541–1573', *Camden Society*, Fourth Series, Vol. 15, 1975.

D. W. Crossley and A. Aberg, 'Sixteenth Century Glassmaking in Yorkshire', *Post-Medieval Archaeology*, 6, 1972, pp. 107–59.

P. J. Drury, 'Post-medieval brick and tile kilns at Runsell Green, Danbury, Essex', *Post-Medieval Archaeology*, 9, 1975, pp. 203–11.

B. F. Duckham, 'Life and Labour in a Scottish Colliery, 1698–1755', *Scottish Historical Review*, 47, 1968, pp. 109–28.

M. S. Giuseppi, 'Rake in Witley', *Surrey Archaeological Collections*, 18, 1904, pp. 11–60.

E. S. Godfrey, *The Development of English Glassmaking, 1560–1640*, 1975.

J. Haslam, 'The Excavation of a Seventeenth Century Pottery Site at Cove, East Hampshire', *Post-Medieval Archaeology*, 9, 1975, pp. 164–87.

N. Lowe, 'The Lancashire Textile Industry in the Sixteenth Century', *Chetham Society*, Third Series, Vol. 20, 1972.

A. Raistrick and B. Jennings, *A History of Lead Mining in the Pennines*, 1965.

W. Rees, *Industry before the Industrial Revolution*, 1968.

H. R. Schubert, *A History of the British Iron and Steel Industry*, 1957.

G. Wills, *English Pottery and Porcelain*, 1969.

Further reading

Chapter 5

M. W. Barley, *The English Farmhouse and Cottage*, 1961.
S. Colman, 'Post Medieval Houses in Suffolk', *Proceedings of the Suffolk Institute of Archaeology*, 34, 1979, pp. 181–90.
J. G. Dunbar, *The Historic Architecture of Scotland*, 1966.
A. Fenton and B. Walker, *The Rural Architecture of Scotland*, 1981.
J. Lees-Milne, *The Tudor Renaissance*, 1951
J. Lees-Milne, *The Age of Inigo Jones*, 1953.
R. Machin, 'The Great Rebuilding: A Reassessment', *Past and Present*, 77, 1977, pp. 33–56.
E. Mercer, *English Vernacular Houses*, 1975.
A. Roussell, *Norse Building Customs in the Scottish Isles*, 1934
M. V. J. Seaborne, 'Cob Cottages in Northamptonshire', *Northamptonshire Past and Present*, 3, 1964, pp. 215–28.
J. T. Smith, 'Lancashire and Cheshire Houses: Some problems of architectural and social history', *Archaeological Journal*, 127, 1971, pp. 156–81.
P. Smith, *Houses of the Welsh Countryside*, 1975.
J. Summerson, 'The Building of Theobalds, 1564–1585', *Archaeologia*, 97, 1959, pp. 107–26.
J. Summerson *Architecture in Britain 1530–1830*, 1953.
J. Summerson, *The Classical Language of Architecture*, 1963.
J. Summerson, *Inigo Jones*, 1966.

Chapter 6

M. W. Beresford, *New Towns of the Middle Ages*, 1967.
J. Evelyn, *London Revived*, ed. E. S. de Beer, 1938.
H. Hurst, ed., 'Oxford Topography', *Oxford Historical Society*, 39, 1899.
S. Lang, 'Cambridge and Oxford Reformed', *Architectural Review*, 103, 1948, pp. 157–60.
A. F. Kelsell, 'The London House Plan in the Later Seventeenth Century', *Post-Medieval Archaeology*, 8, 1974, pp. 80–91.
G. S. Pryde, ed., 'Ayr Burgh Accounts, 1534–1624', *Scottish History Society*, Third Series, 28, 1937.
G. S. Pryde, ed., 'The Court Book of the Burgh of Kirkintilloch, 1658–1694', *Scottish History Society*, Third Series, 53, 1963.
T. F. Reddaway, *The Rebuilding of London after the Great Fire*, 1940.
Register Containing the State and Condition of Every Burgh . . . Miscellany, *Scottish Burgh Record Society*, 1881.
R. Renwick, ed., 'Extracts from the Records of the Royal

Burgh of Stirling, 1519–1666', *Scottish Burgh Record Society*, 1887.

R. A. Skelton, Tudor Town Plans in John Speed's Theatre', *Archaeological Journal*, 108, 1952, pp. 109–20.

H. L. Turner, *Town Defences in England and Wales, 900–1500*, 1971.

I. Soulsby, *The Towns of Medieval Wales*, 1983.

G. Stell, 'The Earliest Tolbooths, a preliminary account', *Proceedings of the Scottish Society of Antiquaries*, 111, 1981, pp. 445–53.

J. W. R. Whitehand and K. Alauddin, 'The Town Plans of Scotland; some preliminary considerations', *Scottish Geographical Magazine*, 85, 1969, pp. 109–21.

T. W. Willan, 'Elizabethan Manchester', *Chetham Society*, Third Series, 27, 1980.

Chapter 7

G. W. O. Addleshaw and F. Etchells, *The Architectural Setting of Anglican Worship*, 1948.

A. G. Dickens, *The English Reformation*, 1964.

G. Donaldson, *The Scottish Reformation*, 1960.

D. Easson, *Medieval Religious Houses: Scotland*, 1957.

W. H. Godfrey, *The English Almshouse*, 1955.

H. J. Habbakuk, 'The Market for Monastic Property', *Economic History Review*, Second Series, 10, 1957–8, pp. 362–80.

G. Hay, *The Architecture of Scottish Post-Reformation Churches, 1560–1843*, 1957.

J. Scotland, *The History of Scottish Education*, 1969.

M. Seaborne, *The English School: its Architecture and Organisation*, 1971.

J. Simon, *Education and Society in Tudor England*, 1966.

M. Whiffen, *Stuart and Georgian Churches outside London*, 1947.

G. Williams, *Welsh Reformation Essays*, 1967.

Chapter 8

B. Gille, *The Renaissance Engineer*, 1966.

E. H. Gombrich, 'Icones Symbolicae', *Journal of the Warburg and Courtauld Institutes*, 11, 1948, pp. 163–92.

D. J. Gordon, *The Renaissance Imagination*, 1975.

R. T. Gunther, ed., 'The Life and Letters of Edward Lhwyd', *Early Science in Oxford*, 14, 1945.

P. Mathias, ed., *Science and Society, 1600–1900*, 1972.

A. Pannecock, *History of Astronomy*, 1961.

W. Shumaker, *The Occult Sciences in the Renaissance*, 1972.

Further reading   C. S. Singleton, ed., *Art, Science and History in the Renaissance*, 1967.

A. G. R. Smith, *Science and Society in the Sixteenth and Seventeenth Centuries*, 1972.

C. Webster, ed., *The Intellectual Revolution of the Seventeenth Century*, 1975.

F. A. Yates, *Giordano Bruno and the Hermetic Tradition*, 1964.

F. A. Yates, *The Rosicrucian Enlightenment*, 1972.

F. A. Yates, *The Occult Philosophy in the Elizabethan Age*, 1979.

Chapter 9

K. J. Bonser, *The Drovers*, 1970.

C. W. Chalklin, 'Navigational Schemes on the Upper Medway, 1600–1665', *Journal of Transport History*, 5, 1961, pp. 105–15.

D. A. E. Cross, 'The Salisbury Avon Navigation', *Industrial Archaeology*, 7, 1970, pp. 121–30.

G. Farr, 'Severn Navigation and the Trow', *Mariners Mirror*, 32, 1946, pp. 66–95.

D. B. Hague and R. Christie, *Lighthouses*, 1975.

A. R. B. Haldane, *The Drove Roads of Scotland*, 1952.

W. T. Jackman, *The Development of Transportation in Modern England*, 1916.

W. Minet, 'Some Unpublished Plans of Dover Harbour', *Archaeologia*, 72, 1922, pp. 185–224.

D. G. Moir, 'The Roads of Scotland II, Statute Labour Roads', *Scottish Geographical Magazine*, 73, 1957, pp. 101–10, 167–75.

M. Nash, 'Early Seventeenth Century Schemes to make the Wey Navigable', *Surrey Archaeological Collections*, 66, 1969, pp. 33–40.

M. Prior, 'The Accounts of Thomas West of Wallingford, a Sixteenth Century Trader on the Thames', *Oxoniensia*, 46, 1981, pp. 73–93.

H. Robinson, *The British Post Office*, 1948.

A. A. Ruddock, 'The Trinity House at Deptford in the Sixteenth Century', *English Historical Review*, 65, 1950, pp. 458–76.

W. B. Stephens, 'The Exeter Lighter Canal 1566–1698', *Journal of Transport History*, 3, 1957, pp. 1–11.

Chapter 10

D. Cressy, 'Levels of Illiteracy in England, 1530–1730', *Historical Journal*, 20, 1977, pp. 1–23.

M. W. Flinn, ed., 'The Law Books of the Crowley Ironworks', *Surtees Society*, 167, 1952.

G. M. Griffiths, 'A Visitation of the Archdeaconry of Carmarthen', *National Library of Wales Journal*, 18, 1974, pp. 287–311; 19, 1976, pp. 311–26.

H. Johnstone, ed., 'Churchwarden's Presentments, Part 1, Archdeaconry of Chichester', *Sussex Record Society*, 49, 1949.

J. P. Kenyon, *The Stuart Constitution*, 1966

A. G. Linney, 'Crowley's Wharf, Greenwich', *Transactions of the Newcomen Society*, 16, 1935–6, pp. 149–50.

F. Ouvry, 'Extracts from the Churchwardens Accounts of the Parish of Wing', *Archaeologia*, 36, 1855, pp. 221–41.

T. Parry, *A History of Welsh Literature*, translated from the Welsh by H. Idris Bell, 1955.

R. G. Schafer, ed., 'A Selection from the Records of Philip Foley's Stour Valley Iron Works, 1668–1674', *Worcestershire Historical Society*, 9, 1978.

W. O. Williams, 'The Social Order in Tudor Wales', *Transactions of the Honourable Society of Cymmrodorion*, 1967, pp. 167–78.

D. J. Withrington, ed., *Shetland and the Outside World*, 1983.

Index

295

Carew, Richard, 273
Carlisle, 42, 149, 182, 244, 248
Carmarthen, 20, 137, 139;
    archdeaconry of, 283–4
Carmarthenshire, 19, 74, 77,
    113, 117
Carmelite order, 176
Carolina, 257
Carré, Jean, 90
Carrera, 128
Carriers, 239, 242–4, 248, 250
Carrington, Mid Lothian, 188
Carthusian order, 173
Cary, George, 258
Cary, Sir Robert, 241
Casa de Contratación, 223
Casaubon, Isaac, 214
Castle Carrock, Cumb., 42
Castle Howard, Yorks., 134
Castles, 60, 103, 142–3, 147,
    152–4, 268–9, 284
Castleton, Derbys., 99
Cattawade, Suffolk, 281
Cauldstone Slap, Mid Lothian,
    245
Caxton, Cambs., 236
Cecil, William, 126–7, 207; see
    also Lord Burghley
Chalfont St Peter, Bucks., 266
Chalk, for building, 115
Chambord, château de, 125
Chancellor, Richard, 223
Chancery, court of, 23, 278
Chantries, 172, 190–2, 198,
    203, 273, 282
Chapels of ease, 17, 181
Chapman, John, 126
Charles I, 25, 67–70, 132, 210,
    239, 265, 276
Charles II, 167, 185, 199–200,
    217, 230, 257, 275–7
Charleville, 164
Charlton House, Greenwich,
    128
Charlwood, Surrey, 108
Charnock, Thomas, 207
Charterhouse, Somerset, 99
Charters to towns, 138–40, 258
Chartres, 172
Chatham, naval dockyard at,
    80, 259, 270
Chat Moss, Lancs., 265
Chatsworth, Derbys., 134
Cheddar gorge, Somerset, 102
Cheltenham, Gloucs., 270
Chepstow, Mon., 139, 238
Cheriton Fitzpaine, Devon,
    199–201
Cherwell, river, 39
Cheshire, 24, 43–4, 113, 117,
    120
Chester, 17, 18, 142–4, 175–6,

244, 248–9
Chicheley, Bucks., 34, 38
Chichester, Sussex, 142, 149,
    197
Chiddingfold, Surrey, 90
Chillesford, Suffolk, 68
Chiltern hills, 5
Chilton by Sudbury, Suffolk,
    109
Chilworth, Surrey, 253
Chipping Norton, Oxon., 138
Chorley Hall, Wilmslow,
    Cheshire, 120
Church ales, 16
Churches, 2–3, 5, 16, 28, 32,
    46, 55, 116, 122, 161, 176–7,
    180–8, 227–8, 233, 266, 268,
    274, 282–4
Church of England, 25, 282
Churchwardens, 17, 182, 283
Cistercian order, 178
Civil Wars, 63, 67, 75, 133, 143,
    153, 161, 181–2, 185, 268–9,
    280, 282
Clachan, 48
Clackmannan, 26, 276
Clapton, Suffolk, 281
Clarendon, earl of, 134; Forest
    of, Wilts., 264
Clarke, Francis, 121
Clarke, Thomas, 121
Classical architecture, 130–2,
    135, 150, 161, 171, 185–6,
    193, 196–7, 199, 203, 267, 277
Classical orders, 125–6, 161,
    170, 194, 197
Clawdd Mwyn, Cardigans., 86
Clay, as building material, 116,
    122
Claymires and Botarie, Banffs.,
    49
Clayworth, Notts., 234
Clement VII, 179
Clergymen, 12, 16–18, 282–3
Clifton Reynes, Bucks., 38
Climate, 3, 5, 8–9, 41, 43, 47,
    117
Clipsham, Rutland, 114
Clocks and watches, 227–8
Clough, Sir Richard, 128
Clovelly, Devon, 258
Clyde, river, 11, 240, 258
Coaches, 245–6, 248, 261
Coal, 5, 15, 52, 79–86, 88–91,
    93, 96–7, 100–1, 182, 236,
    250, 253, 258
Coalbrookdale, Shropshire,
    101
Cob, 116
Cobham, Kent, 198
Coggeshall, Essex, 248
Coke, Sir Edward, 140

Coke, Thomas, 260
Colbert, Jean-Baptiste, 277
Colchester, Essex, 142, 237,
    243, 248
Cold Brayfield, Bucks., 37
Coldingham, Berwicks.,
    179–80
Cole, Humfrey, 224
Coleshill, Berks., 133–5, 268
Colet, Dean, 192–3
Collingtree, Northants., 236
Collyweston, Rutland, 114
Colt, Maximilian, 128
Commendators, 26, 179
Commission of the Peace, 19
Commissioners of Sewers, 251
Committee of the Articles, 25
Common Law, 22
Common Pleas, court of, 23
Commons and wastes, 32, 34,
    40, 42, 46, 49, 60, 62, 67, 69,
    71, 73, 75–6, 85, 263
Commonwealth, 194, 200, 246,
    282
Commote, 19, 74
Company of Mines Royal,
    96–9
Conway, Caerns., 112
Conwy, river, 77
Copenhagen, 220
Copernicus, 219–21, 223
Copper, 5, 86, 96–8, 209
Coppicing, 34, 44–6, 81, 92
Copyhold land, 21
Corbridge, Northumberland,
    245
Corby, Northants., 60
Corby Glen, Lincs., 192
Cornish, language, 273
Cornwall, 5, 15, 40–1, 45–6, 58,
    88, 98, 100, 104, 115, 242,
    273
Corse, Gloucs., 34
Corunna, 258
Cotchett, Thomas, 105
Cotswolds, 5, 105, 112, 114–16,
    261
Cottars, 16, 72, 267
Cottenham, Cambs., 46
Council of the Marches of
    Wales, 19–21
Council of the North, 21
County, 2, 273; administration,
    18–19, 278–9; Parliamentary
    representation, 25–6; towns,
    23–4, 270–1
Cove, Hants., 88
Coventry, War., 10
Cowley, Middx., 87
Cox, Richard, 241
Coxe, Richard, 37
Coydrathe, Forest of, Pembs., 77

Pliny, 211
Plot, Robert, 212
Plymouth, Devon, 270
Policies, 71–2
Pontypool, Mon., 77, 92
Population estimates, 1, 9–11, 30, 48, 137, 180, 269–71; mobility, 234
Porlock, Somerset, 238
Porteynon, Glam., 53
Portsea, Hants., 85
Portsmouth, Hants., 143, 182, 248, 259, 270
Post, 241, 248; General Post Office, 249; Letter Office, 248
Pottery industry, 80–1, 85–8, 101, 242, 256
Povey, Charles, 249
Pow of Inchaffry, Perths., 73–4
Powle, Henry, 80
Powys, 19
Praemunire, statute of, 125
Prague, 207, 221–2
Pratt, Sir George, 133
Pratt, Sir Roger, 133–4, 167
Prestbury, Gloucs., 32
Preston, Lancs., 92
Prestonpans, Mid Lothian, 80, 150
Priddy, Somerset, 99
Printing press, 232, 271
Privy Council, 19, 23, 27, 273, 276, 279
Probate inventories, 37, 45, 86–7, 91, 138, 156–7, 241, 261–2, 281
Proctor, Sir Stephen, 178
Protestant reformers, 16, 191–3, 201
Prutenic tables, 219
Pryse, Sir Carbery, 98
Ptolemy, 208, 232
Puddletown, Dorset, 247
Purbeck, Isle of, 90
Purcell, Henry, 272
Pym, John, 275
Pyramids, 172

Quainton, Bucks., 199
Quakers see Friends, Society of
Quays, 257–8
Queensberry, family vault, 188
Queen's House, Greenwich, 130, 200–1

Radnor Forest, 77
Radnorshire, 19, 54, 76, 80, 117
Raglan, Mon., 83
Railways, 84, 265
Rainow, Cheshire, 121
Raleigh, Sir Walter, 116
Raley fell, co. Durham, 60

Rand, William, 241
Rannochmoor, Perths., 4
Ravenscroft, George, 91
Ravenstone, Bucks., 199
Raynham Hall, Norfolk, 132
Reach, Cambs., 47
Reading, Berks., 148, 170, 176, 181
Reading, Nathaniel, 67
Reed, Charles, 192
Reformation, 24, 172, 180, 182, 187, 189, 191–2, 203, 218, 268, 277, 285
Reigate, Surrey, 237
Renaissance, 107–8, 124–5, 127–9, 161–2, 164, 171, 181, 193, 196–7, 203, 214, 218, 230, 285
Requests, court of, 23
Restoration, 66, 71, 85, 102, 132, 143, 146, 161, 168, 181, 187, 192, 246, 249–50, 268, 275, 279–82
Rhosili, Glam., 53–4, 74
Rhuddlan, statute of, 19
Rhwng Gwy a Hafren, 19
Richelieu, cardinal, château and town, 164
Rievaulx, Yorks., 94
River navigation, 9, 47, 250–1
Roads, 1, 19, 51, 61, 65, 71, 77, 85, 235–7, 242–4, 248, 250, 274, 277; maps, 227, 250, 254–7
Robertsbridge, Sussex, 94
Rochester, 236; diocese of, 17; bridge, 237
Rockingham Forest, Northants., 43
Roman Catholics and Catholicism, 125, 189, 276–7
Romanno, Peebles-s. 245
Rome, 164, 168, 171
Romney Marsh, 40
Romsey, Hants., 176
Ross on Wye, Herefords., 170
Ross-shire, 21, 122
Rous, Thomas, 90
Rousham, Oxon., 58
Roxburghshire, 21, 50, 123, 179
Royal Exchange Assurance, 99
Royal Society, 229–30, 232, 242, 249
Royston, Herts., 274
Rubens, Sir Peter Paul, 210, 275
Rudolph II, 207, 222
Rufford Old Hall, Lancs., 120
Rugeley, Staffs., 104
Runrig, 48, 73, 239
Runsell Green, Essex, 87
Rushall, Wilts., 33

Russell, Lord John, 174, 177
Rustington, Sussex, 283
Ruthin, lordship of, 76
Rutland, 59
Rye, Sussex, 144, 161, 236, 259

St Albans, Herts., 173, 246; earl of, 168, 181
St Andrews, 18, 144, 180, 202
St Asaph, 17
St Catherine's Head, Isle of Wight, 259
St Constantine, Cornwall, 5
St David's Without, Brecons., 134
St Dogmael, Cardigans., 176
St Enodoc, Cornwall, 5
St Germans, Cornwall, 46
St Ives, Cornwall, 5
St Kilda, 50
St Osyth priory, Essex, 173
St Sidwells, Exeter, Devon, 61
St Weonards, Herefords., 90
Salcey Forest, Northants., 43
Salisbury, 10, 62, 149, 207, 246–7; earl of, 68, 126, 128; Plain, 250
Salt making, 52, 85
Sanders, Sir Matthew, 60
Sandford, Oxon., 253
Sandwich, Kent, 40, 144
Sandys, William, 253
Sanquhar, Dumfries, 151
Saturn, 210
Savery, Capt. Thomas, 83
Saxton, Christopher, 223–5
Scarborough, Yorks., 181
Schellinks, Willem, 9
Schools, 150, 161, 176, 188, 191–5, 198, 201–2, 223, 272, 274
Scientific revolution, 204
Scotch brook, Staffs., 89
Scott, Sir William, 73
Seagrave, Leics., 234
Sedan chair, 246
Sedbergh, Yorks., 190, 192
Sedgefield, co. Durham, 104
Sedgemoor, Somerset, 67, 265
Selby, Yorks., 176
Selkirk, 51, 143, 239
Selkirkshire, 21
Selwood, Forest of, Wilts., 69
Session, court of, 22, 71
Severn, river, 7, 10, 45, 68, 77, 84, 89, 244, 251, 256
Seville, 223
Seymour, Lord, of Sudeley, 126
Shaftesbury, Dorset, 149, 173
Shakespeare, William, 271
Shangton, Leics., 60